TIMMON ... h his
family t ... ns at
Buckie ...
of Aber ...
West Yo ...
Timi ...
building ...
then we ... PBI),
editor c ... nder
and dir ... and
executiv ... g for
the Hol ... vork
for Qua ... on of
Program ...
Timi ... iting
or camp ... and
protest ... first
book, S ... was
publishe ...

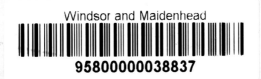

The Truth About Trident

Disarming the Nuclear Argument

DR TIMMON MILNE WALLIS

Luath Press Limited
EDINBURGH
www.luath.co.uk

First published by Luath Press Ltd 2016
in association with

Quakers in Britain

ISBN: 978-1-910745-42-7

The paper used in this book is recyclable. It is made from low chlorine pulps produced in a low energy, low emission manner from renewable forests.

Printed and bound by Martins the Printers, Berwick Upon Tweed.

Typeset in 11 point Sabon

Contents

This book is dedicated to all those people who have worked tirelessly over so many years in so many different ways for the cause of nuclear disarmament. May your efforts finally come to bear fruit in a world free of all nuclear weapons…

List of Abbreviations

ABM	Anti-Ballistic Missiles
ABMT	Anti-Ballistic Missile Treaty
ACTS	Action of Churches Together in Scotland
AWE	Atomic Weapons Establishment
B61	Nuclear weapon dropped from planes and deployed in Germany, Belgium, Netherlands and Turkey
BAE	BAE Systems, (formerly) British Aerospace
BAOR	British Army on the Rhine (Germany)
BBS	British Bombing Survey
CD	Conference on Disarmament
CEP	Circular Error Probable = measure of how close a missile is likely to hit target
CND	Campaign for Nuclear Disarmament
CTBT	Comprehensive Test Ban Treaty
D5	Trident missile used on vanguard and successor submarines
DFID	Department for International Development
DML	Devonport Management Ltd
DOD	US Department of Defence
FOI	Freedom of Information
FMCT	Fissile Material Cut-Off Treaty
G8	Group of eight largest global economies – US, Canada, UK, France, Italy, Japan, Germany
GDP	Gross Domestic Product
GPS	Global Positioning System
HMNB	Her Majesty's Naval Base
HM	Her Majesty
IAEA	International Atomic Energy Agency
ICBM	Intercontinental Ballistic Missile
ICC	International Criminal Court
ICJ	International Court of Justice (World Court)
IISS	International Institute of Strategic Studies
IMF	International Monetary Fund
INF	Intermediate Nuclear Forces
ISIS	Islamic State in Iraq and Syria, also known as Isil, IS, Daesh

KT	Kilotonne, or 1,000 tonnes of TNT equivalent
MAD	Mutually Assured Destruction
MDA	Mutual Defence Agreement
MIRV	Multiple Independently-targeted Re-entry Vehicle
MOD	Ministry of Defence
MORI	Ipsos MORI, a market research organisation in the UK.
MP	Member of Parliament
MSP	Member of Scottish Parliament
MT	Megatonne, or one million tonnes, 1,000 KT, of TNT equivalent
NATO	North Atlantic Treaty Organisation
NDA	Nuclear Decommissioning Authority
NFZ	Nuclear Free Zone
NGO	Non-Governmental Organisation
NNWS	Non-Nuclear Weapon State
NPG	Nuclear Planning Group
NPT	Non-Proliferation Treaty
NSS/SDSR	National Security Strategy and Strategic Defence and Security Review
NWS	Nuclear Weapons State
OECD	Organisation for Economic Cooperation and Development
OEWG	Open-Ended Working Group of the UN General Assembly
OSCE	Organisation for Security and Cooperation in Europe
P5	Permanent five members of the UN Security Council
PRIO	Peace Research Institute Oslo
PSA	Polaris Sales Agreement
PSI	Pounds Per Square Inch
PTBT	Partial Test Ban Treaty
RAF	Royal Air Force
RN	Royal Navy
RNAD	Royal Navy Arms Depot
RV	Re-entry vehicle on a nuclear missile
SDP	Social Democratic Party, later merged with Liberal Party to become Liberal Democrats
SNP	Scottish National Party
SIPRI	Stockholm International Peace Research Institute
SSBN	Strategic Ballistic Missile Submarine
START	Strategic Arms Reduction Talks
STUC	Scottish Trades Union Congress
TNT	Trinitrotoluene, a standard explosive
UNESCO	UN Educational, Scientific and Cultural Organisation

UNGA	UN General Assembly
UNSC	UN Security Council
USSR	Union of Soviet Socialist Republics
USSBS	US Strategic Bombing Survey
VSE	Vickers Submarine Engineering Ltd.
W177	UK-made nuclear weapon
W76	US-made nuclear warhead used on Trident Missile
WMD	Weapons of Mass Destruction
WTO	World Trade Organisation
WWI	World War I
WWII	World War II

Acknowledgements

Special thanks to the following experts and advisors, without whom this book could not have been written: John Ainslie, Martin Birdseye, Frank Boulton, Elizabeth Chappell, Janet Fenton, Steve Hucklesby, Paul Ingram, Bruce Kent, David Lowry, Steven Schofield, Rae Street, Jane Tallent and Phil Webber. As author, I of course take full responsibility for any remaining errors or omissions in the text. Thanks also go to Nora Catlin, Haifa Rashed and Holly Wallis for typing up drafts, and to Ellis Brooks, Izzy Cartwright, Stephen Clement, Roslyn Cook, Helen Drewery, Naomi Engelkamp, James Grant, Claire Poyner, Andrew Rigby, Chris Venables, Emily Wallis and colleagues at the Norges Fredsrad for reading and commenting on earlier drafts, and to Gavin MacDougall, Marigold Bentley, Juliette King and Lotte Mitchell Reford for getting the book into final shape for publishing.

Author's Preface

IT IS QUITE possible that by the time you are reading this book, the British government will have made the 'Main Gate' decision on Trident, committing this country to spending many billions of pounds to maintain its dependence on nuclear weapons well into the second half of this century. It is also possible that by the time you are reading this book, the majority of countries that *don't* have nuclear weapons will have negotiated a treaty banning the development, production, stockpiling, deployment and transfer of nuclear weapons under international law. In either case, the issue of the UK's possession of nuclear weapons will remain relevant and on the political agenda until the last of these weapons has been dismantled.

While the threat of nuclear war between the superpowers has faded away from the consciousness of most people, the world is still awash with nuclear weapons – more than 15,000 of them. Around 2,000 of these remain on high alert and ready to be fired at a moment's notice. The UK's comparatively small nuclear arsenal is fully deployed on submarines patrolling the Atlantic 24 hours a day, 7 days a week, 365 days a year, ready to be fired if the order is given. David Cameron has indicated that he is ready and willing to give that order if he felt the conditions warranted it.

With such important decisions about nuclear weapons being made globally and nationally, it is nothing short of shocking to find so little discussion about this topic and so many people, especially younger people, who know little or nothing about the issues involved. While a number of excellent books have been written on this subject, few are geared to the general reader or readily accessible to them, combining all the arguments for and against into a handy reference.

This book attempts to fill that gap. It is written in the firm belief that the issue of Trident is too important to be left to politicians and generals. It needs to be discussed in the pub, at the school gates and over the kitchen sink so that people are aware of the issues involved and have had the opportunity to think them through.

While I myself have always been opposed to nuclear weapons on moral grounds, I was happy for many of the other arguments in favour of having them to go unchallenged. In doing the research for this book, I was in no doubt that I would be able to make a convincing case that was *on balance* firmly against Trident. Even if as many as 10 of the 20 arguments in favour of Trident could not be easily refuted, I was still confident that the moral case could be made to outweigh the 'lesser' arguments based on finances, jobs, politics, strategic interests, deterrence and so on.

What I never expected to find was that *none* of the pro-Trident arguments stand up to scrutiny. Trident is supposedly the most powerful weapon ever deployed by the UK. But the arguments used to justify having it are themselves exceedingly weak. It therefore takes relatively little effort to effectively disarm whatever force those arguments may have been thought to have. What we are left with is a weapon system that is not powerful at all, but still exceedingly dangerous. Trident does not keep us safe but actually makes us – and the rest of the world – less safe. It is time to disarm not only the arguments, but the system itself.

INTRODUCTION

Getting at the Truth

ANY BOOK WITH the word 'truth' in its title is bound to attract a certain amount of scepticism if not downright ridicule. The idea that there is a single, knowable 'truth' about anything is rightly to be questioned. Even if such a concept exists in any objective sense, perhaps we are each bound by our own set of circumstances to see only our own truth and to claim anything beyond that is a delusion.

And yet, the reality is that none of us would be able to go about our daily lives without some concept of truth as a reference point. Being able to distinguish truth from lies, facts from opinions, evidence from hearsay is part of what makes us human. We all need to be able to establish for ourselves what is true and what is not.

Every witness in a court of law promises to tell 'the truth, the whole truth and nothing but the truth' before giving their testimony. That is a very exacting bar to meet, but if you are caught lying in court, you will go to prison for it. This book attempts to tell the truth, the whole truth and nothing but the truth – as best we are able to ascertain it – about Trident. It is a tall order, and not without its challenges.

Trident starts with a secret

For a start, we are faced immediately with the difficulty that what we are talking about is, at its core, a secret. Julius and Ethel Rosenberg were US citizens found guilty of passing atomic secrets to the Soviet Union, given the death sentence, and executed by electric chair in 1953. Today, vastly more information about the design and construction of nuclear weapons than was available to the Rosenbergs is freely available on the internet and accessible to anyone in the world. Yet the UK remains highly secretive about key aspects of Trident.

This is not just because these are horrifically dangerous weapons that the government doesn't want falling into the 'wrong hands'. It is also because, as we shall see, the whole doctrine of nuclear deterrence depends upon convincing a potential opponent that the British government is deadly serious about this business. Deterrence is all about presentation and perceptions rather than about the reality that may lie beneath these.

It is precisely *because* these are such horrifically dangerous weapons and because the government is so deadly serious about them that there also needs to be much more public discussion about Trident than there is. We need to know why we have these weapons, under what conditions would they ever be used, what would be the impact of their use, how safe are they in the meantime, are they really necessary, can we afford them, are there better alternatives? These are right and proper questions which ought to be discussed openly and publicly in a democracy. And in order to discuss these questions, we need to know a certain amount about the subject matter.

The approach of this book

This book attempts to dig out the truth about Trident by examining the arguments *for* Trident and putting those to the test. Do they hold up under scrutiny? What assumptions are being made and are these valid? What are the facts as best we know them and where are they coming from? What is the logic of the argument and is it valid and reasonable?

Many arguments are used on both sides of this debate, and each argument has many variations. Some are directed to particular audiences, such as the claim that the Labour party would be 'unelectable' if it adopted an anti-Trident position. Others are more general and universal, such as the claim that Britain would not be safe from attack by another nuclear power, like Russia, if it were to abandon Trident at this point.

This book looks at 20 key arguments that are regularly used to present the case in favour of Trident, including some focussed on particular audiences as well as more general ones. In each case, the argument in favour is explained, along with the assumptions and logic behind it. The arguments are then unpicked and examined in more detail, revealing in most cases cracks in the logic, gaps in the evidence and inherent contradictions in what is being asserted. This analysis then forms the basis for summarising the anti-Trident position in each case. The arguments in favour of Trident are given a fair and sympathetic hearing. But this is not a book aiming to present a 'balanced' view, in which each side of the argument is given equal weight and neither turns out to be more 'right' than the other. This is a book about the truth of the matter and trying to seek out and determine what that is.

It will become obvious to the reader, if it is not already, that this book comes down clearly in favour of the anti-Trident position. Whether this is justified on the basis of the arguments and the evidence presented is up to the reader to judge. What most people hear, however, are the pro-Trident arguments. These are presented to us every day by politicians of all the major political parties, the vast majority of journalists and broadcasters, academics, think tank experts, admirals and generals, business leaders, trade unionists, teachers and parents. It is hard to imagine another issue of such importance that is presented in such a one-sided, unbalanced way. This book is one small attempt to redress that balance.

Who this book is for

This book is intended for the general reader who may know little about the subject beyond what they hear on the news. It is also for those who have followed this issue closely over the years but may now wish to refresh their memories in order to more confidently join in the current discussions. While covering in some detail the 20 arguments for and against Trident, this book does not need to be read from cover to cover. Some may want to dip into chapters that are particularly relevant to them or to the discussion at hand. Others may want to review the different arguments for and against Trident by looking at the beginnings and/or endings of each chapter.

The aim of the book is to get beyond the soundbites, headlines and slogans that tend to dominate the debate about Trident. The issues are complex and nuanced. They require more thought and attention than they are normally given. But for people who have neither the time nor the patience to read through a full-length book, there are plenty of short-cuts at hand.

Structure of the book

This book is divided into seven parts. Before looking at the arguments in favour of Trident, the four chapters in part one summarise what it is we are talking about. What *is* Trident (Chapter 1)? What is the fundamental difference between a *nuclear* weapon and any other kind of weapon (Chapter 2)? What is meant by 'deterrence' (Chapter 3) and what does nuclear deterrence mean when other countries *also* have nuclear weapons (Chapter 4)? Following on from this introductory section, the arguments in favour of Trident are grouped into five parts (and then there is a concluding part at the end).

Part two looks at the arguments that centre around the claim that we need nuclear weapons for our security. Did nuclear weapons end WWII (Chapter 5)? Have they 'kept the peace' since 1945 (Chapter 6)? Is Trident protecting us here and now (Chapter 7) and is it needed to protect us from future risks (Chapter 8)?

Part three looks at the arguments which focus on Britain's 'place in the world'. Do we need Trident to be part of NATO and to maintain our 'special relationship' with the US (Chapter 9)? Is it really independent (Chapter 10)? And does it give us our seat at the 'top table' (Chapter 11)?

Part four looks at the arguments relating to Trident in terms of the UK as a sovereign, democratic state. Does it comply with our international legal obligations (Chapter 12)? Is it safe, even if never used (Chapter 13)? What are the real costs of Trident renewal and can we afford it (Chapter 14)? Do we need it to protect jobs (Chapter 15)? And what about Scotland (Chapter 16)?

Part five then addresses the arguments that claim the UK is doing all it can to disarm, we just need to be patient (and hold on to Trident in the meantime). Is the UK committed to 'multilateral' disarmament (Chapter 17)? Has the UK already disarmed as much as it can (Chapter 18)? And even if we got rid of Trident, would it have any effect on other nuclear weapon states (Chapter 19)?

And finally, in part six, we address the set of arguments that say you can't 'disinvent' the bomb, so we need to learn to live with it, however awful that may be (Chapter 20). This includes the claim that Labour would be 'unelectable' if it opposed Trident (Chapter 21), the moral arguments (Chapter 22) and the claim that opposing Trident is not living in the 'real world' (Chapter 23).

In brief, the main arguments for and against Trident and the chapters in which they are covered are as follows:

The main arguments made for and against Trident:

Chapters 1 & 2

FOR	The awesome destructive power of Trident is what makes it effective as a deterrent.
AGAINST	It is a Weapon of Mass Destruction with unacceptable humanitarian consequences.

Chapters 3 & 4

FOR	It is a deterrent and will never be used as a weapon. Having it prevents others using it.
AGAINST	A deterrent is a weapon that will sooner or later be used as a weapon.

Chapter 5	
FOR	Nuclear weapons forced Japan to surrender and ended WWII, saving lives as a result.
AGAINST	The bombing of Hiroshima and Nagasaki was unnecessary and unjustified.
Chapter 6	
FOR	Nuclear weapons have kept the peace since 1945 and prevented WWII.
AGAINST	There is no hard evidence that they have ever 'worked' as a deterrent.
Chapter 7	
FOR	Nuclear weapons are essential to Britain's security in the 21st century.
AGAINST	Nuclear weapons serve no military purpose and do not defend us from 21st century threats.
Chapter 8	
FOR	It is an insurance policy against future unknown risks.
AGAINST	Trident will be increasingly vulnerable and only makes the UK and the world less safe.
Chapter 9	
FOR	We have a duty to share the nuclear burden with the US and to play our part in NATO.
AGAINST	US nuclear weapons do not protect the UK either. NATO nuclear policy makes the world less safe.
Chapter 10	
FOR	Trident gives the UK an independent deterrent in case the US cannot be relied upon.
AGAINST	Trident is not independent from the US.
Chapter 11	
FOR	Trident gives the UK a seat at the top table and status in the world.
AGAINST	The UK does not need Trident to be a key player in the world and would be more respected without it.
Chapter 12	
FOR	The UK can renew Trident without reneging on its international commitments.
AGAINST	Trident is illegal under international law and renewing Trident violates NPT obligations.

Chapter 13

FOR It is kept safe and out of harm's way with little risk.

AGAINST There is a large and increasing risk of accident, miscalculation or unauthorised use.

Chapter 14

FOR The costs are affordable and justified, and do not adversely affect other government spending.

AGAINST The costs are huge and take funds away from other much-needed government programmes.

Chapter 15

FOR Trident provides much needed jobs in shipbuilding and nuclear engineering that cannot be replaced if lost.

AGAINST Jobs are needed for decommissioning Trident but also for developing high tech alternative energy sources and meeting other social needs.

Chapter 16

FOR Scotland is part of the UK and Trident will remain based at Faslane.

AGAINST Scottish opposition to Trident should be taken seriously and is a significant obstacle to renewing Trident.

Chapter 17

FOR The UK is committed to a multilateral approach to nuclear disarmament.

AGAINST The UK continues to block multilateral disarmament because it is not really serious about it.

Chapter 18

FOR The UK has already disarmed to the barest minimum needed for deterrence.

AGAINST The UK has removed obsolete weapons but renewing Trident will be a further upgrade to UK capabilities.

Chapter 19

FOR There's no point in the UK disarming further because it will have no effect on other nuclear states.

AGAINST If the UK took a lead it could break the deadlock on disarmament and speed up the process towards elimination.

Chapter 20

FOR Nuclear weapons are here to stay and they cannot be 'uninvented'.

AGAINST Eliminating nuclear weapons is doable and there is no need to hold onto things that are no longer needed.

Chapter 21

FOR Opposing Trident will make the Labour party unelectable.

AGAINST If the public are given an informed choice, they will choose to cancel Trident.

CHAPTER 22

FOR Nuclear weapons prevent war, which is a greater evil, so they are morally justified.

AGAINST Trident is morally indefensible.

Chapter 23

FOR Nuclear weapons are part of the real world and those who think otherwise are living in cloud cuckoo land.

AGAINST The real world is one in which the majority of countries oppose nuclear weapons. No country can be secure unless all are secure.

Each chapter investigates these issues in detail and at the end of each chapter is a summary of the conclusions reached. At the end of the book is a summary of all the chapters (Chapter 24). For anyone looking for even more information, there is a detailed bibliography of relevant books and other materials, including websites with vast amounts of relevant information. These can all be accessed through the dedicated website for this book: www.TheTruthAboutTrident.com.

PART ONE

The Basics

CHAPTER 1

What is Trident?

'TRIDENT' IS SHORT-HAND for the UK's nuclear weapons system. This system consists of three main components: nuclear warheads that explode when detonated, the missiles that carry the nuclear warheads to their target, and the submarines that launch the missiles from a secret location under the sea. Each of these components in turn consists of a number of sub-components that all together make up the weapon 'system' as a whole.

We know a great deal about some of the components and sub-components that make up the Trident system, but some key information is still a closely guarded secret. We know, for instance, that the UK currently has approximately 215 nuclear warheads,[1] of which 120 are considered 'operationally available'.[2] We know that the UK has access to 58 Trident D5 missiles that are leased from the US naval stockpile in King's Bay, Georgia.[3] We know the submarines have 16 missile tubes each (because these are visible in photos), but the government has said a maximum of 8 missiles are currently deployed on any of the submarines.[4]

We are told by the government that at any one time, there is at least one submarine on 'continuous at-sea deterrence' (CASD) patrol with up to 40 nuclear warheads. This would mean that the 8 missiles on board must have an average of 5 warheads each.[5] We know that each patrol lasts for 2–3 months, during which time a second submarine is being readied for the next patrol, one submarine is on 'R&R' being scrubbed up from the previous patrol and one submarine is in dry-dock for maintenance and repairs.

Theoretically it would be possible to have all four submarines fully loaded with their nuclear weapons, at sea and able to launch them all at the same time. In practice, one submarine is always out of action and would not be deployable even in a crisis. Of the three remaining submarines, only one is considered 'operational' by the MOD at any given time, although at least one more can be made operational in a matter of hours or days.[6]

How powerful are the Trident warheads?

What we don't know from official government sources is how much explosive power is contained in each nuclear warhead on board those Trident submarines. Most nuclear experts believe these are 100 KT[7] warheads of similar design to the US W76 warhead.[8] We know much more about the US warheads because this information is publicly available. The W76 is a 100 KT warhead deployed on most of the US Trident missiles. Some nuclear experts believe that despite the enormous amounts of money being poured into nuclear weapons research and development at Aldermaston, the UK Trident missiles carry warheads that are not just similar to the US W76 warhead but actually *are* the W76 warheads.[9]

According to the 'Rifkind Doctrine' of the late 1980s,[10] the UK's Trident submarines needed to be able to undertake a 'sub-strategic' role that might involve firing a 'demonstration shot' or destroying a more limited military target with a smaller nuclear warhead. For this reason, warheads of much smaller yield were tested at the US underground testing site in Nevada as late as March 1989, just prior to the Comprehensive Test Ban coming into effect and ending underground tests.[11] The official position since 2007, however, is that Trident has only a 'strategic' role and therefore it is unlikely that smaller yield warheads are still deployed, but that is not known for sure.[12]

If a Trident submarine is loaded with 40 warheads of 100 KT each, that would give it the firepower equivalent to four megatonnes of TNT (4 million tonnes) in total, or more than 250 times the firepower unleashed on Hiroshima. This is more than the total firepower of all the bombs dropped during WWII, including both Hiroshima and Nagasaki – all on a single submarine.[13]

What would be the effects of a 100 KT explosion?

The Hiroshima bomb was estimated to be in the range of 12,000–18,000 tonnes of TNT (12–18 KT), or roughly 1,000 times as powerful as the largest conventional bomb in the US arsenal today.[14] The total number killed by the Hiroshima bomb is not known. The original estimate of 68,000 dead and a similar number injured was based on a random survey of households in 1946. However this did not take into account up to 20,000 Korean prisoners of war and an unknown number of refugees from other Japanese cities known to be in the city at that time.

Many of those who were injured by the Hiroshima blast died subsequently from radiation sickness and fatal injuries, in part because medical facilities were destroyed and very little was known about the dangers of radiation poisoning. It is difficult to know how many of the subsequent deaths in Hiroshima should be attributed to the atomic bomb as opposed to other causes. Most sources now use the figure of 140,000 as the total number killed by the Hiroshima bomb, although the city of Hiroshima maintains an official register of deaths from the atomic bomb right up to the present day, and that register now has more than 200,000 names.[15]

The atom bomb which was dropped on Nagasaki was of a different design and estimated to be slightly more powerful at 20 KT. The total death count was initially estimated at 60,000, or slightly less than at Hiroshima. A much larger number were injured but more of these people survived than did in Hiroshima. Other differences between the death tolls in the two cities have to do with weather conditions, the terrain, the type of buildings, the population density of the city and where the bomb was dropped in relation to where people were at the time.

If a single Trident warhead has a yield of 100 KT, it is 6.6 times the size of the Hiroshima bomb. The scale of the destruction and the number of people who would be killed or injured from such an explosion is difficult to determine and depends on many factors, including those just mentioned above. There is not a linear relationship between the size of a nuclear explosion and the numbers killed or area destroyed. The biggest factor has to do with whether the bomb is detonated at, or near, the ground or higher up in the atmosphere (see next chapter). Nevertheless, based on what we know about Hiroshima, it is clear that the effects of a single Trident warhead landing on, or above a city, would be devastating.

The nuclear fireball

The detonation of a nuclear weapon creates a massive fireball as the nuclear chain reaction, or 'fission', breaks down the atoms of uranium and/or plutonium that are the initial fuel of the bomb. The temperature inside this fireball rises to tens of millions of degrees Centigrade. This is hotter than the interior of the sun and thousands of times hotter than a conventional explosion.[16] Inside the fireball, these temperatures trigger the thermonuclear 'fusion' reaction that creates even more destructive energy as atoms of hydrogen are fused into helium and other by-products. The fireball of a 100 KT warhead is a sphere approximately 500 metres (1,500 ft) across in all directions.

If the fireball is 500 metres across and the centre of it is more than 250 metres above the ground, this is called an 'airburst'. With the whole of the fireball in the air, very little else is consumed by the fireball other than the nuclear fuels contained in the bomb and small quantities of oxygen and other gases in the air. If the fireball is detonated below this height, this is considered a 'groundburst'. Everything within that sphere is then turned into radioactive by-products as a result of the explosion, and this is a critical factor which we shall explore in greater detail in the next chapter.

From a basic airburst explosion, already more than 300 different radioactive isotopes are created from the exploding uranium and/or plutonium.[17] Many more varieties of radioactive material may be additionally created from a groundburst explosion, depending on what was on the ground at that precise time and place. If the target of a groundburst explosion was a nuclear missile silo, nuclear weapons store or other nuclear facility, any nuclear warheads or other nuclear materials – as well as living creatures – that end up within reach of the fireball are themselves going to be irradiated and added to the total fireball and subsequent release of radioactive by-products.

Heat and blast effects

Conventional explosives cause death, injuries and destruction of property from the heat and blast of the explosion. This rips through buildings, sets fire to anything that burns and throws shrapnel, bits of building and other debris through the air, all of which is highly dangerous to anything or anybody that may be nearby. A nuclear explosion causes all these same effects, in addition to the unique effects of radiation, which are discussed in the next chapter.

At a distance of 4 km from a 100 KT nuclear explosion, temperatures are still high enough to set papers and other flammable materials alight.[18] Therefore fires are an enormous hazard in the aftermath of a nuclear explosion even at great distances from ground zero. In Hiroshima, the entire city centre was burnt to the ground and many of the injuries suffered by the inhabitants were the result of burns.

Blast is normally measured in pounds per square inch (psi) of 'overpressure.'[19] Ten psi of overpressure is enough to damage lungs and cause widespread fatalities and 20 psi is enough to pull down a heavily reinforced concrete building.[20] Near the nuclear fireball, the shock wave which is created by the explosion reaches 200 psi of overpressure, with winds of more than 2,000 mph, enough to flatten and kill anything, even the most heavily reinforced concrete bunker.[21] At 1 km (0.6 miles) from a 100 KT blast, the overpressure is 20 psi, which is lethal for human beings and still capable of considerable damage to buildings. At 2 km, the overpressure still reaches 5 psi, with windspeeds over 100 mph and up to 50% fatalities.[22]

Nuclear winter and nuclear famine

Another product of a nuclear explosion is the dust and soot that rises up as a result of fires and the intense heat created. Most atmospheric tests took place on Pacific islands, barren atolls or in the deserts of western US, central Australia or Siberia. Under these conditions, even groundburst explosions would not be expected to cause major fires and therefore the soot content has been minimal. If a nuclear explosion took place over dense forest or a densely populated city, however, fires could be expected to burn out of control for some days over a large area. This happened in Hiroshima and Nagasaki as well as in places like Dresden and Tokyo where conventional explosives were used in huge quantities to create 'firestorms'.

During the 1980s there was concern that an all-out nuclear war between the Soviet Union and the West could push so much soot into the atmosphere that it would lead to a 'nuclear winter' – a lowering of global temperatures, causing widespread famine, disease and death of large numbers of people not already killed by the nuclear weapons themselves or the after-effects of radiation.

The US and Russia each had an estimated 2,500 MT worth of TNT in their nuclear arsenals at that time and climate scientists estimated that an all-out nuclear war would therefore put about 150 million tonnes of soot into the atmosphere. Using complex computer modelling of the earth's climate, they estimated that that much soot could lower the earth's average temperature by as much as 8.5 degrees C and reduce annual rainfall globally by as much as 1.4 mm. This in turn would reduce growing seasons worldwide and mean that some key grain-producing regions like Iowa and Ukraine would remain below freezing even in the height of summer and thus unable to grow anything for up to two years.[23]

Using the same modelling techniques, scientists then tried in the 1990s to estimate the climatic effects of just 100 Hiroshima-sized bombs (ie. just 15 of the 40 100 KT warheads on a single Trident submarine), for instance in a regional war between India and Pakistan.

Given the population densities in those two countries and the vulnerability of crops to radiation damage, it was concluded that even a 'small-scale' nuclear war in that region would have hugely devastating consequences for all the countries across the whole Northern Hemisphere and could lead to the death of over two billion people.[24]

Further studies have looked at the effects of 'limited' forms of nuclear warfare, for instance the launching of nuclear weapons from a single Trident submarine. Dr Philip Webber, chair of Scientists for Global Responsibility, has estimated that the simultaneous detonation of 4 megatonnes of TNT, roughly the total firepower of one Trident submarine, could produce between 10 and 38 million tonnes of soot, sufficient to cause a cooling of the earth by 1.5–3 degrees C and a shortening of growing seasons by 10–30 days over a five-year period.[25]

How this might affect global food supplies is hard to estimate, but the implications are clear. Even a comparatively 'limited' nuclear war would cause devastating and long-lasting climactic effects. A major all-out nuclear war would endanger the entire planet.

Targeting Trident

Trident is currently 'de-targeted', meaning the missiles are deployed on submarines without specific targeting instructions. These instructions, however, are very easily and quickly assigned to the missiles once a decision is made to do so. There are two types of target for Trident warheads. 'Counterforce' targets are basically military installations, specifically nuclear missile sites. 'Countervalue' targets are cities or other civilian facilities.

Since the early 1960s, the UK's nuclear weapons have been aimed at countervalue targets in Russia (or rather the Soviet Union, as it was), and specifically at Moscow, with the aim of inflicting 'unacceptable damage' should they ever be used. Unacceptable damage was defined initially as being able to destroy 50% of the buildings and kill 50% of the people in Moscow and in at least four other Russian cities. This was later amended to 40% of buildings and 40% of the population. There have been many discussions and proposals within the British government as to exactly what does or does not constitute 'unacceptable damage', but this basic concept, known as the 'Moscow criterion' apparently still stands and is easily met by present-day targeting assumptions (see below).

Since the 1980s there have been various attempts to tone down the Moscow criterion to make it sound less like mass murder. The 'master' of deterrence theory, the late Sir Michael Quinlan, redefined the Moscow criterion in 1980 as destruction of 'key aspects of Soviet power' rather than the destruction of Moscow and the killing of half its civilian population per se.[26] In 2012, the then Defence Secretary Nick Harvey criticised the MOD's ambitions to 'flatten Moscow' as outmoded but was told that the MOD's aim was 'holding at risk what any potential adversary leadership would value most… In the Russian case, Moscow of course always represented the very centre of state power.'[27]

Altogether, there are four possible target scenarios for Trident to be used against Russia.

- The first would be a 'counterforce' attack against Russian nuclear missiles and delivery systems in order to prevent a retaliatory strike. Although the UK does not have enough nuclear weapons to destroy all the Russian nuclear weapons completely, Trident could be used as part of a massive US counterforce attack against Russian nuclear missiles.
- The second target scenario would be to aim Trident at other purely military targets, such as military command bunkers as well as airfields, missile defences, submarine and naval bases, etc.
- The third set of targets would be military but also including civilian centres of power and control. The revised 'Moscow criterion' seems to fit this scenario most closely, aiming at government buildings in Moscow as well as military command and control centres.
- The final set of targets would be purely 'countervalue', aimed at destruction of Moscow and other large cities.

John Ainslie, in his paper *If Britain Fired Trident,*[28] drew up a list of possible targets in and around Moscow based on publicly available documents in the National Archive and using targeting assumption three above. This list included ten key government buildings in the centre of Moscow, ten key military command centres in outer Moscow and a further 20 military bunkers and other likely military targets on the outskirts of Moscow, for a total of 40 targets for the 40 nuclear warheads on a single Trident submarine.

In fact a nuclear attack by the UK, were it to take place, would almost certainly involve all the warheads on at least two submarines if not three, since these are what the UK considers as 'operationally available' warheads.[29] Such an attack would therefore involve up to 120 nuclear warheads of what we are assuming to be around 100 KT each.

Not all these warheads would necessarily reach their targets, however, since Russia has an Anti-Ballistic Missile (ABM) defence shield around Moscow that would attempt to shoot down incoming missiles before they landed. A certain number of warheads would be expected to be duds and fail to detonate, and there could be other errors and problems that would reduce the total number of actual explosions.

If, however, we assume that 40 Trident warheads hit government and military targets in and around Moscow, what would be the impact? John Ainslie's paper goes into great detail about the impact of fires across the city, destruction of power stations, carbon monoxide poisoning in underground bomb shelters, damage to schools and hospitals, collapsing skyscrapers and chaos of fleeing civilians trying to evacuate and fatal levels of radioactive fallout in different parts of the greater Moscow region, depending on weather conditions. Overall, he estimates that out of Moscow's total population of 11.5 million, nearly five and a half million people would be killed outright and more than one million injured from an attack by one Trident submarine aimed solely at government and military targets. Physical destruction would be severe and long-term radiation effects would continue to cause cancers and other fatal diseases for many years to come.

Under what conditions would Trident ever be used?

The UK states that Trident would only ever be used as a last resort in self-defence. This could mean either in a so-called 'first strike' before any hostile nuclear weapons have been launched against the UK or an ally, or in a retaliatory 'second strike' after one or more nuclear weapons have landed on the UK or an ally. In the first case, let us imagine that the so-called deterrent failed and that Russia was either about to invade, or had already started to invade, a NATO member such as Poland, with their conventional forces. No nuclear weapons have been used yet, but with nothing else to stop Russia from steamrolling across Europe, NATO decides to respond by destroying as much of Russia's war-fighting capability as possible in an all-out nuclear attack.

In such a scenario, the role of the UK's Trident missiles would be exactly as described above. Their job is to 'take out Moscow' as the UK's contribution to a massive NATO assault which would involve US Trident submarines, US Minuteman Inter-Continental Ballistic Missiles (ICBMs) and free-fall nuclear bombs dropped from long-range warplanes from US bases across Europe as well as from mainland USA.

The second set of scenarios in which Trident might be used involves the so-called 'second strike' or retaliatory strike, after the UK or an ally has already been attacked with nuclear weapons. In this case, the UK might be all but destroyed already and there might be no functioning government even to make the decision to launch Trident. Submarine commanders would be left to open the sealed orders from the Prime Minister to know what to do next. Alternatively, perhaps only one or two cities would have been hit with nuclear weapons or perhaps an ally, such as Poland, has been hit but not the UK.

In this second set of scenarios, it is hard to imagine what the point of launching Trident missiles would be apart from as a form of revenge. The 'deterrent' would have failed by that point and the risk of all-out nuclear war, and with it the destruction of human civilisation as we know it, would be extremely high if not already underway. All communications would have been disrupted; no one would likely have any idea what cities were hit, how many people were dead or still alive or what nuclear weaponry was still remaining. Nevertheless, the whole concept of nuclear deterrence, as we shall see in Chapter 3, rests exactly on this scenario.

When David Cameron says that he would press the button 'under certain circumstances', these are the circumstances he is talking about. Unless the UK is ready and willing to launch Trident in retaliation for a nuclear attack against the UK or any of its allies, Trident is not considered to be a credible deterrent. Therefore it is this second scenario in which Trident is primarily designed to be used – as retaliation for a nuclear attack, whether or not such retaliation would make any political or military sense at that point.

Other possible targets

Since 1998, the UK has given what are known as 'negative security assurances' to every country that does not have nuclear weapons, saying that the UK will only use its nuclear weapons against other nuclear weapons states or states believed to be acquiring nuclear weapons.[30] The UK government has also stated repeatedly that it would only use nuclear weapons as a last resort in self-defence.

This means at present that UK nuclear weapons could in theory only be used against the US, France, China, Russia, India, Pakistan, Israel or North Korea were any of these countries to attack the UK. It is unlikely that Trident would be used against the US or France, with both of whom the UK has close relations and shares nuclear secrets and nuclear technologies. Indeed it is doubtful that the UK would be *able* to launch a Trident missile at the US, given that the missiles themselves are US-made and US-owned, together with the software required to fire them (see Chapter 10).

China has a much smaller nuclear arsenal than either the US or Russia, but apart from Russia, China is the only other state against which Trident might realistically be used, were it to decide to attack the UK. India, Pakistan, Israel and North Korea have nuclear weapons, but currently not the means for these to reach the UK. Therefore it would be unlikely that the UK would use Trident in 'self-defence' against one of these countries (see Chapter 12).

Summary

Trident is a nuclear weapon system capable of causing death and destruction on a scale unparalleled in human history. A single Trident warhead can produce temperatures of tens of millions of degrees Centigrade and a shock wave sufficient to flatten skyscrapers, together with everything else that may be standing, or alive, within 500 metres of the blast.

At a distance of 2 km, the blast is still sufficient to bring down buildings and cause many casualties, with wind speeds at over 100mph. At a distance of 4 km from an exploding Trident warhead, the heat is still intense enough to set newspapers on fire.

Each Trident submarine carries on board up to 40 warheads, ready to launch if given the order, 24 hours a day, 365 days a year. Launching all 40 warheads could push millions of tons of soot into the atmosphere and seriously affect global food supplies.

The UK considers three Trident submarines, or a total of 120 Trident warheads, 'operationally available'. The consequences of launching all 120 warheads or the equivalent of more than 800 Hiroshima bombs, would have a devastating impact not only on the country being hit, but also on the entire ecosystem of the planet.

Trident is currently 'de-targeted'. However the missiles can be easily 're-targeted' and traditionally they have been targeted at Moscow. Even if the targets are a combination of military and government buildings and bunkers, aimed at destroying 'key aspects of Russian state power', the result is likely to be over five million civilians killed from the missiles of one Trident submarine. Trident could also be targeted at China, either to destroy cities and/or military targets.

UK policy is to use Trident only against another nuclear weapon state threatening the UK. This is unlikely to be the US or France. Although North Korea, India, Pakistan and Israel have nuclear weapons, none can reach the UK, so it would be difficult to imagine a scenario in which any of these countries would be targeted by Trident in 'self-defence'.

CHAPTER 2

What is Radiation?

THE BLAST AND heat effects of a nuclear explosion are very similar to those of a conventional weapon, just multiplied many times in scale because a nuclear explosion is so much more powerful than the most powerful conventional explosions. Even the environmental effects are not qualitatively different, since extensive fire-bombing of cities with conventional weapons would also push equivalent amounts of soot into the atmosphere, potentially affecting global climate in a similar way.

But nuclear weapons also produce short-term and long-term effects from ionising radiation which are qualitatively different to any effect produced by other types of weapon. These have huge importance in terms of the impact of nuclear weapons beyond the immediate point of detonation, not only in terms of spreading death and injury far and wide geographically, but also spreading it across time to future generations.

The main forms of ionising radiation are alpha, beta and gamma rays, and also neutrons. These are produced in large quantities from a nuclear explosion. All ionising radiations increase the chemical reactivity of the materials they irradiate, by altering the electrical charge of (or 'ionising') their atoms. In living things, these chemical effects can be very damaging.

Alpha radiation comes from helium ions (with two protons and two neutrons) released during decay of uranium and many of its decay products. Alpha particles penetrate matter very poorly – a single sheet of paper can provide effective shielding so external exposure has very little effect on health. But any uranium or plutonium swallowed or inhaled can reach body tissues where their released alpha particles can penetrate, seriously damaging cells in the immediate vicinity.

Beta rays are electrons formed during radioactive decay. They penetrate more than alpha particles but are still particularly damaging if the radioactive source materials are inhaled or swallowed.

The most penetrating and damaging external forms of ionising radiation are the gamma rays. Gamma rays are a form of electromagnetic radiation.

They can behave either like waves or like particles (when they are referred to as 'high energy photons').

When ionising radiation is absorbed by a given mass of material, the received 'dose' can be measured in physical units called 'Grays' (Gy).[31] But the amount of biological damage varies widely according to the type of radiation (alpha, beta or gamma), and to the various organs affected, because these all have different rates of sensitivity to radiation. A Gy of alpha rays inside the body (for example from inhaled uranium or radon) is reckoned to be 20 times more dangerous than the same dose of external gamma rays.

A different measurement, the 'Sievert' (Sv)[32] is therefore used to indicate the biological effect of a given radiation dose. One milli-Gray of gamma rays, for instance, is 'equivalent' to 1 milli-Sievert, but one milli-Gray of alpha rays is equivalent to 20 milli-Sieverts. For humans, the consequences of most concern from even relatively low doses (below 0.1 Sv) are the increased risks of cancer, and of inheritable changes affecting offspring.

Effects of radiation on the human body

Acute radiation poisoning can result from sudden exposure to doses of 1 Sv or more – for example from the first flash of a nuclear detonation. The clinical effects are predictable and depend on the dose and whether the whole or only part of the body was exposed. As the main form of radiation will be high-energy photons (gamma rays), shielding in the hollows of hills (which occurred at Nagasaki) or inside buildings which remain standing can be partially effective in reducing exposure.

All those receiving more than 8 Sv will die, and progressively higher doses will kill more quickly. About half those exposed to 4 to 5 Sv will die after a month or so. The symptoms are progressively of bone marrow failure (anaemia and bleeding), severe diarrhoea and vomiting, to severe brain damage at very high doses resulting in seizures, coma and rapid death.

Up to half the people exposed to between 1 and 2 Sv will develop relatively mild nausea and slight headache after a few hours, lasting a day or so; but after a week to a month their blood cell counts fall giving them temporarily a tendency to bruise and bleed easily after mild injury, and to get infections more readily. About 5% may die of complications. Doses of less than 1 Sv are likely to cause short-term hair-loss or long-term eye cataracts.

Certain radioactive isotopes have particular effects on certain organs of the body. Bone-marrow and lungs are particularly vulnerable to ionising radiation, as are the reproductive organs and thyroid glands.

Strontium-90 is taken up selectively by bones as strontium is chemically very similar to calcium. This has a half-life of 28.8 years and emits beta particles which, being more penetrating than alpha particles, can reach the blood-cell forming tissues of the bone marrow. A large-scale study of baby teeth in the US in the 1960s found that children born in 1963 had 50 times as much strontium-90 in their teeth than children born in 1950. This was attributed to the atmospheric nuclear testing which took place in the South Pacific during the late '50s and early '60s.[33]

Following the Partial Test Ban Treaty of 1963, which ended most atmospheric testing, the levels of Strontium-90 began to drop. Children born in 1968 thus had 50% less strontium-90 in their teeth than those born in 1963. Although further studies of baby teeth have not been conducted since, they should continue to show a steady decline in levels of strontium-90 as it continues its radioactive decay.

What has been studied more recently is the incidence of cancer among adults whose baby teeth had varying levels of strontium-90 in the 1960s. Those who later died of cancer before reaching the age of 50 were found to have twice the level of strontium-90 in their baby teeth at an early age as compared to those who had not died of cancer by the same age. This suggests that the strontium-90 from nuclear fallout in the 1950s that had found its way into children's teeth in the 1960s had also increased their likelihood of getting cancer by the 2010s.[34]

Iodine-131 (half-life eight days) gets into milk from cows grazing on contaminated land, and represents a thyroid cancer risk to children drinking it. Adults appear to be at much lower risk. Administering normal (non-radioactive) iodine can provide some protection but has to be given very early. Ironically, a standard treatment for thyroid cancer is high-dose radio-iodine.

Caesium is chemically very similar to potassium, so its radioactive isotope caesium-137 – half-life 30 years – is also of biological and clinical significance. Most of it decays by beta emission but it also emits gamma rays. It gets deposited on the soil and taken up by plants and crops, entering the human food chain. Potassium and caesium are widely distributed through the body and are integral minerals essential for all cells and get washed out of the body in a matter of days.

Other radioactive isotopes produced by nuclear fission include uranium-237, neptunian-239, sodium-24, manganese-56, silicon-31, aluminium-28 and chlorine-38. Tritium (H-3) has a half-life of 12.3 years and is produced in very large quantities by a fusion ('hydrogen') bomb. Fusion bombs are triggered by a fission reaction to create the very high temperatures required for fusion to occur. Thus most nuclear weapons today are a combination of fission bombs which then trigger the fusion explosion and deposit fission products in the fallout.

Airburst and groundburst

The bombs dropped on Hiroshima and Nagasaki were both detonated at an altitude of about 1,500 feet above the ground. As was mentioned in the last chapter, this is known as an 'airburst' and it causes the maximum death and destruction over the widest possible area. If the bomb is left to reach the ground (or nearly reach the ground) before exploding, more or less half the impact goes into the ground rather than being spread out across a wider area.

If the target is a city and the aim is to cause maximum damage, the weapon is most likely to be exploded above ground as an airburst. A large amount of initial radiation is released by an airburst explosion, but the amount of radioactive fallout downwind of the explosion is much less than for a groundburst explosion, because less earth and other materials from the ground are consumed by the nuclear fireball.

A groundburst detonation means that large quantities of earth and whatever else happens to be on the earth (ie buildings, people, etc) are engulfed in the nuclear fireball and become irradiated. This additional matter creates many more radioactive particles of many more types and these are carried up into the mushroom cloud where they are dispersed with the wind and eventually come down as radioactive fallout.

While a nuclear strike against a city is likely to be an airburst and thus have comparatively less radioactive fallout, a nuclear strike against a military target such as a hardened nuclear missile silo or command bunker is likely to be a groundburst and thus involve much higher levels of fallout.

Radiation effects from a 100 KT groundburst

Anyone within 1,500 metres of a 100 KT nuclear detonation is likely to receive an immediate dose of radiation well in excess of 100 Sv as a result of the 'initial' radiation effects of the nuclear explosion.[35] This is thousands of times more than a lethal dose of radiation but if they are that near, they will have been killed already from the heat and blast of the explosion. Within a radius of 2,500 metres, the instant dose of radiation is still in excess of 3 Sv, but this then falls off quickly to levels of 0.3 Sv at 3,000 metres. This is the initial, or 'instant' dose of radiation.

At distances further than 1,500 metres from the fireball, the *accumulated* dose of radiation starts to have the greater effect on human health. A dose of 3 Sv in one hour may not be fatal, but over a 4-hour period, the continued exposure to that level of radiation, even though it is rapidly diminishing in strength, almost certainly will be fatal. A dose of 0.3 Sv at a further distance may not be fatal, but again, if the dose is sustained over 24-hours or even longer, it can nonetheless prove deadly.

At even further distances, there is the 'delayed' radiation which travels with the wind and comes down as rain or snow at some distance from the nuclear fireball. In the case of a groundburst explosion, the radiation from this fallout can still be at lethal levels even hundreds of miles from the explosion. During one of the largest nuclear tests in the Pacific, islanders 330 miles from the detonation of a 15 MT hydrogen bomb received accumulated doses of radiation that caused birth defects, leukaemias and other fatal cancers.[36]

Then there is the global radioactive fallout resulting from the smallest of radioactive particles making their way into the upper atmosphere where they may traverse the globe for years before coming back down to earth. By this time, the levels of radioactivity are much lower, but alpha particles of very long-lasting isotopes can get into the food chain and be ingested into the human body.

Some 26 years after the Chernobyl nuclear accident in 1986, more than 250,000 sheep in Wales and Cumbria, more than 1,000 miles away from where the accident happened, were still considered unfit for human consumption because of the levels of Caesium-137 they contained.[37] Caesium-137 contamination is now a major problem in the areas of Japan affected by the Fukishima accident in 2011.

Impact of small doses of radiation

The main risk from lower doses of radiation, which may have no immediately apparent effects, is the delayed onset of leukaemia (especially in children and occurring up to ten years after exposure); or of cancers (the onset of which starts after about five years but the risks are life-long). Even very elderly survivors have an increased risk of cancer, a prospect which may have haunted them throughout their lives. It should be recognised that the psychological effects of knowingly being exposed even to relatively low doses of ionising radiation can be profound – and are none the less significant for it.

While it is impossible to predict whether an individual person will get cancer or other complications as a result of sudden exposure to a dose of 0.1 Sv, more people within a given population exposed to 0.1 Sv will get cancer than in a similar population *not* exposed to 0.1 Sv. This implies that *any* increase in exposure to radiation will increase the likelihood of cancer and other diseases.

According to one study, as many as 2.4 million people could eventually die worldwide from cancers and leukaemias as a result of the atmospheric testing in the '50s and '60s – ten times as many as died from the bombs on Hiroshima and Nagasaki themselves.[38] That is a hugely controversial figure if it is true. It would mean that the numbers killed from cancers and leukaemias as a result of the normal radioactive discharges from civil nuclear power stations would also be correspondingly large and create huge insurance problems for the nuclear industry.

What we do know is that the cancer rates in Hiroshima and Nagasaki are higher than the average for Japan as a whole even today, 70 years after the bombs fell and long after both cities have been re-built into the thriving cities they are today.[39]

Summary

Nuclear weapons are not just very large conventional weapons. They produce effects which no other type of weapon has ever produced. It is the ionising radiation that potentially causes the most serious and long lasting effects of a nuclear explosion. This is especially the case if it is a groundburst explosion aimed at a hardened military or government target.

Mild radiation poisoning destroys blood cells and damages the genetic material in human cells. More severe forms of radiation poisoning destroy the linings of stomach and intestines, cause internal haemorrhages, loss of electrolyte balance, and heart failure. Death from radiation poisoning can take from a few days to several weeks, and beyond a certain dose of radiation, even the most modern medical treatments are unlikely to be effective.

Groundburst nuclear explosions produce large amounts of radioactive fallout which can travel hundreds of miles downwind. The smallest radioactive particles rise up into the upper atmosphere and are dispersed across the entire globe. These small radioactive particles can still be fatal if they enter the food chain and are ingested by humans.

Radioactive isotopes produced by atmospheric nuclear testing in the Pacific in the 1950s were found in the teeth of children as far away as the USA. There are no definitive scientific conclusions on the effects of relatively small doses of radiation, however some medical professionals have suggested that as many as 2.4 million worldwide will have died from leukaemia and other cancers as a direct result of radiation from those nuclear tests.

This means that if Trident were ever used as a weapon of war, it would not only cause cruel and unnecessary suffering to those immediately affected by high doses of radioactivity near to, and downwind of, the explosions. It would also, especially if used as a groundburst weapon to target hardened command and control bunkers, cause large amounts of radioactive materials to enter the earth's upper atmosphere and cause leukaemias and other cancers to people hundreds and thousands of miles away.

CHAPTER 3

What is Deterrence?

IN HER STATEMENT to the Third International Conference on the Humanitarian Impacts of Nuclear Weapons, held in Vienna in December 2014, the official UK spokesperson, Susan Le Jeune d'Allegeershecque, told delegates from 158 other countries that the devastating humanitarian consequences that could result from the use of nuclear weapons was 'not new' but was indeed the reason why these weapons were so effective as a deterrent. In fact, the most common response to the humanitarian concerns raised in the previous chapter is 'of course the UK's nuclear weapons would never be used, they are merely a deterrent'.[40]

> The UK's nuclear weapons are not designed for military use during conflict but instead to deter and prevent nuclear blackmail and acts of aggression against our vital interests that cannot be countered by other means... ('The Future of the UK's Nuclear Deterrent' White Paper, 2006)

The government indeed prefers to refer to Trident, not as a weapons system at all, but as 'the deterrent', as if this categorically defines what Trident is. But Trident is not 'a deterrent' in and of itself. Even the BBC acknowledges that in its internal guidance to journalists.[41] Trident is a weapon system that the government *hopes* will act as a deterrent and will never actually be used as a weapon. Whether there is evidence that it has acted as a deterrent up until now is the subject of following chapters. The question at this stage is what does deterrence actually mean?

According to the US Department of Defence, deterrence is 'the prevention from action by fear of the consequences. Deterrence is a state of mind brought about by the existence of a credible threat of unacceptable counteraction.'[42] In other words, deterrence is a psychological term, not a military term. It is about trying to create a sense of fear that you hope will convince someone that they don't actually want to do something they might otherwise choose to do.

As a strategy for controlling someone else's behaviour, deterrence relies on threatening that person with some form of punishment if they do something you don't want them to do. Leaving aside whether coercion through fear is morally palatable, 'successful' deterrence means the punishment never has to be carried out because the mere threat of it is sufficient to control the behaviour. 'Unsuccessful' deterrence is when the threat has to be carried out in order to control the behaviour in question.

Deterrence in everyday life

As any parent knows, deterrence as a strategy for controlling the behaviour of small children is rarely successful – and with older children even less so. Children are not easily deterred from doing what they want to do at that moment, even when they know they will have to suffer the consequences later. When deterrence *does* (apparently) work as a strategy for managing the behaviour of children, it normally does so only when:

1. The actual punishment has been carried out recently enough or frequently enough for the experience of that punishment to be vividly present when the threat is made.
2. The threat is able to be carried out then and there with immediate effect.
3. There is no possibility of evading responsibility for the behaviour in question or of getting away with it undetected.

In the absence of these pre-existing conditions, parents find themselves inflicting punishments to 'teach a lesson' for the next time – assuming there *is* a next time. Whether or not the subsequent punishment is effective, the deterrence has clearly failed by that point.

These same principles also apply to the use of (legal) threats to deter criminals. Deterrence is a well-known, but highly controversial, concept in the field of criminal justice. Although the primary function of arrest and detention is to punish criminal behaviour, it is secondarily aimed at deterring further criminal behaviour. There is an extensive body of evidence to suggest that people are less likely to engage in criminal activity if they know they will be caught. However there is an equally compelling body of evidence to suggest that very few criminals are deterred by the severity of the punishment they can expect to get, much less by the mere threat of being punished.

Even the threat of death apparently does little to deter murderers. One has only to compare the murder rates of countries which still have capital punishment with those which do not to see that the correlation is entirely opposite to what the theory of deterrence would suggest.[43] Almost without exception, countries with capital punishment have *higher* murder rates, higher rates of crime generally, and higher prison populations than those countries which have abolished capital punishment. This is even the case within the United States, where some individual states retain the death penalty while other states have abolished it.

These correlations, it should be pointed out, do not prove that the death penalty increases the likelihood of murder. However, it certainly does not provide evidence to support the theory that murderers are deterred from committing murder or other crimes by being threatened with their own death.

Indeed, reoffending by people who have already served a prison sentence for an offence is commonplace. In the US, 43.3% of released prisoners are sent back to prison for another offence. In the UK, some prisons report a reconviction rate of more than 70%, with an overall national average of 53% – even higher than in the US.[44]

What this means for the criminal justice system is beyond the scope of this chapter. But what it means for deterrence theory is that criminals who know exactly what it means to be incarcerated for committing a crime appear nonetheless undeterred by the threat of being incarcerated again.

Military forms of deterrence

Deterrence in warfare is nothing new. The existence of standing armies are in and of themselves a form of deterrence, meant to warn off any potential invader by making it clear that the country stands ready and willing to inflict serious damage on any invading army. All manner of armaments and fortifications merely add to the deterrent value of being able to threaten retaliation for any attack.

Switzerland, a country of 8 million people surrounded on all sides by much larger and more powerful countries, was last invaded in 1813. Since that time, Switzerland has had mandatory conscription for all males aged 19–34 years of age as a deterrent against any possible aggressor.

Although Hitler never invaded Switzerland, it is doubtful it was the existence of the Swiss Army that deterred him. It is even more doubtful that the Swiss Army would have deterred an invasion, let alone a nuclear attack, from the Soviet Union during the Cold War. And yet the Swiss have carried on with their universal conscription in the belief that they are deterring their enemies from attacking them.

In 1914, the deterrent that was designed to prevent war in Europe took the form of a massive network of military alliances that threatened to drag the whole of Europe into a suicidal war if any one country were so foolish as to attack another one. The deterrence in that case failed spectacularly and Europe was quickly locked into a devastating war which took many millions of lives.

Following the devastation of WWI, the French began construction of the most advanced set of fortifications ever known – designed to inflict heavy damage on any advancing armies from Germany and thus hoping to deter them from attacking. The Maginot Line consisted of 22 underground fortresses, tank traps, tunnels, rail links and 500 smaller buildings constructed along the 280 mile border with Germany. One quarter of France's entire army was stationed along this line and yet it turned out to be completely useless against Hitler's invasion as he simply went around it in May 1940.

The one certainty that can be gleaned from all these examples of real-life deterrence at all these different levels right up to international war is that deterrence, even if it may appear to work in some cases, is never guaranteed to work in all cases. In fact, if history is anything to go by, deterrence is guaranteed *not* to work at some point or other.

Nuclear deterrence

The theory of nuclear deterrence depends upon it working not just most of the time but *all the time* – and *for* all time. There is no room for a margin of error if the consequence of nuclear deterrence not working is an all-out nuclear war that destroys the whole of human civilisation.

The 'credibility' of nuclear deterrence, furthermore, rests completely on the fact that two atom bombs were dropped on Japan more than 70 years ago. While subsequent nuclear tests have shown how enormously devastating the consequences of a nuclear weapon would be, they do not in themselves demonstrate a willingness to use such a weapon. The UK, for instance, has never used a nuclear weapon against another country in anger. This makes it exceedingly difficult to argue that the UK's threat to use a nuclear weapon is a realistic one. It also increases the likelihood that sooner or later a nuclear weapon *will* be used, if only to send a clear signal so some future adversary that the deterrent is backed up by real intention and willingness to use it.

The logic of nuclear deterrence gets more and more convoluted the deeper one goes into it. It is assumed, for instance, that the leaders of Russia, in contemplating an attack on the UK, would be sufficiently sane and rational as to weigh up the consequences of a possible retaliatory nuclear strike from the UK and decide on that basis to refrain from attacking. On the other hand, it is assumed that those same leaders would base their sane and rational decision on the likelihood of their counterparts in the UK acting so insanely and irrationally as to be willing to launch nuclear weapons against Russia that would almost certainly bring about their own total self-destruction.

Furthermore, the theory demands that 'we' must be willing to use our nuclear weapons if necessary and that willingness must be sufficiently convincing to our opponent that they believe we really *will* actually use our nuclear weapons if they dared to attack us. On the other hand, if we are willing 'if necessary' to use our nuclear weapons against another country which also has nuclear weapons, then at some level we are not 'deterred' by *them*. That other country is likewise not deterred by the fact that *we* have nuclear weapons if it is to be believed that they also would use their nuclear weapons 'if necessary' against us.

Ultimately, nuclear deterrence rests on the assumption that no ordinary, sane person would choose to bring death and destruction down upon family and friends and loved ones, and would therefore choose some alternative route other than to invite nuclear retaliation. The problem is that nuclear deterrence does not operate at the level of ordinary, sane people who care about their loved ones. It operates at the level of generals and politicians who make their decisions according to quite different criteria. It was the logic of those same generals and politicians who sent millions to their certain death in the trenches of WWI and authorised the saturation bombing of German and Japanese cities and the dropping of atom bombs in WWII.

The actual use of nuclear weapons would cause wholescale slaughter on an unimaginable scale, but there is no evidence that such a result would necessarily 'deter' generals and politicians from embarking on such a course should they decide the circumstances 'justified' it. Indeed, they have been ready to launch nuclear war on several occasions and it is luck, more than 'deterrence', which has kept us from having a nuclear war up to now (see Chapter 13).

General MacArthur wanted to drop atom bombs on China during the Korean War. President Nixon was considering the use of nuclear weapons during the Vietnam War. Mrs Thatcher apparently threatened to use nuclear weapons during the Falklands War.[45] Plans were readied for the use of nuclear weapons during the first Gulf War. And every day, 365 days a year, Britain's Trident submarines are patrolling the Atlantic ready to launch a nuclear attack at any moment if given the orders.

Pressing the button

> If you ... believe like me that Britain should keep the ultimate insurance policy of an independent nuclear deterrent, you have to accept there are circumstances in which its use would be justified.
> (David Cameron, Andrew Marr Show, 4 October 2015)

What does being willing to press the nuclear button 'if justified by circumstances' actually mean, apart from the obvious result of hundreds of thousands if not millions of people being killed? It means that Trident is only a 'deterrent' to the extent that a British Prime Minister is prepared to actually use it. Trident as a 'deterrent', therefore, is not somehow distinct from the intention to use Trident as a weapon.

In the words of the late Sir Michael Quinlan again:

> We cannot say that nuclear weapons are for deterrence and never for use, however remote we judge the latter possibility to be. Weapons deter by the possibility of their use and by no other route.[46]

We do not know whether David Cameron or any other British Prime Minister really would press the button in the event that Russia or another potential opponent called his bluff and launched an attack against the UK anyway. Saying that he would does not by itself make the threat credible. A Russian leader might calculate that actually, if push came to shove, Cameron wouldn't actually press the button even though he said he would. It all comes to down to psychology and there are so many unknowns it is impossible to know what anyone would do under any number of possible scenarios. That is what makes the whole theory of deterrence so fanciful.

Deterrence and defence

In the case of nuclear weapons, if and when deterrence 'fails', all you can do is launch nuclear weapons at the other side – or not. In neither case are we being 'defended' from attack by having nuclear weapons. This is an important distinction. What would normally be thought of as 'defence' are the strategies and resources need to fend off or resist an attack on the UK, as opposed to merely retaliating against the aggressor after an attack has already happened.

During the 1930s, Britain's air and sea power was strengthened in the hope of deterring Hitler from invading Britain. When this did not work as a deterrent, those military resources were used to actually defend Britain from the impending invasion. The planes and ships were not just a deterrent, they were a form of defence. Nuclear weapons do not work in the same way. It would be literally suicidal to start launching Trident missiles at ships crossing the English Channel, let alone at planes flying over London. Nuclear weapons cannot defend the UK even against incoming nuclear weapons.

If the UK were really threatened with attack or invasion by a foreign power, which at the moment we are not, our only defence against incoming nuclear weapons would be an anti-ballistic missile system, and even that would have limited effect. Our only defence against advancing troops or invading ships would be conventional forces, sea defences and other kinds of fortifications. Nuclear weapons, and Trident in particular, may or may not function effectively as a deterrent. But if the deterrent fails, Trident cannot then function as a form of defence. It is militarily useless in that sense. While it is often assumed that somehow Trident is going to 'defend' the UK from being attacked by Russia or some other large and powerful enemy, the truth is it cannot.

Summary

The theory of nuclear deterrence suggests that nuclear weapons are so effective in preventing war that they are unlikely ever to be used. Their function is to deter aggression against the UK and its allies, and the more powerfully destructive Trident is, the more effective it is as a deterrent.

Deterrence is commonly used as a strategy in all sorts of circumstances short of nuclear war. In all these other cases, it can be seen that deterrence is not effective 100% of the time, and can only be effective if the intention to follow through with the threat is credible, immediate, and realistic. These same principles apply to nuclear deterrence.

Trident cannot be said to act as a deterrent unless there is a credible, immediate, and realistic intention to use it as a weapon. Thus it is a contradiction in terms to say that Trident will never be used 'because it is only a deterrent'. Trident is designed and deployed as a weapon of mass destruction. It is hoped that it will never be used, but if it is claimed to be a deterrent, that can only remain a hope.

Successive British Prime Ministers have claimed publicly that they would press the nuclear button if the circumstances required it. But would they? Is it credible, immediate, and realistic that the UK would launch Trident in self-defence of the UK homeland, let alone in defence of some distant NATO ally?

Since the bombing of Hiroshima and Nagasaki, no country which has had nuclear weapons, including the UK, has ever used one in war, even when they were on the verge of losing that war. That is not to say that they will never be used, because the theory of deterrence merely increases the risk that they *will* be used. However, the fact that they have not been used so far is not itself evidence that deterrence has worked. The fact that wars have continued to be fought and that nuclear weapons have *not* been used actually undermines the theory that these weapons are an effective and credible deterrent.

CHAPTER 4

What is Mutually Assured Destruction?

WE HAVE LOOKED in chapters one and two at the human, physical and environmental consequences which using Trident might have on a country that has been targeted with attack as well as on the rest of the world. But what about the consequences *to the UK* of using Trident? We have already seen that radioactive fallout could end up coming down in the UK, as it did at the time of the Chernobyl meltdown. Are there other likely effects on the UK?

Mutually assured destruction, or 'MAD', is the logical outcome of attacking with nuclear weapons a country capable of striking back with nuclear weapons. It means that despite the enormous amount of death and destruction which one country may be able to inflict on another country with its nuclear weapons, if that second country also has nuclear weapons, it will be able to inflict an enormous amount of death and destruction on the first country in retaliation.

In the 1960s, both the US and the Soviet Union had enough nuclear weapons, and the means to deliver them with long-range bombers and inter-continental ballistic missiles, to utterly destroy each other many times over. US Defence Secretary Robert McNamara made it US policy that such a balance of terror should be maintained, as the best guarantee against either side attacking the other.

The MAD balance of terror was strengthened by the introduction of ballistic missile submarines like Polaris and later Trident. This meant that no matter what one side might do to destroy the planes or missiles of the other, they would still be able to launch nuclear weapons from secret locations under the sea in a devastating retaliatory strike.

The Anti-Ballistic Missile Treaty (ABM), which was signed in 1972, is perhaps the best example of the US and Soviet Union cooperating with each other during the Cold War to maintain the situation of mutually assured destruction. The ABMT limited the numbers and types of anti-ballistic missile defences that each side could maintain. The purpose was very specifically to ensure that one side could not protect itself against incoming missiles to such an extent as to feel it could survive such an attack. If ABM systems became too effective, that might encourage one side to think they could launch a nuclear war without fear of retaliation, upsetting the balance created by the situation of MAD.

To reinforce the concept of MAD and to be confident of overwhelming even the most sophisticated anti-ballistic missile defences, the US, quickly followed by the Soviet Union, developed a whole range of devices designed to ensure that the nuclear weapons would get through. The most important of these was the development of the MIRV, or 'multiple independently-targeted re-entry vehicle'. MIRVs meant that several warheads could be launched from a single missile and land on different targets, making it impossible for radar systems monitoring the trajectory of the missile to know where the warheads were going to end up.

The ABM Treaty was officially abrogated by President Bush in 2002 and both the US and Russia have invested heavily in anti-ballistic missile defences since then. Both sides have significantly reduced the total numbers of nuclear weapons in their stockpiles as well, but they still retain more than enough to utterly destroy each other. The development of technologies designed to defeat and overwhelm the other side goes on.

How does MAD apply to the UK?

The development of MAD as a reality and then as a policy applied in the 1960s to the US and the Soviet Union, who had then and still have now the vast majority of the world's nuclear weapons and vastly more than needed to destroy each other. MAD carried with it the implication of *total* destruction, against which there was no defence except to ensure that nuclear weapons would never be used.

MAD, as a concept however, does not depend on total destruction of two countries with nuclear weapons aimed at each other, but only on the *assured* destruction of those two countries. Another term which could be used here is 'unacceptable damage', since this is the term most often used by the UK government to describe the purpose of nuclear deterrence.

We cannot easily define what level of destruction counts as unacceptable, but as we saw in Chapter 1, successive UK governments have considered 40–50% of the population of Moscow killed, together with 40–50% of the buildings destroyed, to be an unacceptable level of damage to Russia. Would we apply the same criteria to London and say that 40–50% of the people killed and 40–50% of the buildings destroyed in London counts as 'unacceptable damage'?

Just as we have looked in Chapter 1 at a number of possible targets for Trident in Russia, so there are a number of different possible targets in the UK for a retaliatory strike. Instead of destroying only London, perhaps we would consider destruction of Britain's 40 largest towns and cities as sufficiently devastating to count as 'unacceptable damage'? Alternatively, perhaps unacceptable damage in military terms, or in terms of 'centres of state control' would mean destruction of major airfields, submarine bases, NATO command and control bunkers, nuclear facilities, parliament, Whitehall, etc.

How much nuclear firepower would it take to inflict unacceptable damage on the UK under these different scenarios? As we have seen, one 100 KT nuclear explosion can have a devastating impact on a large city, killing tens of thousands instantly, physically destroying an area of several square miles, and depending on whether it is airburst or groundburst, depending on the wind speed and other weather conditions, fatal levels of radioactive fallout could spread over a much larger area.

A study produced by Article 36 in 2013 examined the effects of a single 100 KT nuclear detonation (the size of one Trident warhead) over Manchester. This concluded that 81,000 people would be killed directly and more than 212,000 would be injured. With the destruction of vital infrastructure, including hospitals and emergency services, the injured would not stand a high chance of surviving. Everything up to 1.8 km from ground zero would be completely destroyed and fires would cause severe destruction out to a distance of 3 km. People up to 7 km from the explosion would still receive severe second degree burns and most buildings would be damaged.[47]

The equivalent of one Trident submarine of nuclear weapons, or 40 x 100 KT, striking the UK would cause 'unacceptable damage' to the UK under any of the above definitions. Russian submarines, like their US counterparts, carry much higher yield weapons and they have many more of these submarines than UK has. One modern SSBN Russian sub is normally believed to have 16 missiles, each containing eight warheads of 400 KT each. That is equivalent to 51 MT, or more than ten times the firepower of a UK Trident submarine.

A Trident attack on Russia

What would be the most likely response of Russia to an attack from the UK using Trident missiles, either on its own or as part of a NATO strike? It is of course possible that they would not be able to retaliate or would choose not to, but once the so-called deterrent has failed and an all-out nuclear attack has taken place, what is to prevent Russia from retaliating with a nuclear counter-strike against NATO, including against the UK? Would it not be illogical to assume that NATO could launch an all-out nuclear attack on Russia and not expect an all-out nuclear attack in response? Since Russia, like the UK, maintains a large number of its nuclear missiles on submarines at sea, it is highly unlikely that an all-out attack against Russia would locate and destroy all these weapons. Therefore some form of nuclear retaliation must be assumed in any conceivable scenario involving the use of Trident.

A limited nuclear attack on the UK

A Russian retaliatory attack against the UK might be limited to military targets such as Faslane submarine base or Mildenhall airbase. It might also include, however, nuclear attacks on London and/or other large cities. In either case, the consequences of such an attack would be enormous and devastating. If the Prime Minister were ever to give the order to launch Trident missiles against Russia, he or she would do so knowing that a likely consequence of such a decision would be nuclear missiles landing on the UK – whether or not any such missiles had already landed prior to that.

Let's imagine a more limited scenario, in which Trident missiles were launched against specific military targets in Russia rather than against Moscow itself. Perhaps they are aimed at crippling Russian command and control operations to halt the invasion, or aimed at troop concentrations and tanks amassed on the border of Poland, or perhaps only a single missile is launched as a 'warning' shot to halt the advancing troops. In this case, the fallout coming back to the UK may be much less, the apocalyptic consequences of all-out nuclear war averted (at least for the time being) and Russia would still be standing, as it were. How are they likely to respond to a nuclear attack, however limited, coming from the UK?

Perhaps in this more limited scenario, Russia would respond in a more limited fashion, attacking a specific military target similar to the one attacked by the UK. It is difficult to see how this would not escalate once nuclear attacks have been initiated, since UK military commanders would not want to lose military assets without responding in kind.

Indeed, one of the difficulties in trying to imagine a scenario of 'limited' nuclear warfare is that by firing even one of its missiles, a Trident submarine is thereby giving away its exact location to the Russians and therefore the most likely response from the Russians would be for them to try to destroy the submarine before it can launch any more of its missiles. This risk, in turn, means that a Trident submarine commander is more likely to fire *all* his missiles rather than hold some back for later. It also means that any attack from either side that does not 'take out' as much as possible of the other side's ability to retaliate is risking much greater losses than would be the case if they throw everything they have at their opponent at the outset.

It is impossible to predict how any of these scenarios might play out in real life. However, *any* scenario involving the launch of UK Trident missiles against an opponent like Russia, no matter what the circumstances, is likely to result in nuclear attacks on the UK in retaliation.

Even where a nuclear attack from Russia has already taken place on the UK, a response in kind by launching Trident would still invite further retaliation, unless for instance Russia had already used up all its nuclear weapons in the first attack. Apart from the morality of launching a revenge attack against Russia once it had already launched a nuclear attack on the UK, what exactly would be the point of it, especially given the other considerations discussed in Chapter 1 concerning the environmental and long-term impact of all-out nuclear war and even the more limited impact of radioactive fallout coming back to the UK from a nuclear strike against Russia?

What if Trident were used against a country other than Russia?

As we have noted above, Russia is, and always has been, the number one target for the UK's nuclear weapons. However, seven other countries also have nuclear weapons and more could try to acquire them. We have ruled out for the foreseeable future using Trident against the US or France. A Trident attack against China would risk nuclear retaliation in the same way as an attack on Russia, since China also has nuclear missile submarines. That leaves India, Pakistan, Israel and North Korea.

Theoretically, the UK could launch Trident missiles against any of those four countries without immediate risk of retaliation. For one thing, none of those countries have missiles with a long-enough range to reach the UK. Neither do the UK's Trident missiles have the capacity to reach North Korea, however, unless the submarines were redeployed to the North Pacific.

Let's imagine that the UK does redeploy a Trident submarine to the North Pacific and launches a nuclear attack on North Korea in a pre-emptive strike to destroy its nuclear missiles before they were able to attack the UK or some other country, for instance Japan. We are moving well beyond the realm of 'self-defence' by this point and certainly beyond the claim that the UK's nuclear weapons would only be used 'in the extreme case where the very survival of the state were at stake'.[48] Even if North Korea, or any other country, were to develop the missile capacity to launch nuclear weapons at the UK, why would they do so – unless it is because they believe the UK might attack *them* with nuclear weapons?

If Iran were to obtain nuclear weapons despite the recent agreement reached with the international community or, for instance, Pakistan's nuclear weapons were to fall into the hands of Islamist extremists, the UK and other NATO allies might well feel sufficiently threatened to consider using nuclear weapons against them. It seems bizarre to imagine a scenario in which the UK would be acting alone in such a situation and would use Trident to deal with it, but let's try to imagine the consequences.

Let us imagine then that Islamic State continues to expand across the Middle East and takes control of Pakistan through a military coup. They re-direct Pakistan's nuclear missiles from pointing at India to pointing at Turkey, and threaten to launch a nuclear attack unless the Turkish government submits to Islamic State. Turkey, a NATO member, calls on the UK and other countries to destroy the nuclear missiles of Islamic State. Knowing that that might happen, Islamic State would probably have already launched them against Turkey without waiting for them to be destroyed in their silos, but let's imagine that they have not yet done that.

What, in this scenario, would launching Trident missiles against Pakistan achieve and what would be the consequences? While Pakistan's missiles may not have the capability of reaching the UK, they could certainly reach other targets and if moved into position against Turkey those targets could include the state of Israel. As with the case of Russia and China, it can only be assumed that a nuclear attack against another state, even with a relatively rudimentary nuclear weapons capability, will result in nuclear retaliation since no one can ever be sure to destroy all the opponent's nuclear weapons in a single strike.

Extended deterrence

So-called 'extended' deterrence, or the 'nuclear umbrella' is the idea that if Russia, or another country, were to attack another NATO country, say for example Estonia, then the US or the UK would retaliate with a nuclear attack against Russia. Russia, knowing this would be the result, would therefore be deterred from attacking Estonia in the first place.

This threat, however, could be perceived by Russia as lacking credibility, since it would seem unlikely that either the US or the UK would risk launching their nuclear missiles at Russia merely for the sake of a third country like Estonia, knowing that Russia would retaliate by launching nuclear missiles against *them*. Why would a UK Prime Minister invite the nuclear destruction of the UK for the sake of Estonia, or Poland, or Turkey, or even France?

Indeed, these were the very concerns which led in the 1970s and 80s to the concept of 'flexible response' and to the deployment of a whole range of intermediate nuclear weapons in Europe. These were designed to provide a nuclear response to any invasion by the Soviet bloc without, it was hoped, inviting an all-out nuclear attack against the US mainland. Without this intermediate level of nuclear response, it was felt that the Soviet Union might not be deterred by the threat of a nuclear strike from the US for the very reason that such a strike was not credible if merely for the defence of European allies. A US President is even more unlikely than a UK Prime Minister to order an all-out nuclear attack for the sake of its allies if such an attack is sure to invite a response in kind against the United States itself.

Summary

The use of Trident against Russia or China would almost certainly result in a devastating nuclear attack on the UK, whether or not a nuclear attack on the UK or one of its allies had already taken place. The use of Trident against another nuclear weapons state might avoid the risk of an immediate counter-attack on the UK, but risks nuclear weapons being used in retaliation on some other country, for instance Turkey, Israel or Japan.

With thousands of nuclear warheads potentially pointed at the UK from Russia and China, it is unlikely in the extreme that there would be none left to launch a counter-attack against the UK in the event of David Cameron pressing the nuclear button, no matter how many may have already been launched. Therefore one can only assume that David Cameron is undeterred by the threat of nuclear retaliation should he decide he must press the nuclear button.

Furthermore, it is accepted NATO policy not to rule out the possibility of a 'first use' of nuclear weapons against a conventional attack on a NATO member state. A conventional attack by Russia against the west, for instance, would mean they still had a considerable arsenal of nuclear weapons in reserve. Therefore if NATO were seriously to consider launching nuclear weapons against Russia in response to a conventional attack, they would be doing so in the full knowledge that they were inviting a nuclear retaliation and in such a case they are not 'deterred' by that possibility.

As we have seen in the case of a conflict with Russia, there is no conceivable use of Trident that would not run the risk of nuclear retaliation against the UK. Of course both countries would suffer enormous devastation from a nuclear exchange, but it is hard to see how the UK could come out of such an exchange better off than Russia, given that Russia is many times larger than the UK, has twice the population and at least 20 times as many nuclear weapons. Even in a conflict with a much smaller country or one with fewer and more rudimentary nuclear weapons, nothing good is likely to come out of a nuclear exchange involving the launch of Trident missiles.

The concept of Mutually Assured Destruction, or MAD, means that in the case of the UK, to launch nuclear weapons against another country with nuclear weapons is to invite the assured destruction of the UK in return. Such a prospect makes a mockery of the idea that having nuclear weapons somehow 'deters' those other countries from attacking us. If anything, it is the likelihood of nuclear retaliation against the UK that ought reasonably to deter the UK from ever using Trident.

PART TWO

We Need Trident for Our Security

CHAPTER 5

Did Nuclear Weapons End WWII?

THE THEORY OF nuclear deterrence rests on the notion that no country would attack the UK if it meant the certain destruction of their own cities and civilian populations. This in turn rests on the widely held assumption that it was the atom bombs dropped on Hiroshima and Nagasaki that caused Japan to surrender at the end of WWII. If just two atom bombs, small in comparison with today's nuclear arsenals, could force Japan to surrender unconditionally, then surely today's nuclear arsenals are sufficient to prevent any would-be aggressor from ever considering an attack on the UK. These are the premises on which the whole theory of deterrence has been built. But are they true?

'The Bomb saved lives'

Bill Westwood, the late Bishop of Peterborough, was a strong proponent of nuclear weapons. In the summer of 1945, he was a 20-year-old paratrooper in the British Army, stationed in Sri Lanka and awaiting the orders to invade Japan. He remained convinced to his dying day that more lives were saved by the dropping of the Atom Bomb than were lost, and he was by no means alone in holding that view.

To be fair, Bishop Bill was concerned not only with the lives of British and American servicemen but also with the lives of the countless Japanese military as well as civilians who would have surely died had there been an invasion of the Japanese home islands. The estimates vary widely and there is no way of knowing how many would have died.[49] However, nearly 150,000 Japanese civilians were killed during the invasion and occupation of the island of Okinawa in the spring of 1945, together with as many as 77,000 Japanese soldiers and 14,000 Allied soldiers.[50]

President Truman had already given the go-ahead for 'Operation Olympic' to invade the Japanese 'home' island of Kyushu on 1 November

1945 with a force of more than 750,000 troops. Although the Allies were unaware at the time, the Japanese military had already deployed nearly 1 million of their soldiers to Kyushu by August 1945, ready to fend off the invasion. With nearly 2.5 million civilians living in the southern part of Kyushu at that time as well, there is no doubt that an Allied invasion would have resulted in a very large number of casualties on all sides, with possibly four times as many as were killed on Okinawa, given the numbers involved. Four times the number of deaths as in Okinawa would have meant as many as 60,000 Allied soldiers, 300,000 Japanese soldiers and 600,000 civilians killed.

By the summer of 1945, WWII had been going on for six years. Nearly every country in the world was involved, hundreds of cities were in ruins and at least 40 million people were already dead. Everyone wanted the war to be over. When President Truman announced that the atom bombs had been dropped on Hiroshima and Nagasaki, there was a huge sense of relief – even jubilation – from people like Bill Westwood, whose chances of surviving the war were otherwise probably less than 50–50 at that point.

When the Japanese surrendered one week later, both President Truman and the Japanese Emperor Hirohito claimed it was because of the atom bomb. Every newspaper and radio the world over (with the possible exception of those in the Soviet Union) reported that the war ended because of the atom bomb. Nearly every history textbook and academic historian tells the same story. Why would anyone disbelieve it?

Questioning the impact of the atom bombs

The Japanese surrender in August 1945 meant an end to the most violent war in human history. For that we can all be very grateful. But do we know that it was the dropping of the atom bombs that caused Japan to surrender? What is the evidence to support this, apart from the statements mentioned above and other similar assertions? The media do not always know what is going on behind the scenes and public statements by politicians do not always tell us the whole truth either.

Even before the bombing of Hiroshima and Nagasaki, some senior politicians and military figures in the US were already convinced that Japan was on the verge of surrendering. Others were questioning the need to use the atom bomb out of concern over the potential consequences of unleashing such a deadly weapon. Immediately after the war, there was an increasing realisation that Japan had indeed been thoroughly defeated by this point in the war:

> Based on a detailed investigation of all the facts and supported by the testimony of the surviving Japanese leaders involved, it is the Survey's opinion that certainly prior to 31 December 1945, and in all probability prior to 1 November 1945, Japan would have surrendered even if the Atomic Bombs had not been dropped...[51]

That was the official view of the US Strategic Bombing Survey (USSBS), which conducted an extensive examination into the effects of US and Allied bombing in both Germany and Japan immediately following the war. The editorial board of USSBS can hardly be considered a neutral source of information, since their main intention was to prove the effectiveness of US bombing as justification for creation of a separate US Air Force with equal status to the US Army and US Navy.[52]

Indeed there are many contradictions between the evidence provided in the 330 reports and annexes of the USSBS and the conclusions drawn by the report's editors. Their opinion that the Atom Bombs may not have been necessary to secure the surrender of Japan is all the more significant precisely because this goes against the general presumption of the report that winning future wars will hinge on the quantity and quality of the bombs dropped by American fighting forces.

What else was going on at that time?

Before the bombing of Hiroshima and Nagasaki, the US had already bombed 67 other Japanese cities, killing as many as 300,000 civilians, wounding 750,000, rendering 1.7 million people homeless and utterly destroying more than 50% of Japan's urban centres. The firebombing of Tokyo alone cost as many as 130,000 lives and incinerated 16 square miles of the city centre.[53] In terms of the number killed outright, Tokyo ranks above both Hiroshima and Nagasaki (although the effects of radiation meant many more were killed from the atom bombs in the months and years to come). In terms of area destroyed, Hiroshima ranks sixth among all the cities bombed and in terms of the destruction as a percentage of the total size of the city, Hiroshima ranks 17th if we look at all the cities in Japan affected by Allied bombing.

What does this mean in terms of the impact of the atom bomb? It is of course hugely significant that a single bomb could be developed to have such devastating consequences as the one which was dropped on Hiroshima. Hydrogen bombs more than a thousand times more powerful than the Hiroshima bomb have since been developed. But apart from the radiation effects, dropping one bomb with the power of 15,000 tonnes of TNT is roughly equivalent to dropping 1,000 bombs which each have the power of 15 tonnes of TNT or dropping 15,000 bombs which each have the power of one tonne of TNT.

As far as the Japanese military were concerned in August 1945, it probably made little difference whether it was one big bomb or 15,000 little bombs that were dropped on Hiroshima. The effect was the destruction of a city and the deaths of many civilians and in terms of the overall conduct of the war, neither of those appeared to be of major concern to Japan's war leaders.

What we now know about Japanese military thinking at the time

From the historical records and archives of the Japanese military and interviews with Japanese political leaders after their surrender and the accumulated evidence of the effects of aerial bombing both in Germany and in Japan, we now know a lot more about what was going on in the summer of 1945 than Bill Westwood or anyone else at the time knew or could have known.

Japan was ready to surrender

We know, for instance, that even before the fall of Germany, many in the Japanese government were looking for an honourable way to surrender and that as early as February 1945, the Japanese premier, Kantara Suzuki, submitted an official memo to the emperor saying 'I regret to say that Japan's defeat is inevitable'.[54] This was on the basis of military assessments definitively indicating that Japan was no longer in a position to be able to win the war.

With Germany defeated, the US could now turn its entire resources to the war against Japan. The Japanese economy was in rapid decline due at least in part to the Japanese being surrounded by Allied ships cutting off its supply lines. Rationing was now very severe, well below the average required intake of energy for a healthy diet; meals rarely included staples, even rice, and consisted mainly of watered down miso soup and substitute foods. Government advice included the eating of grasshoppers, plants and even sawdust. Children fell sick all the time, coal was used in car engines as it was impossible to obtain fuel and it was clear to much of the population that Japan was on its knees.

Japan was willing to negotiate

We know that among those running the Japanese war effort at the time there were those who wanted to sue for peace and those who wanted to continue fighting to the end. As is almost always the case in war, and was certainly the case in the US as well at that time, the strength of the 'war party' relative to the 'peace party' depends to a large extent on the behaviour of the enemy – in this case the US, who were right up until the dropping of the Hiroshima bomb not prepared to accept anything except unconditional surrender.

In fact, the Japanese had as their leader at this point Prince Fumimaro Konoe, who as Prime Minister had originally attempted to avoid war with the United States. In February 1945, he advised the Emperor Hirohito to begin negotiations to end WWII. Konoe's recommendation was to sue for peace with the Soviet Union to find a negotiated settlement to end the war and save Japan from unconditional surrender. Although the Japanese never in fact received any audience with Stalin, this didn't deter the 'peace party' and the Emperor from holding out hope against hope that a bargain would be struck, even as far as to offer to give various contested islands back to them, lease out ports, railways and fishing rights that they were asking for. We know there were daily phone calls to the Soviet embassy during this period and a telegramme on 28 June in which Japan said 'we are prepared to make considerable sacrifices... and to settle all the problems the Soviet Union was interested in settling'.[55]

We also know that Japanese experts in the US State Department were advising President Truman that 'Japan would never accept unconditional surrender'.[56] Even as Churchill, Truman and Stalin were meeting in Potsdam to issue what became the final 'ultimatum' to Japan at the end of July 1945, the emperor himself sent a message that he 'desires from his heart that [the war] may be quickly terminated'.[57]

The allies' insistence that the Japanese give up the Emperor system was particularly insensitive. Although the emperor system had been manipulated by the military regime to enforce unity on the nation through for instance the adoption of the imperial state religion symbol to be worn on all outer clothing, the Japanese emperor symbolised the Japanese race and ethnicity itself. For instance the unbroken lineage of Japanese emperors stretching back 2,600 years had recently been celebrated on the Emperor's birthday in 1940. When finally the Japanese did capitulate to the Potsdam declaration on 10 August 1945, the Americans quickly agreed that they retain the Emperor, indicating perhaps that they could have been less hawkish with the Japanese before, had they not been intent on using the atomic weapon in any case.

The Soviet entry into the war

We know that in May 1945, the Supreme War Council agreed that 'Soviet entry into the war will deal a death blow to the Empire'.[58] We know that Truman informed Stalin that he had a working atomic bomb at the Potsdam conference on 27 July 1945 (the Trinity test in the US had just proved successful), and that Stalin did not react to this game-changing news at the time. But by August 1945, we know that the Soviet Union had secretly moved more than 1.5 million soldiers, 5,400 planes and 3,400 tanks from Eastern Europe to the Far East, ready for a surprise attack against Japan on three fronts, air, land and sea.

We know that when the Soviets declared war on Japan on 8 August (Soviet time) and followed with an invasion by land, sea and air, this triggered the scheduling of a Japanese war council meeting for 9 August – the meeting was scheduled *before* the news of the dropping of the atomic bomb on Nagasaki the next day at 11.14 am. The dropping of the bomb on Hiroshima had triggered no such high-level meeting. Thus the invasion of the Soviet Union had a much greater impact on the behaviour of both the peace party and the war party in Japan than did the bombs dropping on Hiroshima or Nagasaki.[59]

It is not difficult to see that the invasion by the Soviet Union would have dashed the hopes of the peace party whose strategy was to use the Soviets as a mediator to end the war. The invasion equally dashed the hopes of the war party to have in one final showdown with the Americans on the southern island of Kyushu. Since they had already moved so much of their manpower and military assets down there, they could not hope to stem the advance of the Soviets coming down from the North and West. It would only be a matter of time before the Soviets would reach Tokyo. One Japanese General estimated it would take them only 10 days.[60]

Alternative explanations

Perhaps the atom bombs offered the perfect excuse to enable Japan to save face and avoid the humiliation of defeat at the hands of the Soviets? Perhaps, in a sense, the atomic bomb played into the Japanese military government's hands as it offered them the chance to blame the need for surrender on this terrible new 'cruel' weapon, thus exonerating them from the blame by a war-weary nation of having brought ruin on Japan and leaving the country vulnerable to invasion on all sides (the US and the Soviets).

We will, of course, never know what *might* have happened had history turned out differently, but we are obliged, at the very least, to *question* the accepted version of events and to weigh up the pros and cons of alternative explanations. There are now at least three alternative explanations for why WWII came to an end in which the dropping of the atom bombs barely feature:

According to the first theory, Japan already knew it was losing the war long before August 1945. Its economy was in ruins, millions of people were homeless and destitute, its ports were at the mercy of US warships and its cities were at the mercy of US warplanes. Its ability to wage war was severely curtailed and its only allies (Germany, Italy and Turkey) already defeated. It was only a matter of time before it would have surrendered.

According to the second theory, if there had been any serious attempt by the Allies to respond to Japanese overtures for peace, negotiations might have ended the war months earlier on terms more or less identical to what was finally agreed by the US. The main obstacle to Japanese surrender was their insistence on retention of the emperor, which in the end the US gave them, despite the 'unconditional surrender'.

According to the third theory, it was the Soviet invasion of Japan on 9 August, rather than the second atomic bomb dropped on Nagasaki that same day, which led the Japanese to realise all was lost and to accept unconditional surrender.

The effects of aerial bombing in WWII

The atom bomb was – and is – uniquely powerful and many thousands of times more powerful than the largest conventional bombs. However, the result of dropping many thousands of conventional bombs on a single city is just as devastating (apart from the effects of radioactive fallout). To understand the effects of dropping the atom bombs on Japan, we need to understand the effects of dropping conventional bombs on cities up to that point.

The deliberate bombing of cities is generally considered to have begun with the bombing of Guernica during the Spanish Civil War in 1937. In that case, the destruction of the 'spiritual capital' of the Basque country appeared to aid the advance of Franco's forces along the north coast of Spain, although the Republican forces fought on for two more years.

The bombing of Warsaw by German forces in 1939 and then the bombing of Rotterdam in May 1940 seemed to be much more decisive militarily, lending support to the myth that bombing of cities was somehow a 'successful' military strategy in WWII. In the case of Warsaw, although it was being bombed by the *Luftewaffe* from day one of the German invasion, the most extensive bombing took place on 'Black Monday', 25 September 1939. German bombers flew 1,150 sorties on that day, dropping 500 tonnes of high explosives and 72 tonnes of incendiaries, causing widespread destruction of the city centre.

Although fighting continued for another week or two in some other parts of Poland, Warsaw capitulated the day after Black Monday. But by this point, German and Soviet forces already occupied most of the country and were already fighting within the city. It is debatable therefore whether the bombing of Warsaw ended the war in Poland or was merely a part of the ongoing destruction that was taking place there.

The Netherlands surrendered to the Nazis the day after the bombing of Rotterdam and the German threat to bomb Utrecht next. A fuller analysis of the conditions which led to both Poland and the Netherlands surrendering to the Nazis is beyond the scope of this book; however it must at least be questioned whether the bombing of those two cities played as large a part in the decision to surrender as has been widely assumed.

The Netherlands, a small, neutral country hoping to stay out of the war, was invaded on 10 May 1940 from the north, south and in several places on the east by a country ten times its size, with a very powerful and fully mobilised war machine which had already invaded several other countries. Half of the Dutch air force was destroyed by a surprise attack on the first day. By 13 May, the German army had already occupied three-quarters of the country and was preparing to enter Rotterdam. In fact the Dutch commander of Rotterdam was already negotiating the terms of surrender with his German counterpart on the morning of 14 May, but the planes had already set off with their instructions to bomb the city.

Sixty-one cities in Germany and 67 cities in Japan were bombed extensively during WWII in addition to Warsaw, Rotterdam and of course London and other cities in England. As many as 1,000 planes were involved in some of the biggest bombing raids, dropping as many as 650,000 bombs in one raid. A total of 500,000 tonnes (500 KT) of TNT was used by the RAF to attack German cities between October 1939 and May 1945. Some 3,600,000 dwellings were destroyed, 7,500,000 people were made homeless, 300,000 civilians were killed and 780,000 injured in Germany alone.[61]

This bombing went on for six years and the destruction was relentless, and yet there is no evidence to suggest that either Germany or Japan were closer to surrendering as a result of it. In fact both the US Strategic Bombing Survey and the British Bombing Survey that was conducted in parallel following the end of the war found to the contrary that war production actually *rose* in Germany throughout the war, despite the bombing.[62]

According to the British Bombing Survey Unit, which devoted a whole separate chapter to the 'Reasons Underlying Failure of Primary Strategic Aim of Offensive Against Cities':[63]

> Hitler himself paid little apparent attention to the destruction of German cities... (p. 164) Area attacks against towns were undoubtedly overdone, in the sense that however successful they were in terms of material destruction and in pinning down defensive forces, they had little effect upon the trend of German war industry. (p. 166)

The unit concluded that:

> The several lines of evidence that have been discussed thus *put it beyond question that in spite of the widespread physical devastation they caused, area attacks against German cities had little effect* either upon the trend of production or upon the morale of the German worker. (p. 97)

And again:

> In so far as the offensive against German towns was designed to break the morale of the German civilian population, it clearly failed. (p. 79)

Given what John Kenneth Galbraith called in his memoirs 'the disastrous failure of strategic bombing'[64] it is somewhat surprising that the US continued with the same policy in the war against Japan and indeed in the many wars it has fought since.

Drawing from other experience

How could it be that such devastating destruction as was wrought on Germany and Japan by conventional bombing of cities as well as by the atomic bombs could have so little effect on the morale of the population or the willingness of the leaders to continue fighting? If we but look at the effect of the Blitz on the British people and British government, we can perhaps get a better understanding of this.

During the Blitz, at least 40,000 and perhaps as many as 60,000 civilians were killed[65] in London and 15 other UK cities. One million homes were destroyed, large areas of London devastated, the population was terrorised night after night and forced to sleep in London Underground stations. Certainly there was fear. But was there defeatism? Did the British people rise up and demand that Britain surrender rather than endure any more of this devastation? Of course not.

Did Churchill ever suggest that Britain should give up under those difficult circumstances? Or did Britain plough on, more determined than ever to beat back the Nazi war machine?

What happened when the planes hit the Twin Towers of the World Trade Centre in New York on 9/11? Did Americans cower in fear and demand that all US forces be withdrawn from Saudi Arabia? No, what happened was that the US immediately went onto a war footing. American flags started appearing all over the country on cars, houses and on people's clothing. Bush's approval rating soared to 90%, the highest of any US president in modern times.[66]

Summary

The deliberate and targeted bombing of civilian populations is most likely to result in a desire for retaliation and a redoubling of efforts to fight back rather than to resignation and surrender on the part of the targeted population.

The evidence from Germany and Japan in WWII as well as from Vietnam, Iraq and other countries which have suffered huge losses from conventional bombing, is that bombing of cities does not significantly reduce the ability or willingness of people to fight back. It is not the response of the civilian population that matters in terms of willingness to wage war, however, so much as the response of political and military leaders. Here the evidence is crystal clear: massive bombing of cities does not deter states from waging war and therefore there is no reason to suppose that the threat of massive bombing of cities would deter them, either.

Japan surrendered shortly after the atom bombs were dropped and the Soviet Union entered the war. It was preferable for the Japanese military to surrender to the US and say it was the atom bombs that made them do it, but it is more likely that it was the Soviet invasion, together with many other factors, which forced them into that decision at that particular time. Many lives could have been saved and the war could have ended months earlier if the Allies had been willing to negotiate the terms of surrender.

Nuclear weapons have enormous power to destroy whole cities and kill large numbers of civilians. However, destruction alone does not win wars.[67] There is no evidence to support the belief that nuclear weapons, any more than conventional weapons, can bring a country to its knees and force it to surrender. Therefore it is a weak argument to suggest that the *threat* of such destruction, ie so-called nuclear deterrence, actually deters anybody from doing what they would otherwise be determined to do, whether that be another Hitler or a more benign opponent that might be expected to be somehow more concerned about their own civilian population.

CHAPTER 6

Have Nuclear Weapons 'Kept the Peace' Since 1945?

IT IS PROBABLY the most common argument used in favour of nuclear weapons to say that they have 'kept the peace' since 1945. This argument claims that Britain's nuclear weapons, along with those of the US, prevented a Soviet invasion of western Europe during the Cold War and prevented that war from becoming 'hot' and turning into WWIII. The more universalist claim of this argument is that the possession of nuclear weapons, not just by the UK and the US but also by Russia, France and China, has somehow created a 'stable' situation in Europe and the world and prevented war between the major powers from breaking out.

'Be careful above all things not to let go of the atomic weapon until you are sure and more than sure that other means of preserving peace are in your hands,' said Winston Churchill.[68] This has been the mantra of British Prime Ministers ever since. If nuclear weapons are the reason we have had a period of relative and sustained peace since WWII, why would anyone wish to destabilise such an arrangement?

We have already looked in Chapters 3 and 4 at the concept of nuclear deterrence. We now need to look at the historical record. Has it actually worked or hasn't it? Do we have irrefutable evidence to back up either claim? And if so, what are the implications of this?

The long peace

It is certainly the case that Western Europe, at least, has had a prolonged period of relative peace since WWII and of that we can all be very grateful. There has not been a nuclear war between the superpowers, for which we can be even more grateful, since if there had been we would probably not be here now discussing it. It is hardly the case, however, that there have been no wars at all during this period.

Throughout the world, there have been well over 100 wars since 1945 and depending on what you count as a 'war', as many as 250 of them.[69] Of these, a few have been civil wars or border wars with no involvement of the major powers. However, the military forces of one or more of the nuclear states have been directly involved in nearly half the wars fought since 1945.[70] Many of the civil wars which did not involve any of the nuclear powers directly have nonetheless involved armed groups militarily supported openly or covertly by one side or other of the Cold War.

Within Europe, there has been the conflict in Northern Ireland, the war in Cyprus, the wars in former Yugoslavia, the invasions of Hungary and Czechoslovakia, military coups in Poland, Greece and Spain. Outside Europe, there have been major wars and military confrontations involving one or more of the superpower blocs in Korea, Vietnam, Angola, Mozambique, Iraq, Afghanistan, Egypt, Lebanon and in South America.

The claim that nuclear weapons have prevented war in the wider sense does not stand up to much scrutiny. More people have been killed in wars since 1945 than were killed in the whole of WWII, so the world has hardly been cleansed of war as a result of nuclear weapons. Perhaps if we look at the more narrow claim, we will find that nuclear weapons have prevented war between the major European powers?

Have there been fewer wars in Europe than there were previously?

In addition to the 'long peace' that we have seen in Europe since 1945, there is an assumption in the 'nuclear weapons have kept the peace' argument that Europe was in a constant state of warfare between the major European powers *before* 1945. It is certainly the case that Europe went through two devastating world wars in the first half of the 20th century, but prior to that was almost a century of relative peace since the Napoleonic Wars of 1803–1815. This was broken by a number of smaller wars in the Balkans and elsewhere, but the only war involving more than two European countries having a brief spat during that period was the Crimean War of 1853–1856.

From the close of the Crimean War to the start of WWI was 58 years. From the end of the Napoleonic Wars to the start of WWI was 99 years. Either way, it is hardly an astounding fact that Europe has not had a major war for the last 70 years.

The fact that there has not been a war between the major powers in Europe since 1945 is no more in need of an explanation, statistically speaking, than the fact that there has not been a major earthquake in Europe since 1945 either, or a major famine or a major outbreak of the plague. In other words, there have *not* been so many wars in Europe prior to 1945 that the absence of war since then requires a historical explanation.

Changing face of Europe

The wars of the first half of the 20th century were fought mainly between Germany, Italy and Turkey on one side and Britain, France and Russia on the other. Why has that configuration of countries ceased fighting each other since 1945? The Cold War created a different configuration of warring parties, pitting Britain and France together with Germany, Italy and Turkey against the Soviet Union. But even more importantly, the central divide in Europe, between France and Germany, was re-engineered so as to make war between them less likely if not impossible.

The European Coal and Steel Community, which eventually became the European Union, consciously and deliberately fused together the economies of Germany and France to such an extent that war and the preparations for war would not be possible for one without implicating the other. Whether the European Union deserved the Nobel Peace Prize in 2012 or not is another matter, but the EU has without doubt been a significant factor in making war less likely between the major powers in Europe since 1945.

Did nuclear weapons prevent a Soviet invasion of Western Europe?

Prior to the 20th century, imperial Russia had invaded Finland and Poland and fought various wars with Sweden, Turkey, Prussia and Serbia. However neither Russia nor the Soviet Union has ever invaded Western Europe, despite being invaded twice by Germany in the 20th century and once by France in the 19th century.[71]

The Soviet Union used its military forces to crush uprisings against puppet regimes in Hungary (1956) and Czechoslovakia (1968) and attempted to do that in Afghanistan (1979–1989), but there is no evidence that it intended or wished to invade other countries not already within its 'sphere of influence'. Unlike Napoleon and Hitler, who had clear and undisguised ambitions to conquer Europe, no Russian or Soviet leader ever claimed such ambitions.

> The Soviet Union had no interest in overrunning Western Europe militarily and would not have launched an attack on Europe in the decades after the Second World War even if nuclear weapons did not exist.[72]

This is according to George Kennan, former US Ambassador to Moscow during the 1950s and a key architect of Cold War 'containment' policies of the US at that time. What he and many others knew at the time, though the general public did not, was that numerous formal and informal discussions between Roosevelt, Churchill and Stalin during the war had thrashed out agreed 'zones of influence' between the three leaders. These discussions, consolidated at Yalta in February 1945, gave Stalin the green light to create a permanent 'buffer zone' between Germany and Russia after the war, comprising the countries of Eastern Europe which would later become the 'Warsaw Pact'.[73]

We do not need the existence of nuclear weapons to explain why the Soviet Union did not invade Western Europe if the Soviet Union or its predecessor had never invaded Western Europe prior to 1945 and showed no intention of doing so after that date.[74] It is certainly possible that had there been no nuclear weapons in Western Europe, the Soviet Union *might* have invaded during that period. But there is certainly no reason to believe that they *would* have invaded under those circumstances and therefore there is no justification for claiming that the existence of nuclear weapons prevented them from doing so.

Post-war world

In fact, the world has changed dramatically since 1945 in so many ways that the existence of nuclear weapons cannot be the only explanation for the absence of a major war in Europe since then. The United Nations came into existence in 1945 and with it a whole body of international law and international institutions that have totally transformed the way nation-states relate to each other, handle disputes and conduct warfare.

For all their flaws and failings, the UN Security Council, the Universal Declaration of Human Rights, the World Court, the Geneva Conventions and a whole host of other treaties have been created to govern and regulate the use of certain weapons, the conduct of war, the laws of the sea, and even the use of outer space. Global trade agreements, global institutions like the IMF and World Bank, and the humanitarian and development agencies of the UN as well as the thousands of civil society organisations have sprung up to address and respond to humanitarian and development needs across the world. UN peacekeeping missions, international diplomacy and mediation efforts, the international protection of civilians and of human rights, the monitoring of early warning signs of war and genocide – all these and many, many more factors have transformed the way conflicts are handled in the post-war world. Perhaps most important of all has been the growth and spread of democracy and the civilian control of military forces, making war between states less likely.

Everyday changes since 1945, like the development of air travel, television, mobile phones, computers and the internet make the world a much smaller and more closely interdependent place. Warfare is a hideously barbaric and increasingly outmoded means of managing disputes in a world in which people can see what is happening in other countries right across the world, where they trade with each other and interact with each other and even make friends with each other transcending countries and continents on a daily basis.

Steven Pinker, in his 2012 book *The Better Angels of Our Nature* takes a broad sweep at the trends in human behaviour over the centuries and millennia of human history and concludes that human beings have been becoming less and less violent with every passing generation. His methodology may be disputed,[75] but his conclusions are inescapable: just because we saw two world wars and untold numbers dead in the first half of the 20th century does not mean that we need an explanation as to why an even more deadly third world war has not occurred by now.

The logical fallacy of this mindset

Imagine for a moment that your home was burgled on a regular basis until one day when you decided to get a cat. Since having that cat, you have not been burgled once. Is it the cat that is protecting you from the burglars? And if everyone had a cat, would all burglary cease?

It *could* be the case that your former burglar was afraid of cats (or allergic to them) and the cat really *is* the reason you are no longer being burgled. But there are quite a lot of other possible explanations, in fact an *infinite number of them*!

In terms of logic, to argue from correlation to causation is known as *post hoc ergo propter hoc* (followed by therefore caused by) and it is one of the most common of all logical fallacies. The fallacy is assuming that if two things are linked chronologically, the former must have caused the latter. But this is rarely the case and the logic is inherently faulty.

This can easily be seen with the common example of the cock and the sun: Every morning without fail, the cock crows just before sunrise, ie the cock crows, *then* the sun rises. *Therefore,* according to the logic of *post hoc ergo propter hoc*, the crowing of the cock causes the sun to rise. Wrong!

If we break down the claim that nuclear weapons have kept the peace since 1945, what this is arguing is that:

1. There have been wars for centuries [between the major European powers].
2. In 1945 the nuclear weapon was invented.
3. Since 1945 there have been no wars [between the major European powers].
4. *Therefore* nuclear weapons must be the reason there have been no wars since 1945 [between the major European powers].

The conclusion that nuclear weapons are the reason for there being no wars between the major European powers since 1945 is a *post hoc* fallacy and therefore logically incorrect. There are an infinite number of other possible explanations for why there have not been any such wars since 1945.

If we go back to the cat-deterrent analogy, we could rule out the cat hypothesis if we were to find that other people *with* cats were still being burgled or that people *without* cats were also not being burgled. These are called 'counterfactuals' and with an infinite number of possible explanations for why anything may or may not happen, it helps enormously if we can rule out some of the obvious explanations by finding examples which would disprove them being the cause in question.

Is there evidence that nuclear weapons have **not** *prevented invasions?*

In 1945 only one country had nuclear weapons (the USA) and that number has by now increased to nine.[76] If, while having nuclear weapons, any of those countries have still been attacked, that would negate the theory that nuclear weapons are the cause of them not being attacked. Similarly, if other countries which do not have nuclear weapons have also not been attacked, that too makes nonsense of the theory that nuclear weapons are what prevent a country from being attacked.

Let's look at the second proposition first. Are there countries and situations in which one might have expected those countries to have been attacked because they were 'defenceless' in the face of nuclear weapons and yet they did not get attacked? In other words, if nuclear weapons were protecting the NATO countries from being attacked by the Soviet Union, for instance, then one would presume that countries not similarly protected by NATO nuclear weapons *would* have been attacked by the Soviet Union.

Countries in western Europe but not in NATO included, during the Cold

War, Finland, Sweden, Austria, Switzerland, Yugoslavia, Spain[77] and Ireland. There is no particular reason why the Soviet Union should have invaded or threatened or 'blackmailed' any of these countries, but the fact is that it did not – despite them not being at all 'protected' by nuclear weapons.

Other countries bordering the Soviet Union and/or China during the Cold War but also without the 'protection' of nuclear weapons included Iran, Pakistan, India, Nepal, Bhutan, Burma and Laos.[78] None of these countries were invaded or threatened or blackmailed, despite not being likewise 'protected' by nuclear weapons. As we have already noted, Afghanistan was invaded by the Soviet Union in 1979 to prop up a pro-Soviet regime that was at risk of falling into the hands of Islamic 'mujahideen' militants, themselves heavily funded and supported by the US.[79]

What about the countries *with* nuclear weapons; what is the evidence that these weapons have 'kept the peace' for all these years? The UK's possession of nuclear weapons did not stop Egypt from taking over the Suez Canal in 1956, they did not stop Iceland from seizing British fishing vessels in 1974 or Argentina from invading the Falklands/Malvinas in 1982. They did not prevent the bombing of the plane which crashed on Lockerbie in 1988 or other attacks which have taken place on British soil.

Possessing nuclear weapons did not save any British lives in Iraq or Afghanistan nor did they in any way affect the outcome of military interventions in Kosovo, Libya, Sierra Leone or anywhere else where British troops have been deployed. UK nuclear weapons did not stop the Provisional IRA from carrying out any of its bombings nor did they have any impact or affect the outcome of the Good Friday agreement. Nuclear weapons did not stop suicide bombers from blowing up trains and buses in London on 7/7 nor have they stopped Somali pirates from seizing British ships in international waters.

At the global level, US nuclear weapons have proven similarly ineffective as a deterrent against military attacks on its allies or the prevention of wars or revolutions in Korea (1950–1953), Vietnam (1955–1975), Cambodia (1967–1975), Cuba (1959), Nicaragua (1979), Iran (1980), Angola (1975–2002), Laos (1975–2007), Somalia (1992–1993) or Iraq/Kuwait (1991).

Cuban Missile Crisis

During the Cuba Missile Crisis in 1962, President Kennedy threatened Khrushchev with nuclear war if he did not turn around his ships loaded with Soviet nuclear missiles heading for Cuba. At the 11th hour, with all US nuclear forces on full alert and ready to launch, Khrushchev backed down and nuclear war was averted.

Proponents of nuclear deterrence showcase this as an example of when deterrence 'worked'. President Kennedy threatened the USSR with nuclear weapons and the USSR backed down. But as Ward Wilson points out in his insightful book, *Five Myths About Nuclear Weapons*, the real story here is that deterrence did *not* work in this example. What worked was behind-the-scenes diplomacy and the American promise to remove nuclear missiles from Turkey which were aimed at the Soviet Union. It was the proximity of those missiles to Russia which almost certainly prompted the reciprocal Soviet placement of missiles in Cuba in the first place.[80]

What worked was also the good sense of Premier Khrushchev not to engulf the world in a nuclear holocaust over a relatively minor incident like this. Was Khrushchev 'deterred' by the threat of American nuclear weapons raining down on his country, or was he simply the more sane of the two? President Kennedy was apparently not deterred by the threat of Soviet nuclear weapons raining down on *his* country, because if he had been, he would not have made ultimatums to Khrushchev that brought the world to the brink of nuclear war.

In order to be able to say that nuclear deterrence 'works', it is necessary for the threat of nuclear annihilation of one's own country to be sufficient to prevent one from attacking or threatening to attack another country. In the case of the Cuba Missile Crisis, the US President threatened the USSR to the point of being willing to initiate nuclear hostilities despite the clear and unmistakable risk that nuclear annihilation of the US could result from that.

The Case of India and Pakistan

India and Pakistan have fought four wars and engaged in a number of military confrontations short of war since they became independent countries in 1947. Three of these wars took place (in 1947, 1965 and 1971) when neither country had any nuclear weapons. The fourth took place after both had officially acquired them.

Serious incidents between India and Pakistan that could have escalated into full-scale war but did not, have been taking place throughout this period, particularly in Kashmir, where armed clashes took place in 1984, 1985, 1987 and 1995. Military stand-offs as a result of heightened tensions between the two countries took place after the terrorist attack on the Indian parliament in 2001 and following the Mumbai attacks in 2008. Other border skirmishes have taken place in 1999, 2011, 2013 and 2014–15.

Between India's first nuclear test in 1974 and Pakistan's first nuclear test in 1998, India had a monopoly of nuclear weapons in South Asia.[81] Interestingly, this period coincides with the longest period of relative peace between the two countries. Does this mean that India's monopoly of nuclear weapons gave it such a military advantage over Pakistan that the latter was 'deterred' from engaging with India's military during this period?

The problem with that theory is that India has always had a military advantage over Pakistan, being a much larger country with a much larger military force. The period of relative peace between 1974 and 1998 also means that India's military did not engage with Pakistan's military, either. In any case, how do we account for the fact that military confrontations – including a full-scale war – resumed after both states had acquired nuclear weapons?

The Indo-Pakistani War of 1999 (the 'Kargil War') was comparatively limited and short-lived. This was primarily a result of the intense international pressure, especially from the United States, to end the war before it could escalate into a nuclear confrontation.[82] Nevertheless the fact remains that a dangerous, full-scale war took place between two countries possessing nuclear weapons. Neither India nor Pakistan were apparently deterred by the prospect of nuclear retaliation from the other side.

Summary

The first half of the 20th century was by most accounts the bloodiest in human history, with two world wars claiming the lives of at least 50 million people worldwide. Thankfully, there has not been a third world war in the last 70 years. But neither was there a full-scale confrontation between the major powers of Europe for nearly 100 years prior to WWI.

We need to go back to the Napoleonic Wars of 1803–1815 to witness battle deaths on a scale equivalent to WWI or WWII. There was the Crimean War of 1853–1856, but most historians consider the 19th century to be one of the most peaceful periods in European history. From a historical perspective, therefore, there is no need to explain why a third world war did not take place in the second half of the 20th century.

The major European and Asian powers fought smaller wars and skirmishes with each other throughout the 19th century, as indeed they continued to do throughout the 20th century. The so-called 'peace' of the last 70 years has in fact been punctuated with more than 250 wars, many of them involving one or more of the nuclear weapon states – including wars which those states lost, despite having nuclear weapons.

Immediately following WWII, the Soviet Union installed puppet regimes across Eastern Europe and maintained tight control over them, blockading Berlin in 1948, crushing the revolt in Hungary in 1956, invading Czechoslovakia in 1968, and imposing martial law in Poland in 1980. These were all seen as signs of Soviet 'aggression' and an intent eventually to invade Western Europe. Yet it was Churchill and Roosevelt who defined the post-war 'spheres of influence' and in effect gave Stalin 'permission' to maintain Eastern Europe as a permanent 'buffer zone' between Germany and Russia.

Following the collapse of the Soviet Union in 1991, it has become increasingly clear that despite all the cold war propaganda at the time, no Soviet leader had any plans, or any intentions, to invade Western Europe. The nuclear arms race, which brought the world to the brink of nuclear war on several occasions, was fuelled by unfounded fears on both sides.

There is, in fact, no real evidence to support the common belief that it was nuclear weapons, rather than any other reason, that prevented the Soviet Union from invading Western Europe or kept the Cold War from turning 'hot.' Indeed, if nuclear weapons were the only thing preventing countries from being attacked by the Soviet Union, one would expect countries without nuclear weapons to have been attacked or invaded during that time, such as Finland, Sweden, Austria, Switzerland, Yugoslavia, or Spain. None of these countries were protected by the NATO nuclear 'umbrella' and yet they suffered no adverse consequences.

Similarly, if nuclear weapons were as effective at deterring attacks and preventing war as they are believed to be, one would reasonably expect that those countries which have had nuclear weapons not to have been attacked or suffered defeat in wars, and yet this is also not the case.

There are many plausible reasons why a third world war has not taken place and there is no need to believe in the theory of nuclear deterrence to explain this fact. For a start, all countries agreed in 1945 to renounce war except in self-defence and to rely instead on peaceful means of settling disputes, especially through the mechanisms of the United Nations. Other explanations include the increasingly interdependent nature of the world economy: this means that attacking another country invariably damages one's own economic interests. We are also an increasingly cosmopolitan world in which people interact with, befriend, and marry each other across national and cultural boundaries as never before. All these and many other factors are what has 'kept the peace' since 1945.

CHAPTER 7

Are Nuclear Weapons Keeping Us Safe Today?

IT IS COMMONLY believed that nuclear weapons put an end to WWII and prevented WWIII. Both of these beliefs must at least be questioned, since there are other plausible explanations for both results (see Chapters 5 and 6). The Cold War ended nearly 25 years ago but we still have nuclear weapons. Have they been keeping us safe since then and are they keeping us safe today?

Britain's highest serving general, Chief of Defence Staff General Sir Nicholas Houghton, is concerned that people understand how important Trident is to the defence of the realm. He refers to Trident as 'the deterrent' and said on the *Andrew Marr Show* in November 2015, 'when people say you are never going to use the deterrent, what I say is that you use the deterrent every second of every minute of every day'.[83]

There is a confusion of language here between 'using' the deterrent (ie the weapon), in the sense of pressing the button and firing a Trident nuclear missile at somebody and 'using' the deterrent (ie the policy), in the sense of preventing somebody from attacking the UK by the threat of striking back at them with a Trident nuclear missile. General Houghton is not suggesting that we fire Trident missiles every second of every minute of every day, but he is implying that we are successfully preventing potential aggressors from attacking the UK because we are threatening every second of every minute of every day to fire Trident missiles at them if they do.

Is that meant to mean that *without* Trident acting as a deterrent every second of every minute of every day, the UK would face an ever-present threat from potential aggressors trying to attack us here and now? Are we, at this present moment, faced with such a threat? According to the government's 2015 National Security Strategy, 'there is currently no immediate direct military threat to the UK mainland.'[84] This has been the assessment produced by successive governments for at least 25 years.

Neither Russia nor China nor any other country is at this precise time threatening to attack the UK. Perhaps General Houghton believes that during the Cold War, the Soviet Union did pose such a threat. Perhaps he believes that Russia or some other country could, in future, pose such a threat. These are issues we look at in some depth in other chapters. But the claim that Trident is here and now 'being used' as a deterrent every second of every minute of every day is difficult to understand and if true, highly dangerous – since it implies the 'deterrent' could also fail at any second of any minute of any day.

Is Trident protecting Estonia?

Perhaps, if the UK itself is not under threat right now, Trident is at least 'protecting' NATO allies in Eastern Europe, such as Estonia or Poland, who might otherwise be facing the threat of imminent attack by Russia? According to NATO, however, 'the Euro-Atlantic area is at peace and the threat of a conventional attack against NATO territory is low.'[85] This was NATO's assessment in 2010 and it has not been changed since then despite heightened NATO activity on its eastern frontiers with Russia.

Nevertheless, members of NATO are supposedly protected by the US 'nuclear umbrella' which includes thousands of nuclear weapons on planes and ships, missiles on submarines and in underground silos, missile defences and a global satellite and radar communications system linking all these together. In what way does the UK's single Trident submarine in the Atlantic contribute to this 'umbrella'?[86]

If there is any sense in which it can be said that Russia is 'deterred' from attacking Estonia, is it likely that the UK's single patrolling Trident submarine is what is deterring it or even *contributing* to that deterrent in some meaningful sense, as opposed to the 7,000 nuclear warheads currently in the US arsenal and making up the NATO nuclear 'umbrella'? Why would Russia even care about the UK Trident weapons when it is faced with an overwhelming arsenal of nuclear weapons from the US?

Perhaps Trident is the *reason* that both the UK and Estonia are so free from direct military threat, and if we didn't have it, the threat would return? As we have seen in the previous three chapters, there is little reason to believe that nuclear deterrence works as a theory and little evidence to support the idea that it has worked up to now. The fact that the UK is not currently threatened militarily is unlikely to be the result of using Trident as a deterrent, since a deterrent by definition can only 'deter' an actor who is already intent on doing something which they then feel prevented from doing as a result of the deterrent.

Current threats facing the UK

If the UK is not facing a direct military threat at the moment, what are the threats that it *does* face and in what ways, if any, can Trident address these more direct threats to national security? The national security risk assessment for 2015 lists six 'tier one' risks that the UK is likely to face over the next five years.[87] These are:

1. Terrorism
2. Cyber warfare
3. International military conflict
4. Instability overseas
5. Public health
6. Major natural hazards

Trident and terrorism

Let us first of all distinguish 'terrorism' as a tactic that is used by certain groups to achieve their objectives and 'terrorist groups' who use this tactic. Terrorism as a tactic, at least as it has been most often used in modern times, is a means by which a relatively weak party attempts to use the strength of their adversary to their advantage. They do this by goading their adversary into committing acts of (indiscriminate) violence and repression which they hope will sufficiently anger and antagonise the victims of that violence and repression as to bring themselves more support and more recruits.

It is not difficult to see how this vicious cycle works in the case of so-called ISIS, for instance. First, a so-called ISIS terrorist beheads a British tourist, guns down holiday-makers on a beach, or blows up a restaurant in Paris. Next, western governments step up their attacks on so-called ISIS strongholds in Syria or Iraq and in the process, kill women and children, destroy homes and disrupt whole communities trying to survive. Those communities then rise up in anger and indignation, vowing to avenge the death of their loved ones. They join ISIS, give money, provide shelter and otherwise support the ISIS cause more than they did previously. And the cycle continues, with ISIS growing in power and support all the while.

In the case of terrorism of this kind, the concept of deterrence does not and cannot apply, since the whole purpose of using terrorism, by a group like ISIS, is to push the US, UK and other Western powers to bring down more violence on their own communities. Imagine that the UK decided the only way to stop ISIS was to launch a nuclear attack on their headquarters in

Raqqa. The whole world would probably recoil in horror and there would be a huge outpouring of sympathy for ISIS, accompanied by a huge flow of funds, weapons and volunteer fighters to avenge the attack, leaving ISIS many times stronger than it was before.

When it comes to terrorist groups like ISIS, it must be remembered that they do not only employ terrorism as their weapon but may also fight their enemies in a more conventional fashion, with armies, weapons and battles over territory. In this sense, a terrorist group is like any other adversary, especially if they hold large amounts of territory, have large amounts of cash and weaponry, operate as a government over their territory and do business with the outside world, even if only on the black market.

ISIS, as a quasi-government controlling large areas of Syria and Iraq is, in this respect, similar to the Taliban when they were in control of Afghanistan. Perhaps they could be defeated and dislodged by other rebel groups with the support of outside powers like the US and the UK. But would nuclear weapons likely be of assistance in this kind of scenario? Apart from antagonising the local population and driving them further into the hands of ISIS, nuclear weapons are unlikely to be of much use in guerrilla warfare settings where the fighting groups are agile and dispersed and where the fighting takes place house to house, neighbourhood to neighbourhood, with fighters intermingling with the civilian population.

Trident is useless as a weapon for fighting terrorism, and for that reason it is just as ineffective as a deterrent against terrorist groups. However, it is itself a weapon of terror, raining down death and destruction like no other weapon on earth. It is therefore a prize which any terrorist group in the world would be glad to get their hands on. Imagine the impact globally, if instead of destroying the Twin Towers and killing 3,000 people, Osama bin Laden had been able to detonate a nuclear bomb, however crude, in the centre of New York.

As we shall see in Chapter 13 the risk of a nuclear detonation, whether by accident or by design, is a very real one and it is our own politicians and generals who pose that risk to the world, not terrorists. Nevertheless, the fact that terrorist groups exist and are forever seeking more lethal forms of terrorism is a sober reminder that nuclear weapons or fissile material getting into the hands of a terrorist intent on using it against random civilians in any city in the world is a very real risk.

A terrorist is unlikely to get hold of a Trident submarine at sea, although even that is not an impossibility. More likely is that a terrorist would attempt to get hold of nuclear material from a submarine that is docked, or while warheads are en route to or from the submarine, or in storage. We look at these safety issues in Chapter 13 but here it is worth noting that far from being a useful tool for combatting terrorism, Trident and the whole nuclear industry that goes with it makes the UK much more of a target for terrorists who want to get their hands on nuclear material. Imagine, not only a terrorist atom bomb going off in New York, but the world then discovering that the nuclear material was acquired in the UK?

Trident and cyber warfare

As modern societies become more and more dependent on computer systems for every aspect of daily life and especially for control of political and military processes, the more at risk we become to the possibility of cyber attacks which might not only inconvenience people but put lives in danger. There is no point in discussing whether Trident can protect us from cyber warfare, because it clearly cannot.

However, as with the threat of terrorism, the threat of cyber warfare raises additional concerns about the safety of having nuclear weapons around. Trident and everything to do with launching and targeting of nuclear weapons is heavily dependent on computer software. There have already been cyber attacks on nuclear facilities, including an attack which actually destroyed equipment at a nuclear reactor site in Iran, believed to be the work of Israeli government hackers. Three nuclear power stations in the US have been shut down in recent years by computer bugs and viruses[88] getting into the system, illustrating the potential danger to civil nuclear facilities.

Former Defence Minister Des Browne claimed in November 2015 that Trident could be vulnerable to cyber attack based on a US Department of Defence study into the vulnerabilities of vital IT infrastructure to cyber attack.[89] The report warned that the US and its allies could not be confident that their defence systems would be able to survive a concerted cyber attack from a sophisticated opponent like Russia or China. Des Browne was quickly dismissed by government officials and a former White House spokesperson who said that the report was not correct because nuclear weapons software was a closed system not accessible from the outside.[90]

Other computer experts have countered this by saying that 'the reality is that *any* defence facility, or national public or private infrastructure service, could be hacked.' They warn that the techniques of cyber warfare are advancing all the time and there are many ways of accessing a closed system using smartphones, memory sticks and other electrical components, as was the case with the cyber attack in Iran mentioned above.[91] However unlikely it may be, Trident, like all other modern weapons systems, is heavily dependent on computer software, making it potentially vulnerable to cyber attack. So instead of helping to fight cyber warfare, once again Trident actually makes the UK more vulnerable.

Trident and international military conflict

What role does Trident play in the UK's military involvement in places like Syria, Libya, Iraq, Afghanistan? These interventions are included as tier one 'risks' facing the UK presumably because the 'risk' is that the UK will get involved in more of these in the next five years – perhaps sending troops and/or fighter jets to Yemen, Bahrain, or even Saudi Arabia?

There are those who argue that the UK has used Trident to bully other countries into doing what we want, and will continue to use Trident in that way.[92] However, there is no hard evidence that nuclear bullying is any more effective than nuclear deterrence. They both assume a certain type of psychological response and rational calculation of costs and benefits which cannot be proven. No doubt the UK government would *like* to be able to get its own way in the world by rattling its nuclear sabre every now and then, but whether other countries respond in the desired way is another matter.

The Falklands War

Britain's possession of nuclear weapons did not deter the generals in Argentina from attacking and occupying the Falklands/Malvinas in 1982. Although many thousands of miles from the UK mainland, these islands were still considered British territory and therefore technically a military attack on the UK took place, despite the UK having a nuclear deterrent at the time.

There are claims that Prime Minister Margaret Thatcher threatened to use nuclear weapons if the war started going badly wrong. It seems unlikely that any British nuclear missile submarines were deployed to the South Atlantic. However, in 2003, the Ministry of Defence admitted to the *Guardian* newspaper that other types of nuclear weapon, probably W-177 nuclear depth bombs, were carried on British ships sailing to the Falklands. None were used, although there remains speculation as to whether any nuclear weapons were on board the HMS Sheffield when it sank after being hit by French-made missiles.[93]

Other recent conflicts

British troops fighting in Iraq and Afghanistan were not at any time helped or protected by the UK having nuclear missiles, nor did those missiles act as any kind of deterrent against armed opponents in those places. It should be remembered that both in the first Gulf War of 1991 and in the second Iraq

War of 2003 onwards, there were many who claimed that Saddam Hussein had nuclear weapons as well as chemical and biological weapons. Yet this possibility was never considered to be a deterrent to US and UK forces (and others) attacking Iraq. It was also well known that Israel had nuclear weapons by this time, and yet that did not deter Saddam Hussein from launching medium-range missiles against Israel. Indeed there were fears that some of the Iraqi missiles might contain chemical, biological or even nuclear warheads. Yet this possibility apparently did not deter any of the warring parties from continuing with their attacks.

What about Russia?

Until 1991, all of the UK's nuclear weapons were aimed at the Soviet Union. When the Soviet Union disappeared, the first Trident submarine was still on the assembly line, but they continued to roll out the programme and the weapons continued to be aimed at what is now the Russian Federation. Officially, the Trident missiles are now 'de-targeted' and could in theory be re-targeted at some other country, such as Iran or Pakistan. In practice the main target is, and always has been, Russia.

As we saw in the last chapter, there is no real evidence that tens of thousands of nuclear weapons from the US, let alone a few hundred from the UK, had any deterrent effect on the Soviet Union during the Cold War. There are many other plausible explanations for why a third world war did not take place during that time. What is the rationale for believing that now, 25 years after the Cold War, the UK's nuclear weapons could have a deterrent effect on Russia?

'Russia has become more aggressive, authoritarian and nationalist,' says the 2015 NSS/SDSR. 'We cannot rule out the possibility that it may feel tempted to act aggressively against NATO allies.'[94] We need to first of all look at what is going on with regard to Russia and NATO, and then secondly look at what, if any, impact Trident may have on this.

Ukraine and the Crimea

Ukraine has been sharply divided politically since its independence in 1991 between those in the more prosperous and westward looking parts of the country and those in the poorer decaying industrial areas of eastern Ukraine. This conflict goes back centuries and mirrors to some extent what happened in Yugoslavia, where the more prosperous western parts (Croatia and Slovenia) were looking westward to the EU as their model while the more traditional Russian-facing parts to the east (Serbia) were looking eastward to Russia. Electoral maps showing voting patterns in Ukraine since independence highlight this sharp east-west divide in Ukraine very clearly.[95]

The 'Euromaidan' revolution of 2014 and the months and years leading up to it have all been about this political divide over the future of Ukraine, with western Ukrainians wanting Ukraine to join the EU and NATO while eastern Ukrainians wanting closer ties to Russia. It is likely that Russia has been providing support to the eastern rebels fighting the present Ukrainian government just as it is likely that the US was providing support to the Euromaidan rebels before the removal of President Yanukovych.[96] But this is not about Russia or other outside parties; it is about the internal politics of Ukraine.

What Russia would find very difficult to accept would be for Ukraine to join NATO and take control of the key Russian naval base in the Crimea. The Crimea has always been of strategic importance to Russia/the Soviet Union because it is home to Russia's only year-round fully ice-free port, Sevastopol. The Russian Black Sea Fleet is based there, along with 15,000 Russian sailors. The naval base itself was leased to Russia when Ukraine got its independence in 1991.

Under the terms of independence, the Crimea was declared an 'autonomous republic' within Ukraine. Crimea has always been predominantly Russian-speaking with only a small Ukrainian minority. After centuries of rule by various other empires, including Greeks, Roman, Byzantines, Mongols and Ottomans, the Crimea was incorporated into the Russian empire in 1783. It was 'gifted' to Ukraine in 1954, at a time when Ukraine was still fully part of the Soviet Union. It was thus not a real transfer of 'sovereignty' as such.

Ukraine and nuclear weapons

It is sometimes suggested that if only Ukraine had kept its arsenal of nuclear weapons inherited from the Soviet Union, it could have deterred Russia from annexing Crimea or from intervening in support of rebels in eastern Ukraine. Since these were actually Russian missiles under Russian control, the idea that they could have been used by Ukraine against Russia is rather absurd. What *is* likely is that had Ukraine still possessed nuclear weapons at the time of the 'Euromaidan' revolution and subsequent war in the east, the risk of nuclear weapons falling into the hands of some rebel group or other would have raised alarm bells across the world. Who can imagine anything more dangerous than a country with nuclear weapons in the midst of a civil war, with military units changing sides and a government that is not fully in control of the military or of all parts of the country?

And where does Trident fit into this picture? What if Ukraine had already been a member of NATO at the time of the Euromaidan revolution? Would the UK have come to the rescue of a NATO ally and threatened Russia with its nuclear weapons if they tried to annex any part of Ukraine? How might that have played out in the event of a referendum taking place and Russian troops seizing control of key facilities in Crimea? Would the UK then have launched Trident missiles at Russia as a result? It is difficult to imagine how Trident could play any kind of role at all in real-life situations like this, let alone a positive or constructive role.

It is not surprising that General Sir Nicholas Houghton presents a confusing picture of the deterrent being used every second of every minute of every day. He and his fellow military professionals are caught in a catch-22 situation that they can't easily get out of. If they admit publicly, or even to themselves, that Trident actually contributes nothing at all to the defence of the realm or to the kinds of real situations the UK faces in today's world, they are themselves undermining the very theory of deterrence they have been trained and taught to regard as the defining doctrine of the nuclear age. If, on the other hand, they try to justify why we have it, they are bound to end up stretching their own credibility to the breaking point, either in terms of describing the nature or extent of the military threats we actually face or in terms of describing their confidence in the ability of Trident to address those threats.

Summary

Since the end of the Cold War nearly 25 years ago, politicians and military figures have insisted that the UK still needs nuclear weapons 'now more than ever before'. If nuclear weapons are keeping us safe today, what are they keeping us safe *from*?

The 2015 National Security strategy lists six 'tier one' security risks facing the UK over the next five years: terrorism, cyber warfare, international military conflict, instability overseas, public health, and major natural hazards.

No one is suggesting that nuclear weapons have any role to play in protecting public health or combatting major natural disasters. Instability overseas is in no small measure a direct result of international military conflict, as are terrorism and the threat of cyber-attacks. It is difficult to see how nuclear weapons contribute to any of these security risks facing the UK today. If anything, Trident makes the UK more vulnerable to both terrorism and to cyber-attack, because of the risk of someone hacking into, damaging or stealing a nuclear weapon.

Trident is utterly useless in terms of deterring a terrorist attack or responding to a terrorist attack if one occurs. Terrorists have no obvious military or political headquarters to attack with nuclear weapons, so the threatening to attack them is meaningless. Terrorism as a military strategy is aimed at provoking a heavy-handed response that will strengthen support for the terrorists among their own population. All military responses to terrorism are counterproductive because they play directly into the terrorist's strategy. A nuclear response would be counter-productive to a correspondingly massive degree.

In terms of the international military conflicts that the UK has been engaged with since the end of the Cold War (as well as before that), there is no case in which UK's nuclear weapons have played a role and it is hard to imagine a case in which they could have done. Nuclear weapons did not protect the Falklands/Malvinas from being invaded by Argentina and they did not protect the Suez Canal from being taken over by Egypt. They did not protect British troops fighting in Iraq or Afghanistan.

Since the end of the Cold War, Russia has remained the principal target of the UK's nuclear weapons, despite posing no direct threat to the UK. Russia's military involvement in Georgia and then more recently in the Ukraine are seen as signs that Russia has become more 'aggressive' and a potential threat to NATO allies. Some have even suggested that if Ukraine had retained its Cold War nuclear weapons and/or joined NATO, it could have successfully deterred recent interferences from Russia.

Like all conflicts, the situation in Ukraine is complex and nuanced. Adding nuclear weapons into an already complex and volatile situation is hardly like to have improved matters. Would the UK have threatened to launch Trident missiles at Russia if it tried to annex from Crimea? What would have been the response from Russia had the UK made such a threat? And what would the UK have done if Russia had annexed Crimea anyway?

These and many other such questions cast considerable doubt upon the usefulness of Trident since the end of the Cold War. It carries out its 'continuous at-sea' patrols day in day out, year after year. But who is it deterring and what is it deterring them from doing? Retired Royal Navy Commander Rob Green describes Trident as 'the emperor's new clothes'.[97] The submariners parade around, pretending to be defending the UK from all sorts of unseen threats when in fact they are doing nothing of the sort. The UK is no safer for having nuclear weapons than, say, Brazil is for having none.

CHAPTER 8

Do Nuclear Weapons Protect Us From Future Risks?

AS WE HAVE seen in previous chapters, there is little evidence for the claims that nuclear weapons forced Japan to surrender in WWII, or that they deterred the Soviets from attacking western Europe during the Cold War or that they have played a role in deterring any other threat since. They cannot be considered 'essential' for the defence of the UK or its allies because we face no clear or present threat. What about the future, though? Surely, as Tony Blair claimed, and as David Cameron reiterated in the 2015 Strategic Security and Defence Review, we need nuclear weapons as the 'ultimate insurance policy' against unknown threats to the UK in the future?

No one can predict the future. We live in a rapidly changing world with many state and non-state actors making decisions that can affect us and our future security here in the UK. Surely some sort of insurance policy against the possibility of future threats is reasonable and prudent under the circumstances.

Using the insurance analogy

It sounds intuitively logical to compare Trident to an insurance policy. It makes it sound like a sensible investment in the future, a protection for the years ahead, something that will be well worth the cost if and when we come to need it one day, and terribly short-sighted to try to do without.

In most cases, the government is careful to argue that Trident is needed now *as well as* being an insurance policy for the future, but logically speaking you cannot have it both ways. By using the insurance metaphor, the government is implicitly undermining the argument that Trident is also needed now, because if it is needed now, it makes no sense to be talking about insurance.

Insurance is by definition something you invest in so as to give you what you might need at some point in the future. If you need something in the present, you're too late to take out insurance. No insurance company will insure you against something you already need at this moment, precisely because it negates the whole concept of insurance to do that. If you miss your flight home, you don't take out travel insurance, you take the next flight. The only time you *can* take out travel insurance is when you don't need it, ie before you travel. The same applies to every other kind of insurance, including, of course, life insurance.

Insurance is also something that normally pays out to 'remedy' a misfortune such as sickness, accident, fire, missed flight, death... In the case of death, the 'remedy' is to provide ongoing support to a bereft spouse or children, while in other cases it is the person who takes out the insurance who benefits from whatever the 'remedy' may be. It is a strange form of insurance indeed which pays out by raining down even more death and destruction as a 'remedy' for being invaded. That is a bit like having fire insurance which burns down your neighbour's house rather than repairs the fire damage on your own house.

But let's continue with the analogy and try to imagine that there is some scenario in the future for which it makes sense to take out nuclear insurance now as a precaution, bearing in mind that insurance is, as we have seen, a misleading analogy. What might such a scenario look like?

Facing down another Hitler

The most common fear driving people to support Trident as an insurance policy is the fear that another Hitler might arise and try to take over Europe and/or the UK. We might call this the '1940 argument' because it harks back to the days when Britain stood alone against Hitler and there was no one to come to our defence. We need not argue here about how likely such an event might be, only whether having Trident would somehow protect us in those hypothetical circumstances.

As we saw in Chapter 6, one of the arguments against the theory that British, French and US nuclear weapons prevented the Soviets from attacking and invading western Europe during the Cold War is that had those weapons been used against the Soviets, they almost certainly would have provoked a counter-strike with nuclear weapons against the UK at least as ferocious as anything we might have launched against them. What would have been the net result of such an exchange? Perhaps the Soviet Union would have been unable to invade Western Europe, but by that point there would have hardly been anything left of Western Europe for them to invade.

Possession of nuclear weapons cannot *prevent* a nuclear attack unless those weapons are used in a pre-emptive first strike with a near 100% success rate in destroying all the incoming nuclear weapons of the opposing side.

We will look in later chapters at the whole question of NATO, the US nuclear 'umbrella' and the UK's special relationship with the US on nuclear matters. But for now, we need only focus on what Trident would contribute to preventing, deterring or protecting the UK from an all-out attack by a major power like Russia.

The honest and difficult truth is that the UK's 200-plus nuclear warheads are no match for Russia's 7,000-plus nuclear warheads. However much destruction Trident could cause in return, they would be unlikely to stop a Russian leader who was determined to attack the UK.

And the even more troublesome truth is that Trident would almost certainly never be used at that point. Why? Because it would mean certain suicide for the whole country, as we have seen in Chapter 4. By launching a nuclear attack against a more powerful and presumably nuclear-armed adversary, we would be inviting a response in kind which would have far more devastating consequences to a small island nation like the UK than it would to a vast superpower like Russia.

Nuclear blackmail

Another possible future threat against which Trident could be claimed to protect us is nuclear blackmail, or the idea that some country might threaten us with nuclear weapons unless we agreed to do their bidding. It is hard to understand the difference between the theory of nuclear deterrence and the concept of nuclear blackmail, other than the fact that when we use our own nuclear weapons as a threat, that is called deterrence, whereas when another country uses their nuclear weapons to threaten *us*, it is called nuclear blackmail.

Let us try to imagine a scenario that could be conceivably defined as nuclear blackmail. Let us say there is another Falklands War, only this time the UK has given up its nuclear weapons while in the meantime Argentina has acquired them. Let us further imagine that Argentina has acquired a lot of other sophisticated military hardware and used these to launch another successful invasion of the Falklands/Malvinas. Once again, a British task force sets sail from the UK to fight a war in the South Atlantic, only this time Argentina announces that it will bomb the British task force with nuclear weapons and effectively wipe out the Royal Navy unless it turns round and sails back to the UK.

From the Argentine viewpoint, they are using their nuclear weapons as a deterrent in exactly the way foreseen by nuclear deterrence theory – as a threat against another country which they hope will not need to be carried out because the other country would see it as inflicting unacceptable damage and decide to desist from their planned course of action. From the UK point of view, this would look like nuclear blackmail, since it is a threat using nuclear weapons to try to prevent the UK from doing what it believes to be its right and duty, namely the defence of British territory from external invasion.

What might happen next is anyone's guess. However, what *should* happen according to international law is quite clear. First, the matter should be taken to the UN Security Council as a breach of international peace and security. The Security Council should then call on the UK and Argentina to negotiate a peaceful solution to the problem, offering to mediate if necessary. They might ask the International Court of Justice for a ruling on who legitimately 'owns' the disputed islands. They might call for an arbitrated settlement or set up a UN trusteeship to put the islands under neutral international control. They might call for a referendum by the islanders to decide their future.

If none of these peaceful means to resolve the dispute are successful, the Security Council would then be authorised to rule who is at fault and to impose sanctions on either or both parties unless they follow the instructions of the Security Council. Even if the Security Council were to rule in favour of the UK being the rightful owner of the islands and victim of an illegal invasion by Argentina, they might still order the British task force back to port until the crisis is resolved.

If all else failed, the Security Council might then authorise the use of force under Chapter VII (see Chapter 12) to remove the Argentine occupying forces. This would not be a British force but an international force, possibly not even including the UK but perhaps including the US and other South American countries, for instance. Would Argentina threaten the US and other neighbouring countries with nuclear weapons, or would it have deferred to the international community long before it reached that point?

The Trident Commission

The independent Trident Commission, in their concluding report in 2014, came down in favour of retaining nuclear weapons on the grounds that

> if there is more than a negligible chance that the possession of nuclear weapons might play a decisive future role in the defence of the UK and its allies... they should be retained.[98]

Nevertheless, they 'reject the case for retaining a military nuclear capability as a general insurance against an uncertain future'. It is difficult to see how the former statement, which the Trident Commission support, differs from the latter statement, which they reject. Surely, saying that nuclear weapons 'might play a decisive future role' is tantamount to saying they do not play a decisive role at the moment but we want to hold on to them in case they might in the future?

In rejecting the 'general insurance policy' approach, however, the Trident Commission states that 'every effort should be made to specify exactly what possible types of threat could arise for which an independent UK nuclear deterrent would be relevant'.[99] They go on to describe three (and only three) cases in which they see the possibility of Trident playing a decisive role in the future:

- Re-emergence of a past nuclear threat (specifically, Russia).
- New emerging state nuclear threats (specifically, Iran).
- Nuclear terrorism, chemical and biological weapons (specifically, biological).

The Commission rejected other possible scenarios where Trident might be thought of as needed in the future, such as in a conflict with China, India, Pakistan, Israel or even North Korea. Nevertheless, the three cases listed above, which they do consider relevant, leave the door sufficiently ajar to allow for many other interpretations of what a 'decisive future role' for Trident might be.

Incitement to proliferation

All of the arguments used to justify the UK having its own nuclear weapons could be just as equally applied to every other country in the world. But no other argument in favour of nuclear weapons is as much an incitement to nuclear proliferation as the argument that we need them as a 'general insurance against an uncertain future' or that they 'might play a decisive future role'. This lowers the bar pretty much to the floor in terms of an argument for 'needing' nuclear weapons since, as we have suggested above, this kind of language implies that they are *not* needed now but only *might* be in the future.

Iran is virtually surrounded by the nuclear weapons of potentially hostile states: Pakistan to the east, Russia not that far to the north, Israel not that far to the west and a US nuclear fleet in the Persian Gulf to the south. On what basis can the UK, which by its own admission does not face a serious military threat from any other country, say that Iran should not have its own nuclear weapons when the UK insists on needing them for an 'uncertain future'? On what grounds can the UK insist that North Korea has no right to its own nuclear weapons? Or for that matter, what leverage does it give the UK with the nuclear weapons of India or Pakistan, when all they have done is to follow their former colonial master's lead?

Unmistakable signs that the UK government intends to hold onto its nuclear weapons for the indefinite future include:

- Signing a nuclear cooperation agreement with France that is supposed to last for the next 50 years.
- Building submarines that are supposed to enable the UK to maintain continuous at-sea patrols until the early 2060s.
- Investing in large-scale infrastructure projects at AWE Aldermaston for the next generation of nuclear warheads that will only come into service in the 2040s.

The argument that Trident might be needed at some unknown point in the future – even if not needed at this precise moment – merely reinforces this picture of a government unwilling to contemplate the elimination of its nuclear arsenal. As we shall see in Chapter 12, this is directly contradicting the UK's treaty obligations as interpreted by the World Court and is an invitation to every other country in the world to develop their own nuclear weapons because they too 'might need them' at some unknown point in the future.

The risks of relying on outdated technology

It is impossible to predict what the international political environment will look like in 10, 20 or 30 years from now. We can confidently assume, however, that technology will continue to advance in the decades to come, especially in the military sphere.

Already, cyber warfare technologies are outpacing the security technologies designed to provide protection against cyber attacks. Underwater drones and advances in sonar technology are making invulnerable submarines suddenly vulnerable to tracking and monitoring even in the depths of the open sea.[100] Anti-ballistic missile defences are also advancing, making ballistic missiles like Trident increasingly vulnerable to being destroyed in mid-air before reaching their target.

With greater targeting accuracy also comes new ways to protect targets from attack, for instance burying nuclear missile silos and command bunkers ever deeper under tonnes of earth and concrete or spreading them out over vast distances which would require many more times the number of missiles in order to 'take them out'.

The nature of warfare throughout human history has been one of advances in offensive capabilities that are followed by advances in defensive capabilities and vice versa. Whatever advantage may have been gained by one side through the latest technological development is very soon offset by technological developments on the other side. Despite the unprecedented destructive power of nuclear weapons, the basic dynamics of warfare remain the same. Trident will be as obsolete in 20 or 30 years time as the bayonet or the cavalry charge is today.

Summary

We live in an unpredictable and rapidly changing world. The claim is that Trident is an insurance policy that protects the UK from those unknown future risks.

Trident is a weapons system designed in the 1970s for a (Cold) War that ended in the 1990s. It is currently being upgraded to the technology of the 2010s, but will that still be relevant in the 2060s, 50 years from now?

From a purely military point of view, the new Trident submarines and their missiles and warheads are likely to be outdated before they even come into service in the 2030s.

What kind of world will they be operating in by the 2050s or 2060s, and what kind of threats would they be protecting the UK from? The Trident Commission identified three specific future threats in which Trident might play a 'decisive role': re-emergence of the 'Russian threat', newly emerging nuclear threat from, for instance, Iran, and the threat of biological terrorism from an unspecified but state-sponsored source.

It is not clear how Trident might play a decisive role in each of these scenarios. In the case of Russia, the UK will always be a minor player in relation to such a large country. It is hard to see how the UK could threaten or use nuclear weapons against Russia at any time in the future without suffering catastrophically as a result.

In terms of Iran or another emerging nuclear power, it is again hard to see how Trident would be more successful at reducing the potential threat than, for instance, international negotiations such as those recently concluded. Terrorism, whether with biological weapons or any other kind of weapons cannot be deterred or successfully responded to by nuclear weapons, as we saw in the last chapter.

In the long term, there are only two conceivable scenarios that can emerge. One is a world that is safe from nuclear weapons because all countries have agreed to get rid of them, or a world that is awash with nuclear weapons because more and more countries decide they need them as an 'insurance policy' against future risks. By arguing that the UK needs Trident as an insurance policy, we are encouraging other countries to follow our logic and our example. A world full of nuclear weapons is a far more dangerous world than the one we live in right now. The insurance argument therefore makes the UK less safe, not safer.

PART THREE

We Need Trident to Maintain Our Place in the World

CHAPTER 9

NATO and the 'Special Relationship'

THERE IS NO hard evidence to indicate that Trident has ever protected the UK from external threats and there is little reason to believe it will do so in the future. But do we have a responsibility to protect other countries, even if that puts the UK at greater risk? In what sense does our 'special relationship' with the US require us to be part of the nuclear club?

Lord Robertson is a former UK Defence Minister and Secretary-General of NATO. He has been responsible for the UK's nuclear contribution to NATO from both sides, as it were. In the run-up to the Scottish referendum vote in 2014, Lord Robertson gave a speech in the US in which he said that Trident was 'part and parcel of the West's security' and that removing Trident would not only render Scotland unwelcome in NATO but would also be 'effectively disarming the remainder of the United Kingdom' – a result he claimed would be 'cataclysmic in geo-political terms.'[101]

Trident, like Polaris before it, is officially 'assigned' to NATO as part of the UK's contribution to the collective security of the NATO alliance. NATO, in turn, is unequivocally wedded to the concept of nuclear deterrence. It is, above all, a nuclear alliance. While this primarily means that NATO members are covered by the US 'nuclear umbrella', the UK's Trident submarines are also considered part of this umbrella.

Britain's moral obligations

Britain supposedly went to war to defend Belgium in WWI, and to defend Poland in WWII. The logic now is that we should be ready and willing to go to war to defend Estonia or Latvia, or any other NATO member, should they be attacked. This is what is meant when the National Security Strategy says 'we would use our nuclear weapons only in extreme circumstances of self-defence, *including the defence of our NATO allies* [emphasis added]'.[102]

To be a responsible world power and to play our part in protecting democracy and freedom against tyranny and aggression means carrying our weight in the world, sharing the burden of responsibility – and cost – for smaller and more vulnerable countries that may be on the 'frontline' in ways that we are not. Trident is simply one of those ways in which Britain contributes to global peace and security as a nation second only to the USA in terms of military technology and capabilities.

'It is wrong for the UK to sub-contract its security to other countries, and to expect... other nations to carry the burdens and the risks...' said David Cameron to the House of Commons in November 2015.[103] He was referring to the bombing of ISIS in Syria, but he could just as well have been referring to continuous at-sea patrols of Trident.

Britain's place in the world

Britain is a small island on the edge of Europe. It contains less than 1% of the world's population and considerably less than that in terms of land mass. It once controlled a great empire spanning almost the entire globe, but those days are long gone. Perhaps it is time to reassess Britain's place in the world and accept that it is not as big or as important as it seems to assume?

And yet, regardless of Britain's size or stature, the UK does have responsibilities beyond its borders. We are part of a global community and we have a role to play, perhaps a rather big one at that. Indeed, because of Britain's imperial past, it has useful and important connections to many other parts of the world. English is fast becoming the most commonly spoken language in the world. Britain's relations with the US are historical but also social and political. They run very deep. The UK is uniquely placed to be a bridge between the US and Europe and to be able to influence both continents.

So let's acknowledge that the UK *does* have responsibilities beyond its borders, that it can and should play its part in world affairs and that there is no 'retreat' from UK complicity in those affairs. Let's furthermore agree wholeheartedly with the concept of 'collective security'. The UK cannot defend itself or its 'vital interests' alone, but only in concert with other countries working together for the security of all.

Collective security and self-defence

There is a contradiction here, however, between the recognition that the security of the UK is intimately bound up with the security of other countries and the claim that the UK needs its own 'independent deterrent' to protect itself. These cannot both be true. We will look in the next chapter at the question of whether, or to what extent, the UK Trident system is actually 'independent'. It is important at this juncture, however, to question the logic of that claim in relation to the concept of collective security.

One of the arguments made in favour of the UK having its own 'independent' deterrent is that the UK cannot necessarily count on the US coming to its defence in a crisis and therefore the UK needs to maintain its own means of 'defending' itself. The US only entered both world wars belatedly and begrudgingly. It has a long history of 'isolationism' which kept it out of European affairs. It took two years of WWII and the bombing of Pearl Harbor before the US came to the defence of Britain in 1941, which had been left on its own in the fight against Hitler up until that point.

We have already looked at the difference between deterrence and defence. We have also looked at the enormous disparity between the nuclear forces of UK and Russia. The UK cannot emerge 'victorious', in any meaningful sense of the word, from a nuclear conflict with Russia. So in what circumstance can it possibly make sense to imagine the UK acting alone against Russia or any other serious nuclear-armed threat, without the US or other allies also being involved?

The UK is, like it or not, dependent on the US and other allies for its defence. It cannot be any other way in the world of the 21st century, where nation-states very much larger and more powerful than the UK can attack, if they chose to do so, with enormous ferocity and speed from thousands of miles away. There is literally nothing the UK, by itself, can do to prevent that from happening, except by working closely with other countries to ensure the whole world is safe from such a scenario.

Why NATO?

To say that the UK can only be secure through some form of collective security is not the same as saying it can only be secure through its membership of NATO. NATO is one form of collective security that was set up in 1949 to protect Western Europe from possible attack by the Soviet Union. Why does it even still exist now that the Soviet Union does not?

During the Cold War, NATO and the Warsaw Pact were two military blocs, locked in an arms race with each other that involved not only nuclear weapons but also steadily improving and more and more sophisticated and deadly conventional armaments arrayed against each other as well. While many believe that the nuclear deterrent is what kept these two great blocs from going to war against each other, no one disagrees that it was a highly dangerous situation for Europe.

Then the Berlin Wall came down in 1989, Germany was unified, the Soviet Union was broken up into 15 different countries and the Warsaw Pact was dissolved. NATO, however, expanded to include increasing numbers of the former Warsaw Pact countries and then countries of the former Soviet Union itself. If the ultimate ambition were to include even the Russian Federation within NATO, that would have been quite interesting. However the reality is that NATO continues to exist in order to be a military counterweight *to* Russia.

It is beyond the scope of this book to look more deeply into the wisdom of encircling Russia with NATO forces and using a new version of the 1950s 'containment' policy to try to keep Russia from expanding its influence beyond its borders. But is it fair to ask whether this kind of approach is making Europe and the UK safer or less safe?

Throughout most of the Cold War period, as we have seen, the US and the Soviet Union each possessed enough nuclear weapons to effectively destroy the other many times over, and it was believed that this 'mutually assured destruction' meant it was very unlikely either side would initiate an attack on the other. However this posed a problem for the European members of NATO, because if the US and Soviets were unwilling to attack each other, what would happen if the Soviets attacked Western Europe? Was a US president likely to initiate a nuclear war with the Soviet Union, knowing it would result in nuclear retaliation against the United States, merely to protect some countries in Western Europe?

The same question can be asked of the UK, since Trident is assigned to NATO and the government claims it would be used not only in the defence of the UK but also in the defence of our allies, ie other members of NATO. Would a UK Prime Minister fire Trident missiles at Russia knowing that Russia would most likely retaliate with nuclear weapons against the UK – even if it were Estonia or another NATO country that was supposedly being protected?

Collective security and the UN

While NATO does have a political structure, including a parliamentary assembly where matters of policy and political strategy are discussed and agreed, it is first and foremost a military alliance. Despite some limited cooperation with Russia, including the 'Partnership for Peace' programme which allows for a certain amount of collaboration on defence-related issues, NATO is *de facto* a military alliance against Russia.

If Russia presents an existential threat against the members of NATO (a rather big 'if' as we saw in Chapter 6), perhaps it makes sense for those countries to band together for their collective defence against Russia. However, in a world which is no longer split into two incompatible ideological camps but instead is more nuanced and more complex than that, collective security is not just about ganging up to protect ourselves from one country or group of countries.

Collective security is the underlying basis of the UN itself, and is sometimes distinguished from collective 'defence' as in the case of a military alliance like NATO. Collective security means that all participating countries treat an attack or an act of aggression against one of their members as an attack against all, and undertake to prevent that happening and if it does happen, to defeat it collectively.

Chapter VI of the UN Charter spells out what the UN and member states must do in order to prevent an act of international aggression and Chapter VII spells out the arrangements for responding collectively to any aggression that does occur. Chapter VII includes provisions for a UN military staff committee and other procedures for pooling of military assets which have never been put into practice. However the principles and procedures for a collective response to international aggression are all there in Chapter VII and have been used, for instance, in UN Security Council Resolution 678, which authorised the first Gulf War in 1991 to evict Iraq from Kuwait.

Chapter VIII of the UN Charter also authorises 'regional arrangements' which may be used to prevent and respond to breaches of the peace without involving the whole international community. These regional arrangements must, however, be in line with the principles of the United Nations and recognised as such by the UN Security Council. NATO is explicitly excluded as a recognised regional arrangement because it was set up as an instrument of 'collective self-defence' under Article 51 of the UN Charter rather than as a regional arrangement under Chapter VIII.[104]

The Organisation for Security and Cooperation in Europe

The Organisation for Security and Cooperation in Europe (OSCE) is, however, the UN-recognised regional arrangement for the collective security of the European continent. Every country in Europe, including Russia and each of the other states of the former Soviet Union, is a member of the OSCE. The OSCE grew out of the Helsinki process which finally 'ended' WWII with a set of treaties and agreements in 1975.

The OSCE has played a hugely important yet relatively unknown role in resolving disputes, protecting civilians, preventing conflict and negotiating peace agreements all over Europe, from the Baltic states to the Balkans to the Caucasus, as well as dealing with disputes, human rights issues and elections as far away as Kyrgyzstan and Mongolia.

Could the OSCE fill the role that NATO now fills in terms of providing military protection for Western Europe and specifically for the UK? Since the OSCE is not a military alliance, let alone a nuclear alliance, it certainly cannot fill a role that *looks* like the role NATO fills. However it could be argued that the OSCE has already done more to protect the UK and Western Europe from war than NATO has ever done.

It is the OSCE, not NATO, which currently has monitors in Eastern Ukraine and has so far successfully kept that conflict from escalating further than it has done. It was the OSCE, not NATO, which brokered agreements in the Baltic states to protect Russian minorities and prevent violent conflict that almost certainly would have involved Russian troops in the immediate aftermath of the break-up of the Soviet Union. It was the OSCE, not NATO, which was successfully monitoring the return of Albanians to their homes in Kosovo prior to the Kosovo War, which pitted NATO against Russia and led to a situation where even today Kosovo is not a recognised member of the UN because of the animosities which remain.

The future of NATO

The public is told that we must have Trident in order to contribute to the defence of our NATO allies. France, of course, has nuclear weapons and is also a member of NATO. Although France was a founding member of NATO, it withdrew from the integrated military structure in 1959 and has never put its nuclear weapons under NATO command. Denmark, Norway and Iceland prohibit NATO nuclear weapons to be stationed on their territory in peacetime and do not allow NATO's nuclear-capable ships to visit their ports. Spain and Lithuania also have legislation prohibiting NATO nuclear weapons on their territories.[105]

Greece and Canada both used to host NATO nuclear weapons, but they have ceased to do so. At the present time, the only NATO countries allowing nuclear weapons on their soil as part of NATO nuclear-sharing arrangements are Germany, Italy, Turkey, Belgium and the Netherlands. In 2005, the Belgium senate voted to negotiate the eventual removal of US nuclear weapons and in 2015 the Flemish parliament voted to have them removed.[106] There have also been calls for US nuclear weapons to be removed from Germany but in September 2015 the US began deploying a new generation of B61–12 nuclear bombs at its airbase in Buchel, Germany.[107]

What if?

What would NATO look like without nuclear weapons? Would it look any different to most NATO countries or to the citizens of those countries? Norway, a NATO member, hosted a conference on the 'humanitarian impacts of nuclear weapons' in Oslo in 2013. This led directly to what is now known as the 'humanitarian pledge' (see Chapter 12), signed by over 120 countries and calling for an international treaty to 'fill the legal gap' that would make possession of nuclear weapons illegal under international law. Although Norway is not currently a signatory to this pledge, there is nothing in the NATO charter that prevents its members from deciding to be an alliance without nuclear weapons if it so chose.

What would Europe look like without NATO? If NATO had disbanded in 1991 along with the Warsaw Pact, would any tears have been shed? A military alliance that was set up to protect Western Europe from the Soviet Union could have gone down in history as an unqualified success story once the Soviet Union had come to an abrupt and unexpected end. Subsequent NATO missions in Bosnia, Afghanistan and elsewhere could just as easily have been conducted by ad hoc coalitions of countries if they had wanted to provide a military presence. More importantly, these missions might have been handled by the UN or through the UN structures such as the OSCE if NATO had not existed.

Summary

It is accepted by most British politicians and military leaders that the UK's place in the world is secured by being the closest and most reliable ally to the US. Having Trident demonstrates a commitment that no other US ally has ever offered – that of sharing the nuclear burden with the US.

In practice, this means that Trident is assigned to NATO, and a US General decides when, and against what, Trident would ever be used (except in the case that UK 'supreme natural interests' are at stake). This potentially means that Trident could be used against Russia in response to a Russian attack on another NATO country, for instance, Estonia.

By offering to share the nuclear burden with the US in defence of NATO, the UK is putting itself in mortal danger on behalf of other NATO countries, since the Russians would almost certainly retaliate with nuclear weapons against the UK if they were attacked by a (UK) Trident submarine. This might save the US from direct nuclear retaliation and prevent all out nuclear with Russia, but the UK would be destroyed in the process.

Rehearsing such scenarios is ultimately futile, since no one knows what would happen once nuclear weapons are unleashed in a war situation. It is difficult, however, to imagine how such a scenario could remain 'limited' and not end with all out nuclear war, no matter who fired the first shot.

NATO came into existence as a defensive military alliance of Western countries, against a perceived threat from the Soviet Union and its allies in the Warsaw Pact. When the Soviet Union collapsed NATO, instead of disbanding as the Warsaw Pact did, continued to expand, taking in not just former Warsaw Pact countries, but countries formerly part of the Soviet Union itself.

NATO military power now dwarfs that of present day Russia and its reach extends deep into the former Soviet Union. NATO war games, including the simulated use of nuclear weapons, take place right by the border of Russia in the Baltic States, Poland, and on the Balkan Peninsula.

Whether NATO as it is now configured makes Europe safer or less safe is beyond the scope of this book. However, tying the UK's defence to the US and to NATO does not require the UK to possess nuclear weapons.

NATO's nuclear policies are subject to continual review by NATO member countries. Although France has its own nuclear weapons, these are not assigned to NATO and France does not take part in NATO nuclear policy. Denmark, Norway, and Iceland explicitly prohibit NATO nuclear weapons on their soil. Spain and Lithuania also refuse to allow nuclear weapons. Greece and Canada used to host NATO nuclear weapons but have since withdrawn from that arrangement.

Out of 28 NATO member states, only five allow nuclear weapons to be stationed on their territories. Three of these, Belgium, Netherlands, and Germany have large popular movements opposed to this arrangement. While NATO remains a 'nuclear alliance' at present, there is no requirement that it will continue as one. Ultimately, the UK's security rests not on its relationship only with the US, but on its relationships with all other countries, through the United Nations.

CHAPTER 10

Is Trident Really 'Independent'?

GIVEN THAT TRIDENT is officially assigned to NATO, as we have seen in the last chapter, in what sense is it the UK's 'independent deterrent'?

'Only the Prime Minister can authorise the launch of nuclear weapons...'[108]

The government is always at great pains to stress that it and it alone has the final say on when or how Britain's nuclear weapons would be used. This is defined as 'operational independence' as opposed to other aspects of Britain's nuclear relationship with the US, where the UK is clearly dependent on them.[109]

There are two basic treaties – the Mutual Defence Agreement and the Polaris Sales Agreement, together with some other practical and technical arrangements, which determine the level of dependency on the US which the UK has in relation to Trident.

The Mutual Defence Agreement (MDA)

The Mutual Defence Agreement (MDA) was signed in 1958 and sets out the overall terms of cooperation between the US and the UK regarding nuclear weapons technology. The MDA has been renewed every ten years or so and was debated in parliament for the first time in December 2014 before its most recent renewal, which now runs until 2024.

The MDA allows the US and the UK to share classified information about nuclear weapons design and production. It gives the UK access to US nuclear testing facilities and to a vast amount of data from US nuclear tests.[110] It also provides for exchange of highly-enriched uranium and plutonium needed for production of nuclear weapons.

A number of crucial components for Trident nuclear weapons are directly transferred from the US to the UK. These are described as 'cost-saving measures' in the NSS/SDSR[111] as they save the UK millions of pounds in research and development costs as well as production costs for highly specialised and technical components.

Polaris Sales Agreement (PSA)

The Polaris Sales Agreement was a separate agreement with the US, signed in 1963. This gave the UK access to the entire Polaris missile system (minus the nuclear warhead) at a knock-down price. This agreement also allowed the UK to subsequently lease Trident missiles from the US on the same basis.

The precise details of the PSA arrangement have been controversial since they were first negotiated. The condition under which the US agreed at the time to make these missiles available to the UK was that they be assigned to NATO and therefore remain under US military command.[112] Harold MacMillan, who was Prime Minister at the time, managed to obtain an exception from President Kennedy in the extreme case 'where Her Majesty's government may decide that supreme national interests are at stake'.[113] What this means in practice, however, is unclear.

According to Prime Minister Thatcher, when she reported to parliament on the Trident agreement in 1982,

> Like the Polaris force, and consistently with the agreement reached in 1980 on the supply of Trident I missiles, the United Kingdom Trident II force will be assigned to the North Atlantic Treaty Organisation and *except* where the United Kingdom Government may decide that supreme national interests are at stake, this successor force *will be used for the purposes of international defence of the Western alliance in all circumstances* [italics added].[114]

The challenge in interpreting the precise wording of the PSA is that for the UK government there was the assumption that the UK would retain its own political control over these nuclear weapons, since it otherwise made little sense to be spending large amounts of money on a weapon that does not belong, ultimately, to the UK. For the US government, on the other hand, the assumption was that by giving the UK access to its most valuable nuclear missile system, it was not thereby compromising its own security by simply handing something like that over to an independent third party to do whatever they might want to do with it.

In legal terms, the UK has control over its own nuclear warheads, while the US has control over its own nuclear missiles. These missiles are merely 'leased' to the UK under the terms of the PSA. They remain the *property* of the US government.

Technical cooperation and dependency

We have already noted the fact (in Chapter 1) that some nuclear experts believe the warhead on the UK's Trident fleet is actually a US warhead (the W76). Whether or not this is the case, there is ample evidence to suggest that the UK warhead is at the very least a close 'replica' of the W76 and based on the same design and technology. In Chapter 1 we also reviewed some of the main components that go into making up the Trident nuclear weapon system. Many of these components, apart from the missile itself, are also bought off-the-shelf from the US rather than built from scratch in the UK. These include, most crucially, the Mark 4 re-entry vehicle (RV), the Arming, Fusing and Firing System (AF&F), the Fire Control System and the Missile Guidance System. These components include both hardware and software elements, and the software in particular is heavily dependent on US maintenance and upgrades on a regular and ongoing basis.

The Trident D5 missile is currently being upgraded in the US through what is known as the Trident 'life extension' programme (D5LE). This involves adapting the missile to fit the new Mark 4A RV, an upgrade from the Mark 4 RV which the UK has already purchased.[115] The Mark 4A RV in turn includes a new AF&F system which allows the Trident warheads to be more reliably used as groundburst weapons (see Chapter 2).[116]

The guidance system for getting the warheads to their intended target is of crucial interest in relation to the question about Trident's independence. When the Trident D5 missile was first deployed in 1982, it had a state-of-the-art guidance system that claimed to be accurate enough to hit a target to within 1,200 feet CEP (see Chapter 2) when fired from a distance of up to 7,000 nautical miles away.

This was made possible through a technology known as 'inertial guidance', which tracked by computer exactly where the missile was in space throughout its flight and automatically adjusted the rocket motors to keep it on track as it went along. Midway through its trajectory, another guidance technology known as 'stellar guidance' kicked in to take a reading from the stars and re-calibrate the tracking system to its actual location according to the position of the stars at that moment.

A CEP of 1,200 feet was at the time a major breakthrough in missile accuracy but it is still not considered sufficient to guarantee destruction of hardened missile silos protected by several feet of reinforced concrete. For that, a CEP of 300 feet or less was considered necessary and the only reliable way of achieving that is through satellite tracking via GPS (Global Position Satellites).[117] Although GPS is now made available to the general public on mobile phones and other navigation devices, this remains a US military system and public access can be switched on and off by the US military whenever they want to.[118]

It is not clear whether UK Trident missiles now rely on GPS satellite tracking for their missile guidance as the US missiles do. We are told they can be used without it, as per the original specification. However, GPS provides real-time weather and other technical launching data required for the accurate targeting of the missiles. Therefore, in terms of the ability of a Prime Minister or a submarine commander to target the Trident missiles at specified targets and expect the missiles to reach those targets, it is probably the case now, and almost certainly the case in the near future, that this ability is dependent on access to US military satellites. According to Navy sources, without ongoing US support, the UK Trident system would only limp along for a matter of months.[119]

Summary

So how 'independent' is Trident? In theory, a British Prime Minister has the final say on whether to fire Trident missiles and where to fire them. In practice, the US owns the missiles and produces many of the warhead components. It controls the software for firing the missiles, targeting them and detonating them. And except in an undefined emergency situation, Trident is assigned to NATO and under the command of a US general.

If it ever came to the point where the UK was considering launching its nuclear missiles at the US, there would be multiple ways in which the US could prevent this from happening and almost certainly *would* prevent this from happening. Could or would the US President prevent the UK from launching its missiles against a non-US target that was nonetheless considered to be in US vital interests to protect?

Say, for example, that the UK felt threatened by a nuclear-armed Iran and feared a nuclear attack by Iran on the UK was imminent. For the sake of argument, let's imagine that the US had meanwhile decided that Iran must at all costs be protected because it was needed as an ally against a resurgent Islamic State or perhaps against hostile governments in Iraq and Afghanistan. The UK is nonetheless determined to launch nuclear missiles at Iran. Would the US allow this to happen and could they technically prevent it from happening? Most probably they could and they would.

Trident, therefore, is independent only to the extent that we define that term as meaning the British Prime Minister can, in theory, make the final decision about launching British nuclear weapons. What that means in practice is, as we have illustrated here, quite another matter.

CHAPTER 11

Does Trident Give the UK a Seat at the Top Table?

IN THE GOVERNMENT'S official report proposing renewal of Trident, it specifically rules out 'status' as one of the reasons for retaining Trident. However, this is one of the most common reasons given when the issue of Trident has been debated in hustings and union halls around the country. During the Scottish referendum campaign in 2014, former Prime Minister John Major claimed on Radio 4 that scrapping Trident would lose Britain its place on the UN Security Council:

> If we lost Trident not to an enemy but to the actions of a neighbour – that would be just extraordinary. Our role in NATO would be reduced. Our relations consequently with the US would be damaged. The United Kingdom would be weaker in every international body it attends. It would certainly be weaker in the EU in the forthcoming negotiations. We would lose our seat at the top table in the UN.
> (John Major, on the *Today* programme, BBC Radio 4, 9 Sept 2014)

In his memoirs published in 2010 Tony Blair claims that, having looked at the pros and cons of renewing Trident from a military point of view, 'in the final analysis I thought giving it up too big a downgrading of our status as a nation…'[120]

So what is the relevance of Trident as a status symbol and does it have any basis in fact?

A brief history of UK's nuclear weapon status

At the end of WWII, Britain was still the dominant imperial power in the world, ruling over one-fifth of the world's population including great swathes of Africa, Asia and the Middle East. The US was the most powerful country militarily and in 1945 was the only country with the atom bomb.

The Soviet Union had taken control of Eastern Europe and was growing rapidly as a superpower. The Cold War was already well under way.

At the end of the war and following the election of the first majority Labour government in the UK, the US unexpectedly cut off all nuclear collaboration with Britain. This convinced Prime Minister Clement Atlee and his Foreign Secretary Ernest Bevin that they needed to develop a British bomb that in Bevin's words 'would have the bloody union jack on top of it'.

Nuclear weapons have remained an issue within the Labour Party ever since (see Chapter 22), but successive British governments (including Labour ones) have continued to assert the importance of being in the 'nuclear club'. Nuclear weapons became identified as the status symbol that would keep Britain 'great' despite its loss of empire.

Where does the belief that nuclear weapons bestow such an important status on the UK come from? As we shall see below, it does not seem to come from any rational analysis of the different international forums in which Britain plays a leading role or might aspire to. Perhaps having giant, powerful missiles somehow compensates certain British politicians for their lack of power and influence in other spheres. Perhaps nuclear weapons give them the closest intimacy with the superpower status of the US that they believe is achievable.

The UN Security Council

Before we look at how the UK's nuclear weapon status affects the role it plays or could play on the world stage, let us first of all dispense with the claim that nuclear weapons give the UK its seat on the UN Security Council. The structure of the UN, including the Security Council and who would sit on it as permanent members (the 'P5'), was agreed by the allied powers at the Dumbarton Oaks conference in 1944 and ratified by the founding members of the UN in June 1945. This was all before any country had nuclear weapons and before WWII was even over (in the Pacific). The decision as to who would sit as permanent members on the UN security council was based on the assumption that the allies would win the war and that the major parties in that war, barring the defeated Axis powers, would be the key players in the post-war world order.

From 1945 to 1949, the US was the only P5 member with nuclear weapons, and from 1949 to 1952, only the US and the Soviet Union had nuclear weapons. In 1952 the UK was added to the nuclear club and in 1960 France was added. Until 1971 the Chinese seat on the security council was held by Taiwan, which did not (and still does not) have nuclear weapons. So only from 1971 have all P5 members had nuclear weapons.

But by 1974, India had tested its first nuclear weapon. Israel is suspected of having tested its first nuclear weapon in 1979.[121] Pakistan then joined the nuclear club in 1998 and North Korea in 2006. Therefore it was only between 1971 and 1974 that all the P5 countries had nuclear weapons and that only these countries had them. There is, of course, nothing in the UN charter referring to nuclear weapons, since, as we have established, the UN charter predates the invention of nuclear weapons.

Whether the UK 'deserves' to have one of only five permanent seats in the UN Security Council in today's world is something which requires serious consideration. There have been many proposals over the years for reform of the structure and voting system of the Security Council, and these have included removing or restricting the veto power of the P5, giving the EU a permanent seat and then giving the seats of UK and France, who would be represented by the EU, to other emerging powers like India or Brazil, or radically changing the whole structure of the Security Council to better reflect the different regions and power dynamics in the world today.

None of the proposals so far mooted or discussed among UN members has ever included the suggestion that only countries with nuclear weapons should have permanent seats on the Security Council. In fact, such a suggestion would go against so many fundamental principles of the international system that it would be laughed out of court if ever proposed.

For starters, such an idea would encourage countries to develop their own nuclear weapons and reward them for doing so, in utter contradiction to everything the Non-Proliferation Treaty stands for (see Chapter 12). It would also mean that existing pariah states like North Korea would be catapulted into positions of enormous power and influence on the world stage, which probably not a single other country at the UN would support. Israel is likewise a very controversial UN member for having ignored, violated or broken more UN resolutions than any other country by far, including at least 32 binding Security Council resolutions.[122]

Simply put, Israel would never be allowed a permanent seat on the Security Council without a huge row that could split the UN apart as an institution. So the suggestion that P5 membership be linked in any way to possession of nuclear weapons is a non-starter.

UK *status as a nuclear weapon state*

Officially, the Non-Proliferation Treaty, or NPT, defines the UK and the other four countries which had nuclear weapons as of 1967 as 'nuclear weapons states' or NWS. All other state signatories to the treaty are defined as 'non-nuclear weapons states' or NNWS.

Some have tried to suggest that this means the UK and other NWS cannot legally change their status from being a NWS to being a NNWS without re-negotiating the treaty. This, however, contradicts the intention of the treaty, which is aimed not only at preventing the proliferation of nuclear weapons but at achieving their total elimination.[123]

Unfortunately, it has become the practice to refer to the five nuclear weapon states acknowledged by the NPT as the 'P5', since as we have seen above, they happen to be the five permanent members of the Security Council at the moment. Strictly speaking, they should be called the 'NPT5' or the 'NWS5' or just the 'N5' to distinguish them politically from the P5, even if at the moment they are one and the same countries.[124]

The US–UK 'special relationship'

We have already looked at key dimensions of the 'special relationship' in the last two chapters. We will come back to it again in Chapter 19 when we look at the effect Britain giving up Trident might have on the US. But how does Britain *having* Trident affect the UK's relationship with the US at a political level?

The UK is in a privileged position to be able to discuss and share top secret technical information with the US about nuclear weapons. No other country has that level of access to US nuclear scientists, technicians, weapons designers or nuclear war planners. How does that translate into access at a political level? There is no real way of knowing how effectively the informal links established at lower levels of government and military do or do not 'grease the wheels' for higher political level cooperation.

In terms of NATO, the UK is the only NATO member working directly with the US at a military level to integrate Trident into the NATO nuclear 'umbrella'. Turkey, Belgium, Netherlands, Italy and Germany are the only NATO members with nuclear-sharing arrangements with the US which involve technical and military cooperation in terms of handling and potentially using the nuclear weapons stored on their territory. But at the political level, NATO policy and decisions regarding nuclear weapons are taken within the Nuclear Planning Group (NPG), which consists of all Defence Ministers of all NATO members (apart from France). Unless the UK decided to withdraw from this Group as France did, it would remain part of this NATO political-level nuclear decision-making whether or not it had nuclear weapons – just as the other 25 NATO members who do not have their own nuclear weapons are nevertheless a part of the NPG. Any decision to use nuclear weapons on the part of NATO would go to the NATO heads of state, and again, this level of decision-making involves all NATO members and not just the US and UK, who are the only NATO members with nuclear weapons assigned to NATO.[125]

The UK *in other international forums*

Other international forums in which the UK plays a significant part include the G8, the G20 and the OECD.[126] The G8 includes the US, UK, France and Russia, so four of the 'N5', but also includes Germany, Italy, Japan and Canada as four other large and 'important' world economies. Is there any reason to suppose that the UK would be expelled from this club for giving up its nuclear weapons when only half the club currently has them and the other half does not?

The G20 is a larger grouping of 20 industrialised countries, as is the OECD, which includes 34 industrialised or industrialising countries. These larger groupings include many more states which do not possess nuclear weapons, so once again it is hard to argue that the UK would be penalised in some way if it were to renounce its status as a nuclear weapons state.

The UK plays an important, and often leading, role in many other international forums, including the EU, NATO, the OSCE, the Commonwealth, the IMF, the World Bank, UNESCO and many others. None of these organisations, apart from NATO, have any interest at all in whether the UK possesses nuclear weapons or not. The majority of countries in these organisations do not have nuclear weapons, and it does not enhance UK's status thereby to have them.

Summary

National status is not something that is easily quantified or even put into words. When politicians talk about national status being enhanced by having Trident, they most often mean status with the US government above all else. But even this changes with a change of US President, a change of mood, a change of public opinion. The US is a very big country with a wide diversity of views, including many who are opposed to nuclear weapons or who see no point at all in the UK having its own nuclear weapons.

When it comes to France or Germany or other countries in Europe, what is it that enhances or diminishes the national status of the UK? Usually this is influenced most by the UK's willingness to cooperate – or not – with its

European neighbours on an equal and fair basis.

What are some of the things have actually enhanced the UK's status in the world in recent years? Playing a constructive role in the treaty to eliminate landmines gave the UK some kudos in terms of its standing in the world, as did its constructive role in creating the International Criminal Court, playing a positive role in promoting and standing up for human rights around the world, constructive work in the Millennium Development Goals and the subsequent Sustainable Development Goals and perhaps most of all, its generous ongoing contribution to international development through the work in many developing countries funded by the Department for International Development (DFID) and the government's commitment to meet the OECD target of 0.7% GDP spent on overseas development aid.

These kinds of contributions to a better, fairer and more peaceful world are what give a nation-state like the UK 'status', not the number of missiles it can launch from submarines or the numbers of people it can kill and cities it can annihilate with those missiles. It is a sad reflection on the state of the UK that it is apparently run by people who not only believe Trident bestows status but that whatever kind of status it is that they think Trident offers is a kind of status worth aspiring to.

PART FOUR

We Can Manage Trident Legally, Safely, Responsibly

CHAPTER 12

Are Nuclear Weapons Legal?

IN THE GOVERNMENT'S recent NSS/SDR, published in November 2015, it is repeatedly asserted that the security of the UK depends upon adherence to a 'rules-based system of international relations'. In the same report, the government claims that renewal of Trident is 'fully consistent with our legal obligations under the NPT...' The NPT defines five countries, including the UK, as 'nuclear weapons states' (NWS) and all other countries as 'non-nuclear weapons states' (NNWS). This gives the UK and the other 'N5'[127] special obligations that are different from those assigned to the NNWS.

In 1996, the World Court (officially the International Court of Justice, or ICJ) gave an 'advisory opinion' on the legality of nuclear weapons. One of their conclusions was that a decision could not be reached on whether use of nuclear weapons would be legal or not 'in the extreme case of self-defence when the very survival of the state is at stake'. This language is used in the most recent SDR to define the only circumstances under which the UK would ever use its nuclear weapons, adding weight to the claim that its use of nuclear weapons under those circumstances would be legal.

In 2006, when parliament was debating the 'initial gate' decision to build a new set of Trident submarines, the Attorney General gave his opinion to parliament that such a renewal would be legal under the NPT. Unlike the upgrade from Polaris to Trident, which as we will see in Chapter 18 was a major enhancement of the UK's nuclear capability, the then Foreign Secretary, Margaret Beckett, assured parliament that the replacement of Trident 'would not involve any upgrade or increase in capability'.[128] Indeed this was one of the specific commitments given at that debate which we shall come back to in Chapter 18.

The government has also been at pains to explain that UK maintains only 'the minimum deterrent necessary' and that it has unilaterally removed more than half the number of warheads held during the height of the Cold War. This enables the government to claim it is the 'most compliant' of all the nuclear weapon states when it comes to meeting the legal requirements of the NPT.

So what exactly does the NPT require of the UK, legally, and how compliant is the UK with these requirements? Are there other legal responsibilities which the UK is bound by in relation to nuclear weapons? And what exactly does the World Court ruling on legality of nuclear weapons mean, particularly in terms of Trident?

The Non-Proliferation Treaty

The NPT was signed in 1967, ratified in 1968 and came into force in 1970. It is important to note that the UK was not only a founding signatory to the NPT, but one of the 'depositories' of the treaty and in fact played a key role in the negotiations that created the NPT. There exists a full transcript of those negotiations where it is clear that the UK helped to formulate and frame the 'grand bargain' at the heart of the treaty as well as many of the specific points which must be interpreted legally not only in terms of the 'letter' but also in terms of the 'spirit' of what was intended by those who created the treaty.

The grand bargain at the heart of the NPT was this: in order to convince countries which at that time did *not* have nuclear weapons to renounce ever developing them, the countries *with* nuclear weapons were agreeing to get rid of theirs.[129] This would mean that eventually *no* country would have nuclear weapons rather than ending up with *all* countries having them.

This legal commitment of the NWS to eliminate their nuclear arsenals is enshrined in Article VI of the Treaty:

> Each of the Parties to the Treaty undertakes to pursue negotiations in good faith on effective measures relating to cessation of the nuclear arms race at an early date and to nuclear disarmament, and on a treaty on general and complete disarmament under strict and effective international control.[130]

As with all treaties and conventions, the wording is open to interpretation and has been claimed to mean different things by different people. During the NPT negotiations, however, the UK ambassador to the UN made it very clear that the UK was committed to Article VI and to negotiations leading to total nuclear disarmament:

> As I have made clear in previous speeches, my government accepts the obligation to participate fully in negotiations required by [NPT] Article VI and it is our desire that these negotiations should begin as soon as

possible and should produce speedy and successful results. There is no excuse now for allowing a long delay to follow the signing of this treaty.[131]

The NPT agreement was that NWS will negotiate nuclear disarmament 'at an early date'. That was a commitment made in 1967 and yet 48 years later the UK government has still not put its nuclear weapons up for negotiated settlement in any nuclear disarmament treaty. The other phrase in the text of Article VI is 'in good faith'. As we shall see in Chapter 17, the UK government can hardly claim to have acted in good faith when it comes to their stated commitment to multilateral nuclear disarmament and fulfilling this particular obligation under the NPT.

We will come on to look at the ICJ Advisory Opinion in a moment, but it is useful to note at this stage that they did clear up one point that the UK and other NWS have used to hide behind in the past. The ICJ clarified that Article VI of the NPT gives the NWS an obligation not merely to 'negotiate' nuclear disarmament – which could go on indefinitely, and so far has done – but to negotiate 'and bring to a conclusion' an agreement for the total elimination of their nuclear weapons.[132]

International treaties are only as effective as their signatories wish to make them, and there is no enforcement mechanism in place to make countries abide by their treaty obligations. Since the UK and the other N5 have veto powers in the UN Security Council, they can always prevent any international enforcement action being proposed against them. Nonetheless, the UK is more conscientious than some when it comes to international treaties and, as already mentioned, is committed to a 'rules-based system' of international relations. What is a 'rules-based system' if it does not first and foremost involve countries abiding by the treaties to which they themselves have signed up?

Nevertheless, the UK government continues to get away with the claim that renewing Trident is 'fully consistent' with its NPT commitments when it knows full well what those commitments actually mean. In fact, the UK is currently in the dock at the ICJ for precisely this reason.

Marshall Islands v UK: on trial at the World Court

The Republic of the Marshall Islands is a tiny country of 70,000 inhabitants spread across a thousand small islands which cover nearly a million square miles of the South Pacific. It also happens to be where 67 open air nuclear tests took place between 1946 and 1962, causing a significant rise in birth defects, cancers, radiation burns and a host of other health and environmental effects which are still affecting the country's population.

In 2014, the government of the Marshall Islands lodged cases at the ICJ against all nine nuclear weapons states (the 'N9'), claiming that they were violating Article VI of the NPT. The basis of their argument is that by continuing to develop and improve their nuclear arsenals and by failing to even discuss the complete elimination of their nuclear arsenals, the nine NWS are in breach, not only of the NPT but of customary international law.

Of the nine countries in the dock, only the UK, India and Pakistan accept the compulsory jurisdiction of the ICJ. All three have lodged counter-proceedings to have the cases thrown out on technical grounds. The court will rule on these in 2016.

If the case against the UK is not thrown out, it will then proceed to submissions of expert testimony and hearings which could go on for three or more years. At that point the World Court may rule in favour of the UK or against it. If it is the latter, and if at that point the UK is still pressing ahead with modernisation of its Trident fleet, this would be in clear breach of the World Court and illegal under international law.

ICJ Advisory Opinion

In the meantime, is Trident legal? The aforementioned Advisory Opinion of the ICJ declared that in the extreme case of self-defence, they could not reach agreement as to whether it would be legal or not to use nuclear weapons. Note that they did not rule that it was *legal* in the extreme case of self-defence, merely that they could not decide whether it was legal or not. This is an important distinction.

According to Justice Bedjaoui, who was presiding judge of the ICJ at the time, the advisory opinion has been widely misunderstood and misused on this point. What the ICJ clearly *did* say was that nuclear weapons are illegal in all other circumstances. What it also clearly said was that the use or threat of use of nuclear weapons can *only* be legal if it is in conformity with all other existing international law. We shall look at what constitutes existing international law relating to war and weapons of war below. First, we need to clarify what is meant by 'self-defence'.

The right of self-defence

The inherent right of self-defence, when it comes to countries, was enshrined in the UN Charter as Article 51. This article supersedes all previous legal definitions of self-defence and has, once again, been constantly misunderstood, misinterpreted and misquoted more times than not.[133] Article 51 of the UN charter does not provide for an unlimited and unconditional right of self-defence, no matter what the circumstances or however a state may wish to define their actions as 'self-defence'. Instead, it places the right of self-defence within the overall framework of the United Nations as the only body which is now legally authorised to use force. It reads in full:

> Article 51: Nothing in the present Charter shall impair the inherent right of individual or collective self-defence if an armed attack occurs against a Member of the United Nations, until the Security Council has taken measures necessary to maintain international peace and security. Measures taken by Members in the exercise of this right of self-defence shall be immediately reported to the Security Council and shall not in any way affect the authority and responsibility of the Security Council under the present Charter to take at any time such action as it deems necessary in order to maintain or restore international peace and security.

If it *were* a genuine situation of self-defence where the UK or an ally was under attack (ie not 'imminently' facing attack or 'possibly' under attack, but *actually* under attack, as stated in Article 51) and before the UN Security Council could act, it might be considered legal to use nuclear weapons against the attacking forces *provided* that all other legal requirements had been met.

The ICJ opinion states very clearly that the use of nuclear weapons would be illegal under all circumstances other then the extreme case of self-defence when the very survival of the state is at stake. But it also says that even in that extreme case of self-defence, it would only be legal to use nuclear weapons if all other legal requirements could be met under international humanitarian law and the laws of war as laid down in numerous treaties, conventions and protocols.

The laws of war which apply to nuclear weapons

What are these other legal requirements? The laws of war have developed over many centuries but are mainly codified in the Hague and Geneva Conventions of 1899, 1907, 1922, 1948 and 1977.

These conventions and protocols set down the conditions under which weapons of war can be legitimately used. The ICJ Advisory Opinion of 1996 sums up what it calls the 'cardinal principles' of international humanitarian law coming out of the various Conventions and Protocols listed above:

> The cardinal principles contained in the texts constituting the fabric of humanitarian law are the following. The first is aimed at the protection of the civilian population and civilian objects and establishes the distinction between combatants and non-combatants; States must never make civilians the object of attack and must consequently never use weapons that are incapable of distinguishing between civilian and military targets. According to the second principle, it is prohibited to cause unnecessary suffering to combatants: it is accordingly prohibited to use weapons causing them such harm or uselessly aggravating their suffering. In application of that second principle, States do not have unlimited freedom of choice of means in the weapons they use...[134]

In other words, when it comes to nuclear weapons,

> The methods and means of warfare which would preclude any distinction between civilian and military targets, or which would result in unnecessary suffering to combatants, are prohibited. In view of the unique characteristics of nuclear weapons, to which the Court has referred above, the use of such weapons in fact seems scarcely reconcilable with respect for such requirements.[135]

The ICJ additionally refers to the 'Martens Clause', which was first included in the Hague Convention of 1899 and continues to be referred to in subsequent conventions, including for instance the Geneva Additional Protocol I of 1977. This extends the protection of both combatants and non-combatants under international humanitarian law to new forms of warfare that may not already be foreseen, by specifically stating that:

> In cases not covered by this Protocol or by other international agreements, civilians and combatants remain under the protection and authority of the principles of international law derived from established custom, from the principles of humanity and from the dictates of public conscience.

According to the ICJ, the principles of international humanitarian law are so fundamental and 'intransgressible' that they form a body of customary international law, that applies to all countries, whether they have signed up to the various treaties and conventions or not.[136]

In addition to the two basic principles of protecting civilians and avoiding unnecessary suffering to combatants, a number of other specific protections are defined in international law. The most important of these for the purposes of nuclear weapons is the inviolable right to neutrality, which includes not only the right of neutral countries not to be attacked or invaded but also not to be adversely affected by warfare that may be going on in neighbouring countries.

Finally, there are specific treaties and commitments to which the UK and other nuclear weapons states are bound. These include all the treaties establishing nuclear-weapon-free zones in, for instance, Latin America, the Pacific region, Africa and some parts of Asia. Except where the UK has signed a specific protocol giving it the right to abrogate those treaties under certain circumstances, it is obligated not to use or threaten countries in those regions with nuclear weapons.

At the NPT Review Conference of 1995, all five NWS furthermore gave a written undertaking to all NNWS signatories to the NPT that they would not use or threaten any of them with nuclear weapons 'except in case of invasion or attack on them or their allies'.

When would use of nuclear weapons be legal?

There is really only one conceivable circumstance in which the UK could use nuclear weapons 'legally', and that would be in the case of Russia or China or some other nuclear weapon state launching an invasion of the UK by sea and the UK attacking the invading warships while on the high seas with a low yield nuclear weapon. Such a case might be deemed legal so long as it involved comparatively few civilian casualties, no radioactive fallout landing on neutral countries and no unnecessary or prolonged suffering to the combatants on board the ships.

How such conditions could apply to any other conceivable use of UK nuclear weapons is difficult to imagine. The deliberate targeting of cities or civilians, as in the case of the 'Moscow criterion' discussed in Chapter 1, is clearly illegal under international law. The targeting of government buildings is similarly illegal, since these are by definition occupied by civilians rather than by military personnel. Even the targeting of 'legitimate' military targets within or near to a large city like Moscow would be illegal because a nuclear weapon would not be able to distinguish combatants from non-combatants and the human suffering would be out of all proportion to the military targets chosen.

As we have seen in Chapter 2, the use of nuclear weapons to attack hardened military targets away from population centres, such as Russian missile silos, would require groundburst detonations to be effective. This would result in much more serious radioactive fallout and depending on wind direction and speed is more likely to affect civilian populations at some distance from the intended target, including potentially neutral third countries. It might furthermore result in high altitude fallout traversing the globe before coming down and therefore affecting many more civilians in many more parts of the world. All of this would render such an attack illegal under international law.

The use of nuclear weapons against an attacking ground force crossing Europe would similarly affect civilians, whether airburst or groundburst detonations were used. Even if it were possible to target only military personnel in such a situation, it is hard to imagine that they would not be subject to unnecessary and aggravated suffering due to the effects of radiation.

Any use of Trident not directly related to the immediate self-defence of the UK or its allies would, of course, likewise be illegal according to the ICJ ruling. This includes all 'sub-strategic' roles that might involve protecting trade routes or other 'vital interests', engaging in military interventions to contain or prevent the spread of terrorist organisations or any other role short of the immediate defence of a country from attack that threatens 'the very survival of the state'.

Use and threat of use

The ICJ ruling refers to the 'use and the threat of use' of nuclear weapons. In legal parlance, there is no distinction between use and threat. If committing some act is illegal, like murder, to threaten to commit that act is also illegal. In England and Wales, the maximum penalty for threatening to kill someone is life imprisonment, just as it is for actual murder.[137] The ICJ made it clear that in the case of the legality of nuclear weapons, any situation in which the use of nuclear weapons would be illegal under existing international law, the threat to use nuclear weapons in that situation would also be illegal.[138]

That means that in all of the cases just mentioned, where the use of nuclear weapons would be illegal, the threat to use nuclear weapons in those cases is also illegal. The ICJ did not rule on the concept or practice of nuclear deterrence as such. However, as we have seen in Chapter 3, deterrence is nothing other than a threat, and to be credible it must involve a willingness or 'intent' to follow through on the threat if the deterrence 'fails'.

Thus it is illegal not only to use nuclear weapons in any case other than the remote example of a ship on the high seas clearly in the process of attacking the UK (or an ally) and destroying it as a state, but also to *threaten* to use nuclear weapons under any other circumstance. This actually negates the whole concept of nuclear deterrence, since having the capacity to destroy a few ships on the high seas under very limited conditions is not very credible or even particularly threatening to a potential aggressor about to attack the UK.

There are also critical implications here for the targeting of Trident missiles, the yield of the warheads, the fusing options (see Chapter 1) and other technical details that determine how a nuclear weapon might be used and whether such use would be legal. If the whole Trident system is configured so as to destroy half of Moscow rather than a ship on the high seas, it follows that such a configuration is inherently illegal.

The legal obligation to disarm

Before we leave the issue of legality, we need to return to the legal obligation to disarm as defined in Article VI of the NPT and described above. At the 1995 NPT Review Conference, the UK and other nuclear weapons state made an 'unequivocal undertaking' to seriously meet their obligations under Article VI and to work towards the complete elimination of their nuclear arsenals. The ICJ advisory opinion also referred to this obligation as 'without any doubt an objective of vital importance to the whole of the international community today'.[139]

This legal obligation overrides all the pro-Trident arguments given in Chapters 5–16 of this book, since there really can be no justification for maintaining Trident if the UK is legally committed to getting rid of all its nuclear weapons. To argue that Trident is necessary for UK security, even in the remote example of being able to destroy a ship on the high seas, contradicts the legal obligation to disarm. To argue that Trident is necessary for maintaining the UK's place in the world is even less of a justification if the UK is already legally committed to getting rid of it. The claim that the UK somehow has a 'right' to maintain Trident because it is a democratic country capable of looking after nuclear weapons safely and responsibly is in direct contradiction to the claim that the UK is working for a 'rules based international order' and is committed to international structures and the rule of law.

Filling the legal gap

Even before the ICJ rules on the Marshall Islands case as to whether or not the UK is violating the NPT by continuing with Trident renewal, it is possible that other international developments will have taken place that affect even more conclusively the legality of nuclear weapons.

In December 2014 the Austrian government, hosted the third international conference on the humanitarian impacts of nuclear weapons. At the conclusion of that conference, the Austrian Foreign Minister read out what came to be known as the 'Austrian Pledge'. This was a commitment by the Austrian government to 'fill the legal gap' with respect to nuclear weapons and to invite other countries to join them.

By the end of 2014, just a few weeks after the close of the Vienna conference, more than 30 countries had signed up to the pledge. By spring 2015 this number had reached 70 and by summer 2015 it had exceeded 100. In September 2015 the number of countries signed onto the Austria Pledge stood at 121, just one shy of the number of countries who initiated negotiations leading to the landmines treaty in 1997.

At the UN General Assembly in December 2015, 139 countries voted in favour of resolution A/C.1/70/L.38, which was based on the Austrian Pledge and called for negotiations to fill the legal gap on nuclear weapons. A UN Working Group was set up to consider how to move this forward. It meets in Geneva during 2016 and reports back to the General Assembly in September 2016.

Whatever legal gap there is which still allows countries like the UK to claim that the use of nuclear weapons can under any circumstance ever be considered 'legal' is likely to be filled in the coming years. There are three generally accepted categories of 'Weapon of Mass Destruction' (WMD): nuclear, chemical and biological. Biological weapons were banned by international treaty in 1972. Chemical weapons were banned by international treaty in 1993. There is no reason to think nuclear weapons will not be next.

Anti-personnel mines and cluster munitions were banned by international treaties in 1997 and 2008, respectively, because of their disproportionate and indiscriminate effects on non-combatants. Dum-dum bullets and exploding bullets were banned by international treaties back in the 19th century because of the unnecessary and disproportionate suffering caused to combatants themselves. Nuclear weapons are weapons of mass destruction. They also cause disproportionate and indiscriminate suffering to combatants as well as to non-combatants. They invariably violate the neutrality of third countries. They disproportionately endanger the environment and other species.

Summary

The UK is, at the time of writing, on trial at the International Court of Justice (ICJ), accused of breaching the Non-Proliferation Treaty ((NPT) of 1968 by failing to eliminate its nuclear weapons, obstructing multilateral disarmament efforts and planning for another 50 years of nuclear weapons deployment by renewing Trident. By signing the NPT, the UK agreed to pursue negotiations for the elimination of its nuclear weapons 'in good faith' and 'at an early date'. That was 48 years ago.

While the UK clings on to its nuclear weapons, it does so claiming that it is legal to use them as a last resort 'in the extreme case of self-defence when the very survival of the state is at stake'. This is a reference to the ICJ opinion in 1996 that it could not rule 'whether it would be legal or not' to use nuclear weapons in that extreme case.

However, saying they could not rule whether or not it was legal is not the same thing as ruling that it would be legal in that case. The ICJ made very clear in their 1996 opinion that use of nuclear weapons would be legal, even in the extreme case of self-defence, only if all other international laws of war could be met.

The cardinal principles of international law as they relate to warfare and weaponry are that to be legal, warfare must never be waged against civilians nor cause unnecessary suffering to combatants. Weapons which by their very nature cause unnecessary suffering or are unable to distinguish between combatants and non-combatants are therefore illegal under international law.

The sole case given to the ICJ as a possible legal use of nuclear weapons was the case of a low-yield nuclear weapon being used against an invading armada on the high seas.

On top of this, the ICJ opinion of 1996 made clear that if a particular use of nuclear weapons cannot be legal, then the threat to use nuclear weapons in that particular case is also not legal.

The policy of deterrence amounts to a threat to use nuclear weapons not against ships on the high seas, but against the population centres and government buildings in Moscow and elsewhere. This threat is therefore illegal under the terms defined by the ICJ in 1996.

CHAPTER 13

Are the UK's Nuclear Weapons Safe?

> The Naval Service operates its submarine fleet under the most stringent safety regime, which is subject to independent scrutiny. The Naval Service does not put a submarine to sea unless it is safe to do so, and there are appropriate procedures in place to deal with any issues that may arise during its deployment. There are robust regulatory mechanisms, both within the Ministry of Defence (MOD) but independent of the Royal Navy and, externally with the Office of Nuclear Regulation, to ensure this.[140]
> (Secretary of State for Defence Michael Fallon, 28 May 2015)

THE UK PRIDES itself in having the highest standards of safety and security for its nuclear weapons, nuclear facilities and ballistic missile submarines. Safety measures relating to nuclear materials include multiple layers of redundancy so that if one system fails, other measures will kick in to prevent errors or accidents. But does this mean the risk is zero? As we saw in Chapter 4, the risk of any kind of deterrence failing at some point cannot be zero, which means in the long term the risk of it failing is actually quite high. Does the same apply to the safety and security of nuclear weapons held by the UK, even if they are never intended to be used?

Thankfully, in 70 years there has never been an accidental detonation of a nuclear weapon by the UK or any of the other nuclear weapons states. That is an important statistic in itself although, as we shall see below, the number of times a nuclear weapon *could have* detonated by accident during that period is alarmingly high. Even once would be alarmingly high, but UK officials would be first to point out that none of those close shaves involved the UK's own nuclear weapons (although at least one serious nuclear accident took place on UK soil).[141] Therefore it would be reasonable to conclude that the UK's safety record when it comes to nuclear weapons is better than that of some of the other nuclear weapons states.

The UK's nuclear weapons safety regime is seemingly robust and, at least in terms of the accidental release of nuclear materials, 100% successful so far. The UK government is working closely with other nuclear weapons states, including India and Pakistan, to continually improve nuclear safety and especially to safeguard against the theft or sabotage of nuclear materials by terrorist groups. Any country which possesses nuclear weapons makes itself not only a target for nuclear attack by potential enemies but also a target for terrorist attack by those who want to get hold of nuclear materials for their own purposes.

US record on nuclear weapons safety

The US has had considerably more nuclear weapons over a longer period than the UK and has thus had more opportunity to face a range of safety challenges with regard to the mere possession of this type of weapon. It could be argued that the US has less stringent safety requirements and procedures than the UK, but in comparison to some of the other nuclear weapons states, the US systems and procedures are extremely good. The US also relies on multiple safety mechanisms that would all need to fail simultaneously for there to be a serious accident or mishap. Yet the history shows that multiple simultaneous failures have indeed happened on several occasions.

Eric Schlosser, in his 2014 book *Command and Control*, recounts some chilling moments when some of the largest and most powerful ICBMs ever produced, carrying multiple nuclear warheads each a thousand times more powerful than the Hiroshima bomb, have suffered multiple simultaneous malfunctions and come dangerously close to exploding. Simple human errors like dropping a spanner into a missile silo coupled with a malfunctioning valve that had been reported but not yet fixed, inexperienced operators on duty pressing the wrong buttons, etc have led to uncontrollable fires inside a missile silo, accidental but luckily aborted launch of a missile, release of fatal amounts of radioactivity without actual detonation of a nuclear warhead and other very serious accidents.[142]

In 2013, 17 serving airforce personnel responsible for guarding America's ICBM nuclear missiles were stripped of their duties because of 'a pattern of weapons safety rule violations, possible code compromises and other failings' over an extended period.[143] This followed a number of incidents where personnel responsible for nuclear weapons were caught sleeping, drunk on duty, working whilst under the influence of drugs or unable to pass basic tests about their job. In 2003, half of the Air Force units responsible for nuclear weapons in the US failed their safety inspections despite being given a three-day warning that the inspections were coming.[144]

The most serious accidents involving nuclear weapons took place in the 1950s and '60s, when US bombers were routinely flying around the world with nuclear weapons on board. In 1961, a B-52 bomber on routine patrol crashed after running out of fuel because of a leaky fuel tank. Two massive 3 MT bombs were on board and landed in fields outside Goldsboro, North Carolina. On one of the bombs, five out of six arming mechanisms had been activated but the sixth prevented it from exploding.[145] The other bomb plunged into muddy ground at 700 mph and broke up without detonating. Parts of the second bomb were recovered, but the rest of it, including most of its radioactive fuel, is still 180 feet underneath a field in North Carolina.[146]

In 1966, another B-52 collided in mid-air with a fuel tanker over Palomares, Spain. Four hydrogen bombs were released on that occasion; one fell into the sea and was later recovered, one landed intact with no explosion and two exploded but only with the outer conventional explosives and a release of radioactive materials inside. Fortunately a full nuclear explosion did not take place. In 1968, a B-52 crashed in Thule, Greenland, after some foam cushions caught fire in the navigator's compartment. Four hydrogen bombs were released but again, the final arming mechanisms prevented them from detonating, although large amounts of radiation were apparently released, requiring a major clean-up operation. Parts of at least one of the bombs were never recovered.[147]

Other accidents have involved nuclear weapons lost and never found again. In 1959, a US Navy aircraft dropped a nuclear depth bomb by mistake off Puget Sound, Washington. The bomb sank to the bottom of the sea and was never recovered.

The US has also had a number of nuclear accidents involving submarines. In 1963, the USS *Thresher*, a nuclear-powered submarine of the US Navy (but one not carrying nuclear weapons) broke up in deep water and sank to the ocean floor with all 129 crew on board off the coast of Cape Cod, Massachusetts. In 1968, the USS *Scorpion* sank in mid-Atlantic and was never recovered. This was another nuclear-powered submarine but had nuclear-tipped torpedoes on board. Altogether, as many as 50 nuclear warheads have been lost at sea and never recovered.[148]

Nuclear safety record of other countries

The worst accident involving a nuclear missile submarine took place on 12 August 2000 when the Russian submarine, *The Kursk*, suffered an explosion on exercise off Norway, probably due to leaking torpedo propellant. The ensuing fire then caused seven other torpedoes to detonate in a massive explosion detected as far away as Alaska and measuring 4.2 on the Richter scale.

The Kursk was one of the most advanced submarines in the Russian navy at the time, with two nuclear reactors for propulsion instead of a single reactor, 24 cruise missile tubes capable of being fitted with 500 KT nuclear warheads, plus an array of torpedoes and other sophisticated equipment designed to target and destroy a US aircraft carrier and associated ships. Russia claimed at the time that no nuclear weapons were on board, but this has since been disputed.[149] The wreckage of the *Kursk* was eventually recovered after an enormous salvage operation at a cost of US$65 million, but none of the men on board survived.

In October 1986, the Soviet submarine *K-219* sank in mid-Atlantic following an explosion in one of the missile tubes, probably caused by a leaky seal that let salt water mix with the missile fuel, creating an explosive chemical reaction. The *K-219* apparently had 15 nuclear missiles on board, each of which probably contained two or three 200 KT warheads. All were lost at sea.[150]

Collision of HMS Vanguard *and* Le Triomphant

The UK's most serious accident involving a nuclear missile submarine is minor in comparison to those described above, but it illustrates that the UK is not immune to naval accidents even when nuclear weapons are on board. The Trident submarine HMS *Vanguard* was on routine 'CASD' patrol in February 2009 when it collided with the French nuclear missile submarine, *Le Triomphant* in the North Atlantic, also on its routine patrol. Both subs were submerged and travelling at 'very low speeds'. They each had a full complement of up to 48 nuclear warheads.

The French sub apparently suffered extensive damage to its sonar system, while reportedly HMS *Vanguard* experienced only 'scrapes and dents'. According to Quentin Davies, MP, in a written answer to parliamentary questions, the repairs to *Vanguard* took seven weeks at a cost of £1 million.[151] Earlier estimates of the damage to *Vanguard* were of another order of magnitude, but since ongoing maintenance and repair of the submarines was already covered by existing contracts, the real cost of repairing HMS *Vanguard* after this particular incident may never be known.

UK nuclear safety record

According to Bob Ainsworth, MP, in written answers to parliamentary questions, there were a total of 14 accidents involving British nuclear-powered submarines between 1988 and 2008. These include nine cases of grounded subs, one collision with an iceberg, two snagging of fishing vessels and one collision with a yacht.[152] Between 1987 and 2008, there were 213 'small' fires on board British nuclear-powered submarines, mostly related to electrical faults, 21 'medium-scale' fires requiring 'significant on board resources' to extinguish, and three fires requiring external resources to be extinguished, which luckily all took place while the subs were docked at port.[153]

Nuclear warheads for the Trident missiles are regularly transported by road between the Royal Ordnance factory at Burghfield in Berkshire and the Faslane naval base in Scotland. They go up and down the M25, M1, M6, M74, A1 and other busy A-roads and motorways, past London, Birmingham, Manchester, Glasgow and many other major cities and towns in England and Scotland. Highly radioactive nuclear waste is regularly transported across the UK by rail, and some nuclear shipments are transported by air. There has not been a serious release of radioactivity involving any of these nuclear shipments so far, but according to the Ministry of Defence there were 70 'safety lapses' involving nuclear convoys between 2007 and 2012. There were 67 such incidents between 2000 and 2007. These included vehicle break-downs, fuel leakages, malfunctioning alarms and other system failures.[154] In at least one case, the lead vehicle of a 20-vehicle convoy took a wrong turn and the whole convoy strayed off route before being guided back to where they belonged.

In a rare admission of the scale of risk involved in transporting nuclear weapons on British roads, the MOD has stated that a terrorist attack on one of these convoys:

> has the potential to lead to the damage or destruction of a nuclear weapon within the UK and... the consequences of such an incident are likely to be considerable loss of life and severe disruption both to the British people's way of life and to the UK's ability to function as a sovereign state.[155]

Nuclear design flaws?

Bob Peurifoy is a former director of weapon development at Sandia Labs in the US. He worked on nuclear weapons designs and especially on safety features of US nuclear weapons systems for more than 30 years and is an acknowledged expert in the field. He told Eric Schlosser, when being interviewed for Schlosser's book, *Command and Control*, that he felt confident about the safety features of all the nuclear weapons currently in the US stockpile, except for two: the W76 and W88. These are the two warheads used in the US Trident submarines and they sit atop the Trident D5 missile.

The Trident D5 missile used in US Trident submarines is exactly the same missile used in UK Trident submarines. They come from the same shared missile pool in King's Bay, Georgia. Bob Peurifoy's concern, which has apparently been discussed for more than 20 years in the US, is that in order to save space on the submarine and increase the range of the missiles, the US Navy insisted on using conventional explosives in the warhead and locating the warhead inside the third stage of the missile rocket motor, surrounded by high-energy rocket propellant. This combination makes the W76 warhead on top of a D5 missile more susceptible to accident than other US warheads, and if one were to happen it would be more likely to result in serious consequences. According to Peurifoy:

> An accident with one missile could detonate the third-stage propellant, set off the high explosives of the warheads and spread a good deal of plutonium around...[156]

There are also known generic defects in the nuclear reactors that run the Trident submarines. Cracks in the cooling system were discovered on HMS *Warspite* in 1989 and similar cracks have subsequently been found on other submarines with the same nuclear reactor design.[157] As of December 2015, HMS *Vanguard* has been taken out of service for a second 'deep maintenance period'. This is to include a complete replacement of the reactor core at an additional cost of £120 million. This is because of generic problems in the reactor core identified in 2012 and not dissimilar from those found on previous nuclear subs.[158]

The revelations of Able Seaman William McNeilly

In May 2015, a young submariner training to be a missile technician on board the Trident submarine, HMS *Victorious*, wrote an 18-page report of what he considered to be the 'shockingly extreme conditions that our nuclear weapons system is in right now'.[159] He sent his report to a number of journalists and peace activists and it eventually made its way into the news, prompting the official response quoted at the opening of this chapter and sparking a heated debate in parliament about the safety and security of Britain's nuclear weapons.

McNeilly was briefly detained and then discharged from the Royal Navy, but to date he has not been charged under the Official Secrets Act or imprisoned for the information he disclosed.

McNeilly describes fires being started because toilet paper was being stored in the wrong place, flooding onto electrical equipment caused by blocked toilets not being cleaned, electrical faults due to people throwing wet towels on machinery, people not following the correct operating procedures, lax security arrangements, leaky valves, alarms that don't work or are ignored because they go off too often and other safety and security concerns. Following McNeilly's allegations and media attention they received, the MOD conducted their own investigation into the safety and security breaches being described. They concluded that:

- The claims were factually incorrect or result of misunderstanding or misinterpretation.
- Much of what he claimed was based on historic events or hear-say about things he did not witness.
- There is no evidence McNeilly had raised any of his concerns through the chain of command as he claimed, or even privately voiced his concerns to other crew members.
- Concerns about base security were confined to one part of Faslane and did not take into account the complex layers of security around the whole site.
- Ministers, the MOD and the RN is satisfied that the deterrent is viable, safe and secure but are not complacent and will continue to test and develop procedures.
- Not all the claims made can be refuted in public as they are too sensitive from a security point of view.[160]

Despite these denials, the safety and security concerns raised by McNeilly sound all too plausible given what we know about other naval accidents and especially about the lack of due care and attention found among personnel responsible for nuclear weapons in the US (see above). Lack of due care and attention is perhaps the most serious of all the problems relating to the safety of nuclear weapons. All mechanical systems eventually break. It requires competent and alert human beings to notice when things are not working and to take corrective action before worse things happen.

Reports from nuclear regulatory bodies have consistently raised concerns that the level of experienced personnel is not sufficient for safe handling of nuclear weapons. The Navy cannot find enough recruits to fill specialised places needed to run nuclear equipment.

Miscommunication, misunderstandings, misperceptions and miscalculation

So far, we have looked at the safety of the UK's nuclear weapons in terms of the risk of accidents and mechanical failures. These are exacerbated by lack of experienced personnel handling those weapons and the systems needed to keep them safe. But there is also another element of the human dimension to take into account; the people at the tops of the chains of command, decision-makers, politicians, generals, policy advisors and so on, can also make fatal mistakes of judgement.

The 2014 Chatham House report, *Too Close for Comfort: Cases of Near Nuclear Use and Options for Policy*, focuses on this aspect of nuclear risk.[161] The report examines 13 incidents between 1962 and 2002 when the world came close to all-out nuclear war. Although the UK was only directly involved in one of these incidents, the implications for UK leaders are no less relevant than for US or Russian leaders. All of these cases illustrate the same kind of simple human errors that are compounded by multiple failings into a dangerous scenario that can quickly spiral out of control. In these cases, however, we are not talking about the possible accidental detonation of a single nuclear warhead somewhere, but the deliberate, calculated launch of all-out nuclear war involving thousands of nuclear weapons and the certain destruction of modern civilisation as we know it.

We have already looked at the Cuban Missile Crisis in Chapter 3, so let us leave that one aside for the moment. Whereas that crisis brought the world to the brink of nuclear war in a very public way which most people even today have heard about, almost no one has heard of the 12 other times that human civilisation almost ended in a nuclear conflagration.

For instance, in January 1995 a research rocket was launched in Norway and mistaken on Russian radar screens for an incoming Trident missile aimed at the Kola Peninsula where Russia's nuclear submarines are based. The radar operators immediately informed the commander of Russian Radar Forces, who immediately informed President Yeltsin. Yeltsin was handed the nuclear 'briefcase' and was on the phone with another general to decide the response when it was calculated that the rocket would land outside Russian airspace and therefore not pose a threat. In this case, the Norwegians had officially informed the Russian government about a research rocket launch, but the message had not been passed on to the appropriate people by the time the launch took place.[162]

In November 1983, a large NATO exercise called 'Able Archer' took place in central Europe. It involved a simulated NATO attack on the Soviet Union with nuclear as well as conventional forces. This was a period of heightened tensions between the Soviets and the west. A Korean airliner had been shot down after straying over Soviet territory, the first nuclear cruise missiles had arrived at Greenham Common in Berkshire and US President Reagan had recently made his famous quip about the Soviet Union being an 'evil empire'. The Soviets were especially nervous about a possible 'first strike' by NATO against the Soviet Union.[163]

What was not known by NATO planners at the time was that because of the heightened tensions and specific nervousness of the Soviets, they had deployed an intelligence gathering ring to NATO capitals with specific warning signs to look out for and report back immediately if seen. These warning signs would indicate to the Soviets that this was more than just an exercise but actually a cover for a surprise first-strike attack against the Soviet Union.

Two of the signs the Soviets were looking for were the raising of the alert status of NATO bases and the use of new communication channels not previously used. Both of these took place during Able Archer. New 'nuclear weapons release procedures' were also in use, which would have raised the level of Soviet concern. In the end, a Soviet double-agent in London warned NATO commanders to tone down the exercise before it led to a nuclear war. Some Soviet forces had meanwhile been raised to high alert, other military operations suspended and the Chief of Soviet General Staff was reputedly already based in a wartime command bunker ready to issue instructions.[164]

A Trident submarine commander is duty bound to launch nuclear missiles only on the direct instruction of the Prime Minister. But what if the submarine loses radio contact with London? In that case, the submarine commander is apparently instructed to tune into the BBC. If the BBC is no longer broadcasting, that is supposed to be a definitive signal that a nuclear war has begun and therefore the commander must open and read the 'last orders' of the Prime Minister stored in a sealed envelope in the ship's safe. But what if there is a fault with the radio signal *and* the BBC signal goes down for some entirely different reason at the same time? It may be down to the judgment of a submarine commander as to whether Moscow and London are reduced to radioactive cinders…

Summary

The 'doomsday clock' on the cover of the *Bulletin of Atomic Scientists* indicates how close its editors think the world is to a nuclear war. It currently stands at three minutes to midnight. It was moved forward by two minutes from five minutes to midnight in January 2015 and now stands at the closest it has been to midnight since 1983. How, 25 years after the end of the Cold War and with more than 85% of the total nuclear stockpiles at the height of the Cold War now dismantled, is it possible that we can be *more* at risk of nuclear war than we were 25 years ago?

> In 2015, unchecked climate change, global nuclear weapons modernizations, and outsized nuclear weapons arsenals pose extraordinary and undeniable threats to the continued existence of humanity, and world leaders have failed to act with the speed or on the scale required to protect citizens from potential catastrophe. These failures of political leadership endanger every person on Earth.

This is what the atomic scientists are saying.[165]

In 1975, the Nuclear Regulatory Commission in the US produced a detailed study of the probability of a major accident at one of the 100 civil nuclear power stations in the US. On the basis of detailed calculations of the stress factors of different materials used, the likelihood of different parts malfunctioning, the redundancy built into the system to ensure that if one part failed another part would kick in to the rescue and so on, they came up with a figure. The report concluded that the probability of a major nuclear accident occurring in the United States in any given year, with 100 nuclear power stations operating at once, was 1 in 5 billion.[166] Four years later, the worst nuclear accident in US history happened at the Three Mile Island nuclear plant in the USA (and since then there has been Chernobyl in Ukraine and Fukushima in Japan).

The chance of an accidental nuclear detonation in the UK in any given year may likewise be 1 in 5 billion or some other wildly large number. But that does not mean it can't happen. In fact, if the chances are greater than zero, then sooner or later it *will* happen.

Risk is normally defined in terms of likelihood and consequences. If the likelihood is very, very low (not zero) but the consequences are catastrophic, the overall risk is high because a non-zero probability means that something that is potentially catastrophic is going to happen sooner or later. This is the case with nuclear weapons.

No matter what precautions are taken and no matter how many failsafe systems are in place to prevent a catastrophe, no government can guarantee that sooner or later a catastrophe will not happen.

CHAPTER 14

Is Renewal of Trident Affordable?

CONSIDERABLE CONTROVERSY SURROUNDS the expected cost of Trident renewal and what impact that might have on other government spending. For those who believe Trident is essential for national security, the cost is more or less irrelevant. For those who feel Trident is important more for maintaining Britain's place in the world, cost is more of an issue. And for those who see Trident more as something the UK is lumbered with until such time as it can be safely negotiated away, paying a large amount of money for it to last another 50 years puts the whole issue into stark relief.

> To those who say we cannot afford a nuclear deterrent, I say that the security of our nation is worth the price.
> (David Cameron, *Daily Telegraph* 2 April 2013)

When the renewal of Trident was first floated in 2006, the cost of replacing four submarines was estimated to be £11–14 billion at 2006 prices. This price tag had risen to £15–20 billion (in 'outturn', or actual figures) by the time of the 2010 Strategic Defence and Security Review. In the most recent NSS/SDSR, published in December 2015, the figure had risen to £31 billion (in actual figures), with a further £10 billion as 'contingency'.

Other estimates, meanwhile, have put the figure variously at £76 billion,[167] £87.4 billion[168] or as high as £100 billion.[169] These higher figures include running costs and other capital costs in addition to the submarines themselves. On the basis of answers to parliamentary questions in October 2015, the Conservative MP and chair of the Defence Select Committee, Crispin Blunt, estimated the total cost had now risen to a staggering £167 billion.[170]

What are we to make of these widely diverging figures and what is the true cost of renewing Trident? Is it a cost that Britain as a nation can afford? And what are the opportunity costs in terms of programmes that will not be funded as a result of spending this money on Trident, both in the defence budget and in the government's budget at large?

A world of cost overruns

Most people have to balance their books at the end of each month to make ends meet. They work for companies whose profits can suddenly evaporate because of what financial markets are doing on some distant stock market, or work in the public sector and are suddenly faced with cuts that have to be implemented in their department, or work for the charity sector and don't know if funding for the next phase of their project is going to come through or not. In contexts like these, it is hard to fathom the sheer scale of a military project like Trident, let alone the kind of culture where money is simply not an issue. Who has ever worked on a project where huge cost overruns are simply accepted as the norm, let alone a project where the cost overruns could amount to £10 billion?

The original estimate for the current Trident Vanguard submarines, for instance, was £4–5 billion in 1980,[171] when the decision was made to replace Polaris. In the end, the price tag for the submarines alone was more than £12 billion, or more than twice the original estimate.[172] The multi-billion pound programme to build Astute submarines (which are nuclear-powered but not nuclear missile submarines), also ended up costing nearly 50% more than was originally estimated.[173]

The cost of new submarines

The simple answer as to why the current cost estimates for renewing Trident vary so widely is that they are including different things in their costings and using different methods to count the cost over a different number of years. Let's look first of all at what is being counted.

As we noted in Chapter 1, Trident consists of three main components and a number of sub-components. The submarines are one component, and these are what the government is counting as the cost of renewing Trident, since the missiles have already been renewed (and paid for) under the D5LE project (see Chapter 1) and the warheads are not yet ready for renewal and will be costed separately when they are.

The cost of each of the current submarines came to approximately £2.2 billion apiece at 1980s prices. The new submarines could end up costing as much as £10 billion apiece (assuming the £10 billion contingency is added to the £31 billion figure in the 2015 SDSR report). Since there are no longer any competitors in the submarine construction business, there is even less incentive than in the 1980s to keep prices down. BAE Systems in Barrow-in-Furness is the only firm that can build the Trident submarines and will presumably do so at whatever price they can negotiate with the UK government.

So far, costs of the assessment phase of the project have already overrun by £600 million, with £3.9 billion to be spent by the middle of 2016.[174]

The major components of the submarine include the Common Missile Compartment, which is built in Groton, Connecticut by the US firm, General Dynamics, because this is the part of the submarine that houses the Trident D5 missiles and was chosen to be identical between the US and the UK versions of the submarine. The nuclear reactor that runs the submarine is probably the most complex and costly part of the submarine and £1 billion has already been invested in the Rolls Royce Derby plant for reactor construction. Other components, including the hull, are assembled at Barrow shipyard. The steel for the hull has already been ordered.

Given the cost-overruns on the Vanguard and Astute submarines, even a contingency of 32% might not be enough. The main point, in calculating the costs, is that the submarines are not the only component of the system.

The cost of missiles and warheads

In addition to the costs of the submarines as such, the government has invested hugely in the Barrow shipyard to enable it to undertake the construction of the Trident submarines. Other investment to extend the facilities at Faslane has also begun. The biggest investment programme by far, and apparently not included in these figures, is the ongoing development of Aldermaston and Burghfield, where the Trident warheads are designed, developed and manufactured.

As already stated, the Trident D5 missiles have already been upgraded to the D5LE. Since the Polaris Sales Agreement gives the UK a cut-price deal on these missiles, the extra cost of upgrading was not great: approximately £250 million. However, these upgraded missiles will also need replacing before the expected lifespan of the new submarines is completed, and that could add a further £2 billion to the cost.[175]

Although the warheads themselves are not expected to be upgraded for another 10 years or more, research and development work at AWE Aldermaston has already begun. Five billion pounds were invested in capital projects at Aldermaston between 2010 and 2015. Actual production of a new warhead is expected to cost £2–3 billion when work begins in the 2020s.176 Altogether, total capital costs at Aldermaston could come to as much as £16.7 billion between 2012 and 2062, based on current investment plans.[177] This means that altogether the *capital* costs of renewing Trident could be as much as £50.6 billion at outturn prices.[178]

Running costs

If the plan is to continue deploying Trident for the indefinite future, it matters little what the running costs are, because these are simply part of the military budget, along with maintaining other ships, planes, bases, munitions, etc. However, to see what the total costs of the new Trident submarines will be over the period which they would be in service, as well as the costs of the current Trident submarines until they retire and are decommissioned (see below), it is of interest to know what the *total* costs are, including capital and running costs, since these represent the opportunity costs which could theoretically be used elsewhere if Trident were cancelled.

The 'in-service' or ongoing running costs of the existing generation of Trident submarines was estimated to be around £1.7 billion per year in 2007. This includes servicing and maintaining the submarines, running support facilities including all the security required to look after nuclear weapons, plus the ongoing nuclear weapons research and development taking place at AWE Aldermaston. Some estimates put this annual figure at about £2 billion in 2015 and this is likely to continue rising with the new generation of Successor class submarines.

Officially, the government has stated that the running costs of Trident come to approximately 5–6% of the MOD budget and it is expected that will remain the case throughout the lifespan of the Successor programme. There are different ways of interpreting the MOD budget, however, because different items may be included depending on the how the budget is presented. At the low end of the scale, the present MOD 'departmental expenditure limit', excluding depreciation, is only £27.2 billion in 2015/16 and 5% of that would be £1.7 billion. At the upper end of the scale, total MOD 'request for resources' is currently closer to £38.2 billion in 2015/16. Taking 6% of that would put annual running costs of Trident at £2.3 billion. Presumably the real figure is somewhere between £1.7 and 2.3 billion, but by how much this is likely to rise over the coming decades is anyone's guess.

Decommissioning and other costs

All nuclear-powered and nuclear missile submarines, together with all other nuclear-related facilities (including civilian nuclear power stations) must be fully decommissioned at the end of their useful life, to safely remove and dispose of all irradiated materials that pose a threat to human health. Official MOD accounts include a line for 'nuclear liabilities' that cover the anticipated costs – over the next 100 years or so – of decommissioning all existing nuclear-related estate, including facilities at Aldermaston and Burghfield as well as all nuclear-powered submarines currently awaiting decommissioning.

In 2006, the MOD's nuclear liabilities were estimated at nearly £10 billion. This included £3 billion for research and development at Aldermaston and Burghfield, £1 billion for eventual 'deep waste' disposal, plus £500 million for the berthing of 27 submarines still awaiting decommissioning and £330 million for eventual berthing of the four Vanguard subs (plus eventual decontamination of other naval sites).[179] In the latest 2014–2015 MOD accounts, total nuclear liabilities have been reduced to approximately £4 billion, of which decommissioning of Polaris and Vanguard subs apparently comes to approximately £1.3 billion.[180]

However, these figures do *not* include the costs of 'deep disposal' mentioned in earlier accounts. Responsibility for what is now referred to as 'geological' disposal has passed to the Nuclear Decommissioning Authority (NDA), which comes under the Department for Energy and Climate Change. The NDA has responsibility for finding a permanent solution to the disposal of nuclear waste from *all* nuclear facilities in the UK, civilian and military. The total cost of dealing with all this nuclear waste has been estimated at nearly £70 billion over the next 100 years or so.

The so-called permanent solution to nuclear waste, which must be kept safe from humans and out of the environment, not just for the next 100 years but for the next 100,000 years, is expected to be in place by the 2040s. Until that time, the decommissioning of nuclear submarines involves little more than keeping them tied up at a safe mooring at Rosyth naval dockyard. If berthing and eventual disposal of eight Polaris and Vanguard subs is expected to cost £1.3 billion, we can safely assume that berthing and disposal of four additional Successor subs would be another £650 million or so. It is likely to come to much more than this, especially if the final 'deep disposal' costs are included.

Inflation and spreading of the costs

When calculating the costs of a multi-year project like this, we first of all have to take into account the impact of inflation and the fact that a pound sterling in 2030 or 2060 may be worth much less than a pound sterling in 2015. At the moment, inflation is near zero, but this is not historically the case and so estimates must be made of how much inflation is likely to be over the coming 15 years or more. This is not an exact science.

There is also the issue of which years, and how many years, over which we should legitimately spread the total costs. The building of the new submarines started in 2011 with the 'design phase' and is expected to take 20 years in total. However, the lifetime of the submarines is expected to be 25 or 30 years beyond that, and it is perfectly acceptable accounting practice to apply a discount rate that attributes the cost of building the submarines over the lifetime of the submarines once they are actually in service. This makes it very difficult in practice to understand what the cost of the submarines actually is.

The truth is no one really knows how much Trident will cost over the next 50 years. According to US sources,

> unlike the US, Britain does not report how much it spends on nuclear forces. Budgets for nuclear research and development, testing, procurement and operations are presented in such a way as to hide the real costs and obfuscate the issue.[181]

Total costs

The figure of £167 billion for the total cost of Trident was calculated by Crispin Blunt on the basis of the estimate he received from the Ministry of Defence that in-service costs of Trident would continue to come in 'at around 6% of the annual defence budget'.[182] Blunt then combined this percentage with the government's commitment to maintain the NATO target of 2% of GDP spending on defence, and the GAO's estimate of 2.48% as the rate of GDP growth over the period 2020 to 2060. No other inflationary or discount rate was applied to these figures.

This is an inexact science, especially over such a long period of time. No one can reasonably predict what GDP growth will actually be during that period, nor whether the government will stick to the 2% GDP for defence spending. Estimating that 6% of the defence budget will go on Trident is also highly speculative, since the costs of Trident are not dependent on what the overall defence budget is, but rather the reverse. However, what Crispin Blunt is accurately pointing out is that on the basis of the government's own assumptions, this is the kind of figure they themselves are assuming for the total cost of Trident over the full period of its service.

In fact, the £167 billion figure was based on capital costs of £25 billion and in-service costs, rising gradually to reach a total over 40 years of £142 billion. As we have seen, the NSS/SDSR announced in November 2015 that the capital costs for the submarines alone had risen to £31–41 billion. Taking the higher figure as the more realistic, given the history of cost overruns, would add a further £16 billion to Crispin Blunt's figures, bringing it to £183 billion. If other capital costs are also included, including the expected £16.7 billion investment into facilities and new warhead design at AWE Aldermaston, that would further increase this figure to nearly £200 billion. Adding another £1 billion or so for eventual decommissioning of the new submarines puts the total cost of replacing Trident and keeping the UK's nuclear weapon system going until at least 2060 easily over £200 billion, or more than £4.4 billion each year, on average, over the next 45 years.

Even if we were to assume that total running costs remain constant over the next several decades at roughly £2 billion per year, and only count 30 years as the lifespan of the new submarines, that comes to roughly £60 billion in running costs. We could further assume that there will be no cost overruns on the submarine construction, so that it remains within the £31 billion budget. And finally, if we remove the £3 billion already spent on submarine design plus the £5 billion already spent on infrastructure at Aldermaston, the total cost of renewing Trident still takes us well over the £100 billion mark.

Opportunity costs

Prior to 2010, the costs associated with the UK's nuclear weapons programme were treated separately from other capital expenses. That allowed the MOD to budget for other high-cost military items such as aircraft carriers and fighter jets without these having to compete with Trident for limited MOD resources. Since this is no longer the case, every £1 billion spent on Trident is £1 billion that is no longer available for these other big military projects, all other things being equal.

In the 2015 Spending Review and Autumn Statement, George Osborne announced major increases to the MOD budget over the next five years, including an additional £3.5 billion to meet the NATO target of spending 2% GDP on defence for the whole of that period and £11 billion of investment in new military capabilities.[183] The MOD capital budget is set to rise from £7.1 billion in 2015/16 to £8.7 billion by 2020/2021. By 2020, the capital costs of Trident renewal are expected to be more than £2 billion per year, so that is approaching 25% of the total MOD capital budget at that point.

The autumn statement included generous increases to other departments as well as to the MOD (in addition to cancellation of the planned cuts to tax credits for low income families). However, the government's spending priorities are still dominated by the 'austerity' narrative, with deep cuts forecast, for instance in government grants to local authorities. These will be cut by over £6 billion between 2015 and 2020, leaving local authorities with less than half the funding from central government that they have at the moment.[184]

All government expenditure is a matter of political choice. The total pie is determined by how much governments are willing to raise in tax and other revenues, and how the pie is divided up is on the whole determined by governmental priorities, with some exceptions over which they have little or no control. If the government chose to spend between £100 and £200 billion over the next 45 years on early childhood education instead of on Trident, they could do so. They could also choose to raise taxes and have Trident *as well as* an early childhood education programme.

Cancelling Trident would not automatically make more money available, either for other defence expenditure or for the budgets of other departments. However, the government is making a clear choice if it opts to spend £100–200 billion on Trident as opposed to spending it on other programmes.

Summary

The total cost of renewing Trident and maintaining 'continuous at-sea' patrols for an additional 30 years or more is considerably more than £31 billion. The government's estimate of £31 billion is for building four new submarines and extending the life of the current missiles. It does not include the ongoing costs of running the new subs until the 2060s, the costs of decommissioning them when they are retired or the additional nuclear facilities and materials required to keep the whole system going that long, including new missiles and new warheads at some point.

While the government has added a £10 billion 'contingency' to the £31 billion figure, cost overruns in the nuclear weapons industry have often been much higher than that. Thus, a total figure of £200 billion is not an unreasonable estimate of the costs of extending the life of existing submarines, missiles, and warheads for an additional 30 years beyond their current life expectancy. A figure of £100 billion is probably an unrealistically conservative one.

These figures do not include the costs of the existing Trident programme. Even if Trident renewal were cancelled today, there would still be a further £40 billion in expenditure between now and 2030. This includes £3 billion already spent on preparations for Trident renewal, £30 billion to maintain the existing boats, missiles, and warheads until 2030 and up to £9 billion on decommissioning costs to shut down the whole programme.

CHAPTER 15

Do We Need Trident to Protect Jobs?

FOR SOME, ESPECIALLY in the Labour and trade union movements, the issue of jobs is paramount and the need to protect highly specialised positions in the nuclear engineering and submarine industries is a reason given for retaining Trident. How many jobs are we talking about here, and what jobs in particular are dependent on Trident? Is there viable and suitable alternative employment for these people? What other considerations should be taken into account?

John Woodcock is MP for Barrow and Furness, and he is concerned about jobs in the nuclear submarine industry. He has every reason to be concerned about these jobs in particular, because the BAE shipyard in Barrow-in-Furness is the only shipyard in the UK that is capable of building nuclear submarines and the town of Barrow-in-Furness and surrounding district is heavily dependent upon the employment from this one shipyard.

The town of Barrow-in-Furness has a population of 57,000 people and the local district has a total population of 69,000. The Barrow shipyards have been making ships since the 19th century, and its first submarine was built for the Ottoman Empire in 1886.

At its peak in 1990, the shipyard employed 14,500 people, although this had shrunk to 5,800 by 1995. BAE Systems Submarines currently employs a total of 5,000 employees at nine UK sites, including 3,500 at Barrow. While other naval ships are also built there, Barrow has become the sole shipbuilding yard for nuclear-powered submarines: the Trident ballistic missile subs (SSBNs) as well as the *Astute* class nuclear-powered but conventionally armed 'killer' subs.

According to the House of Commons Defence Committee in 2006, 'without a new SSBN it is possible that there would be insufficient demand for nuclear submarines to sustain the industry'.[185] In other words, as John Woodcock himself has put it, 'without further investment in Trident, we will lose our entire submarine industry'.

Jobs currently dependent on Trident

In addition to the 3,500 jobs directly affected at Barrow, there are sub-contractors spread around the UK who produce parts for the Trident submarines. These include Rolls-Royce, who produce the nuclear reactors for the subs at Raynesway in Derbyshire and employ 930 engineers to do that. There is also Devonport Management Ltd (DML) who handle the refitting and maintenance on the subs and employ 4,700 permanent staff and about 500 contract staff in Devonport, Plymouth. There is Babcock Naval Services who employ 6,500 people at HM Naval Base, Clyde, of which 1,400 work specifically on the Trident submarines.

Roughly another 1,500 people are employed making parts and supporting the construction of Trident submarines at firms such as Weir, Strachan and Henshaw, Thales Optronics, MacTaggart, Scott and Co, Alsthom, L3, Sheffield Forgemasters and Henshaw and York.[186] That's roughly 12,500 people in total, working directly or indirectly on construction and maintenance of Trident submarines.

The Trident missiles themselves are leased from the US, so no jobs in the UK are directly affected. Of course there are the Royal Navy servicemen and women who staff the subs, the support ships, the base at Faslane and the nuclear weapon store at Coulport. These are military jobs but they are supported by 1,080 MOD civilian staff at Faslane and 670 at Coulport plus approximately 2,500 external contractors.

In terms of the design and construction of the nuclear warheads, this all takes place at the two Atomic Weapons Establishments (AWE) at Aldermaston and Burghfield in Berkshire. Some 4,230 staff are employed at AWE Aldermaston and 340 at AWE Burghfield, plus approximately 2,000 contract staff and a 'few hundred' at support facilities in London and Bristol.[187] That means roughly 7,000 people are employed in the nuclear warhead 'industry' on top of the 12,500 in the nuclear missile submarine industry, or nearly 20,000 in total.

According to the trade union, Amicus, a further 13,500 jobs at Barrow, a further 6,000 jobs at Faslane and a further 1,200 jobs at Coulport are directly dependent on the nuclear submarine industry. These are people employed in catering, cleaning, transport and other support roles which provide services to the Trident workforce. If Trident were cancelled, it is impossible to know exactly how many jobs would be lost, since many of these jobs are supporting other programmes as well. However, it is certainly possible that as many as 40,000 jobs are directly or indirectly affected by the ongoing deployment of Trident out of a total UK workforce of approximately 30 million.

That is not to say that a total of 40,000 jobs is insignificant or that we should not care about those people, their jobs, their families or their communities. In fact, one might have thought that the British government would have a plan for what to do with these people, given that they signed a legal commitment in 1968, in the form of the Non-Proliferation Treaty, to see the (eventual) elimination of all its nuclear weapons. There has been ample opportunity since 1968 to devise a strategy and develop a plan for the alternative employment of people whose livelihoods depend on a weapon system that we are legally committed to getting rid of.

Impact on jobs of cancelling Trident

Even if Trident were abolished tomorrow, however, it would take many years to fully and safely remove, disarm, decommission, dismantle, decontaminate, and dispose of the radioactive materials that go into the warheads, submarines and weapons facilities that make up the Trident system. Only highly skilled and specialised nuclear scientists, engineers and technicians can do that work, so by deciding to cancel Trident, we would already be committed to keeping a number of those people in their jobs for the rest of their lives and probably still requiring at least another full generation of nuclear experts to carry through to completion the long-term decommissioning process.

If we take this one step further, we can already see the potential for Britain becoming a global expert in the disarming of nuclear materials, much as it has become a global expert for the disposal of chemical weapons following the conclusion of the chemical weapons convention which banned all chemical weapons in 1993.

The UK's secret chemical weapons base at Porton Down in Sussex used to be where the UK tested, developed and stored its stockpile of chemical weapons. Instead, it is now a centre for researching and carrying out the safe disposal and disarming of chemical weapons and it provides expertise to other countries around the world who are seeking to dismantle their chemical weapons stockpiles in accordance with the chemical weapons convention.

Britain's nuclear bomb factory at Burghfield and the nuclear research and production facilities at Aldermaston could become major centres for the research and development of safe disposal of nuclear weapons. The

UK Nuclear Decommissioning Authority is already heavily involved in supporting the civil nuclear power industry in other countries and raises more than a third of its income from advising and handling the nuclear waste of other countries.

In addition to the safe disposal of nuclear weapons and all their accompanying material is the need for advanced and sophisticated monitoring and verification systems to ensure compliance with any agreements reached on nuclear disarmament. The recent international deal signed with Iran calls for strict monitoring and verification that still needs further development. The UK has already been working with scientists and nuclear experts in Norway to develop such systems and take a lead in this area.

Given the considerable ongoing investment in the nuclear weapons facilities at Aldermaston and Burghfield, the UK could easily take and maintain a lead in this field, meaning that these facilities would be needed for many decades to come just to deal properly with any nuclear disarmament processes that may follow our own. In terms of the 7,000 jobs at Aldermaston, Burghfield and related facilities, it is therefore likely that a large number of these would be needed whatever happens to Trident. Were the UK to take a global lead in the nuclear decommissioning industry, even more jobs at these facilities could be created.

Most of the jobs at Faslane support not just Trident but also the Astute submarines and other surface ships of the Royal Navy. Some would go if Trident were cancelled, along with many of the 1,200 jobs at Coulport, since this site relates only to Trident. The Scottish Trades Union Congress, however, estimates that of the total workforce at the two sites, a total of 520 people would be at risk of redundancy if Trident were cancelled, assuming other naval activities continued.[188]

The dismantling and safe disposal of the existing Trident submarine fleet will take place mainly at Rosyth dockyard, which means the Barrow shipyard would not be likely to benefit from ongoing jobs involved in that work. However, nearly all the personnel currently employed at Barrow are involved in the construction of Astute submarines. In the past, Barrow shipyard also produced submarines for the navies of other countries. Therefore the effect on jobs of a cancellation of Trident is more to do with the lack of other submarine orders – and the decision to focus only on submarine construction at Barrow – than to do with Trident itself.

Future for jobs in the nuclear industry

In the long run, new jobs will need to be created to replace those currently in an industry that cannot be continued indefinitely under any reasonable scenario. A Defence Diversification Agency as proposed by Jeremy Corbyn, Leader of the Labour Party, would need to research and plan for that eventuality by looking at the skill sets and technical expertise of those currently employed in the nuclear submarine and weapons industry and proposing alternative work that would be commensurate with the kind of skills and experience involved. It does not require that much imagination to see that numerous applications already exist in parallel fields, even without considering the contentious issue of nuclear power generation or other nuclear technologies where the transfer of skills and know-how might be almost seamless.

The challenges we face globally in the 21st century require us to be investing in research and development to replace fossil fuels with renewable energy sources in all forms of transport, industry, heating, electricity production and many other applications which current rely on oil and gas products. This amounts to a revolution comparable in scale to the first introduction of steam-powered machinery or the advent of computers. It will require the technical skills and expertise of an entire generation devoted to this challenge, and will undoubtedly dwarf the investment in jobs and infrastructure that has gone into development, production and deployment of nuclear weapons.

In fact, one of the largest off-shore wind farms in the UK is already located right by Barrow-in-Furness and there have been proposals for an electricity generating tidal barrage across Morecambe Bay, starting at Barrow. These and other low-carbon, alternative energy projects would require serious government investment, but if such investment were forthcoming, they could easily employ the 3,500 people currently working on submarines at Barrow.

The 'arms to renewables' project of the Campaign Against Arms Trade looked at the job prospects in the renewable energy field and the investment that would be needed to meet the UK's climate change targets over the coming decades. They estimate that with an initial government investment of £7 billion, over 300,000 jobs could be created across the UK in the wind and marine energy fields, including at least 22,000 in the Barrow region. These would be mostly high-tech engineering jobs that match the kinds of skills involved in nuclear submarine construction.[189]

Looking at the bigger picture

Suitable jobs can undoubtedly be found for those currently employed in the nuclear weapons and submarine industry. This may require government investment, but it would be miniscule in comparison to the total costs of renewing Trident. In the broader perspective, arguing that any weapon system should be maintained in order to safeguard the jobs involved in making and using that weapon system is nonsensical.

Weapons, like all other products that are produced, come and go as other products are invented or created to replace them. No company and no country can safely remain reliant on an outmoded product just because people's livelihoods have depended on it up to now. Maybe there are some who would argue that Britain should have kept all its typewriters and touch-type secretaries and paper filing systems and all the administrators whose jobs depended on that level of technology rather than move over to the computer age. We would not have survived long as a thriving economy had we done so.

When it comes to jobs dependent on nuclear weapons, there are additional ethical considerations to take into account. When parliament abolished the transatlantic slave trade in 1807, many jobs were immediately at risk, especially in cities like Liverpool and Bristol which were hugely dependent on the slave trade at that time. Does anyone seriously suggest today that Britain should have kept the slave trade going in order to protect those jobs?

When WWII ended, millions of men were demobilised and sent home with no jobs, while millions more (mostly women) who had been working in the munitions factories and other war-related industries were suddenly out of work as well. No one at that time or since has ever suggested that the country would have been better off keeping all those people employed and not ending the war. It may have been a difficult transition, but people found jobs, families survived, communities were rebuilt.

Compared to the ending of the transatlantic slave trade or of WWII, the number of people kept in employment directly or indirectly by the Trident programme is miniscule – as already mentioned, perhaps as many as 40,000 people out of a total workforce of 30 million. Of these, at least 8,000 direct jobs and presumably a similar number of indirect support jobs would likely remain for many years or even decades to come even if Trident were cancelled tomorrow. That leaves approximately 12,000 jobs directly affected and another 12,000 support jobs potentially affected. Alternative employment could easily be found for these people at similar salaries and skill levels in other industries, such as renewable energy, if the political will was there to do so.

Summary

Barrow-in-Furness is historically a ship-building town. Out of a total population of 67,000, however, only 3,500 are currently employed at the shipyard. A further 13,500 jobs are potentially affected if the shipyard closes but already more that 10,000 jobs have been lost since peak employment at the shipyard in the 1980s and 90s.

At Faslane and Coulport, 1,400 jobs are directly connected to Trident, together with 1,000 civilian staff working for the MOD and approximately 2,500 external contractors. A further 7,200 are potentially affected if the submarine base were to close.

In addition to these jobs at Barrow and Faslane, there are 4,700 permanent staff at Devonport involved in the refitting and maintenance of the submarines and another 500 or so contract staff. There are 4,230 staff at AWE Aldermaston and 2,300 or so Burghfield. There are another 2,500 or so working for main contractors like Rolls-Royce, and involved in Trident renewal.

In total, there are perhaps 20,000 people whose jobs are directly affected by the renewal of Trident and another 20,000 who could be indirectly affected. That is a lot of jobs in a particularly high-skilled engineering sector. Out of a total UK workforce of some 30 million it is still a relatively manageable problem.

At the end of WWII, millions were de-mobilised and millions more stopped working the munitions and weapons factories. Even if Trident is renewed, these jobs will go at some point or other.

Even highly skilled workers need to be re-trained and found alternative employment when the industry they are in ceases to need them. This has happened over the course of the last 50 years in industry after industry. It achieves nothing to cling onto a dying industry for the sake of jobs.

What the UK could benefit from is a massive investment in alternative energy sources to reduce our carbon footprint and meet the international targets for limiting climate change. This will require high-tech and highly skilled engineers among many others. The time to address the jobs issue is now, rather than in 20 years when the same jobs will be lost even if Trident is renewed.

CHAPTER 16

What About Scotland?

FASLANE NAVAL BASE (HMNB Clyde) is about 30 miles from the centre of Glasgow and is the home base for Trident submarines when they are not at sea. Just across the loch is RNAD Coulport, where the UK's nuclear weapons are stored when they are not on board the Trident submarines.

For those who argue in favour of retaining and renewing Trident, the location of the submarines is not an issue. So long as Scotland remains part of the UK, it is not considered relevant what the Scottish parliament, or indeed what Scottish public opinion, thinks about Trident or where it is located. This is purely a matter for the government in Westminster.

That, in any case, is the official line. However, in the run-up to the independence referendum in 2014, it became clear that a 'yes' vote would have huge implications for the future of Trident. Whether or not another referendum takes place any time soon and regardless of the outcome, the political landscape of Scotland has dramatically changed since 2014. Does this, or could it, affect the renewal of Trident? What are the implications for Trident remaining in Scotland against increasingly strong and powerful opposition?

Impact of a nuclear attack

In the event of a nuclear war with Russia, this part of Scotland would almost certainly be the first to be attacked in order to try to destroy the UK's capacity to fire back any more nuclear weapons than those already at sea. This could involve detonation of as many as six sea-launched missiles of 100 KT each (similar in firepower to the UK's Trident missiles) or perhaps two ground-launched missiles of up to 800 KT each. Even if such an attack did not detonate or release radiation from the Trident missiles in storage or docked at the base, which of course cannot be ruled out, the explosions from a Russian nuclear attack on these two bases would be massive.

The impact of such an attack on Scotland's largest city would depend very much on wind speeds and wind direction. The prevailing winds are from the southwest, so most of the radioactive fallout would hopefully land on the relatively sparsely populated Scottish highlands. If the wind speed was slow to moderate and coming from the west or northwest, however, the entire central belt of Scotland could be severely affected. Since roughly 70% of Scotland's 5.3 million people live in this densely populated area, as many as 3.7 million people could receive a radiation dose of up to 1 Sv per hour in this worst case scenario.

As we have seen in Chapter 2, 1 Sv per hour is a potentially lethal dose of radiation if accumulated over a relatively short period of time. An absorbed dose of 4.5 Sv is enough to kill you. Anyone not sufficiently protected from radiation at a rate of 1 Sv an hour will suffer acute radiation sickness within a matter of hours. It is hard to predict from this how many casualties might result, but clearly it would be a catastrophe for Scotland of unprecedented proportions.

It is the government's hope that there would never be such an attack on the UK. Indeed, for those who fervently believe in the effectiveness of nuclear deterrence, the very fact that the UK's nuclear weapons are based at Faslane is meant to *ensure* that such a scenario will never happen. That hope and belief is not necessarily shared by those who would be affected.

Public opinion in Scotland

A public opinion poll in 2013 purported to show that 53% of Scots were in favour of Trident while only 36% are opposed.[190] This, however, was a misleading interpretation of results that actually showed that only 24% of Scots supported Trident while a further 29% supported some unspecified but less powerful and less costly system to replace it.[191] In fact, all other polls by YouGov, MORI/Ipsos and others have consistently shown strong majorities against Trident in Scotland. As is the case with all polling data, results depend very much on what question is asked and in what context. An earlier YouGov poll, for instance, indicated that while only 25% of those in UK overall think Trident should be scrapped altogether, the equivalent figure in Scotland was 48%.[192] The most reliable indication of public opinion comes from the votes cast at elections.

In 2007, the Scottish parliament voted against Trident replacement, with 71 MSPs voted against, 16 in favour with 39 abstentions (from the Labour Party). In 2014, MSPs again voted on Trident and this time it was 68 against and 47 in favour (with Labour voting along with the UK party line at that point). On 3 November 2015, following a policy decision by the Scottish Labour Party to vote against Trident, the Scottish parliament voted for a third time on Trident renewal, this time with 97 opposed and only 17 in favour.

In Westminster, 58 of Scotland's 59 MPs are poised to vote against Trident renewal, including all of the SNP's 56 MPs plus the one remaining Labour MP and the one remaining LibDem MP. That leaves only the single Conservative Party MP in Scotland, David Mundell, likely to represent a pro-Trident position from Scotland. This strength of opposition in the Westminster parliament follows not only the meteoric rise of the SNP in the aftermath of the independence referendum but also the growing opposition to Trident from many other sections of Scottish society.

In short, everything that could be done to address the Trident issue through democratic channels in Scotland has been done at this point. This includes through the Scottish Parliament, the Scottish Executive, the Scottish legal system (see below) and Scottish representation at Westminster.

A long history of opposition to Trident in Scotland

The degree of opposition to Trident in Scotland cannot be explained simply by reference to the proximity of Faslane and a potential nuclear attack to Scotland's largest city. After all, the second most likely target to be hit in a nuclear attack against the UK is probably the joint military headquarters at Northwood, which is even closer to the centre of London than Faslane is to the centre of Glasgow, with many millions more people potentially affected from the fallout of a nuclear attack on Northwood.

Scotland has in fact had a long and consistent record of anti-nuclear campaigning that stretches back to the origins of the Campaign for Nuclear Disarmament (CND) in the late 1950s. Prior to Trident, it was the US Polaris nuclear submarines, also based on the Clyde, which were the focus of anti-nuclear protests. When the Cold War began to heat up again in the 1980s, 'peace camps' appeared at nuclear bases all across Europe as focal points for permanent protest. Faslane Peace Camp was set up in June 1982 and recently celebrated its 33rd anniversary – still going, decades after all the other peace camps have long since disappeared.

Decades of colourful and creative protest at Faslane, including 'Faslane 365', a full year of daily protests and direct action at Faslane during 2006–2007, have brought tens of thousands of people to the gates of the base, to see the nuclear submarine base for themselves and to put their bodies on the line in opposition to it. This in turn has enabled many tens or hundreds of thousands more to hear first-hand accounts of what has gone on at Faslane and why so many oppose it. In a country the size of Scotland, this level of engagement has meant that Trident is much more known about and talked about than it has ever been in England.

Trident then became a major issue in the Scottish referendum vote in 2014, when a new level of political engagement, especially among young people, was achieved for the first time in any part of the UK. People in Scotland were discussing political issues, including Trident, openly and attentively, at dinner parties and church fairs and in village halls, pubs and shopping centres. This process, more than anything else, contributed to a level of awareness about the issues surrounding Trident that has not been attained in other parts of the UK.

Trident has always been the number two issue for the SNP, after independence. Together with Scottish Greens, Scottish Labour, Scottish LibDems and a host of smaller political parties now all opposing Trident and the Conservatives marginalised with just one MP and a handful of MSPs, the political landscape is now overwhelming anti-Trident. This is the position also supported by the Church of Scotland, Action of Churches Together in Scotland (ACTS), the Scottish Trades Union Congress (STUC) and numerous other civil society organisations in Scotland.

Implications of political opposition

What does it now mean, politically and constitutionally, that a weapons system wholly based in Scotland is so strongly opposed in Scotland, as evidenced by public opinion, the Scottish parliament and 58 out of 59 Scottish MPs at Westminster? As long as Scotland remains part of the UK, the Scottish institutions have no legal say in defence policy. However, the Scottish parliament and the Scottish Executive do have control over many other areas of responsibility which could directly impinge on the viability of Trident remaining at Faslane.

First of all, Scotland has control over planning permissions and environmental controls which could be used to prohibit or slow down work done at Faslane, including plans for ongoing expansion of the base into the surrounding hillsides. Holyrood also has control over policing and emergency services, which affects not only the planning and execution of any emergency response to a nuclear attack at Faslane, but also affects how public demonstrations and direct action at Faslane might be handled and ultimately the extent to which public opposition to Trident is allowed to obstruct the operation of the base itself.

Scottish authorities control the roads and waterways leading into and out of Faslane, which again could create difficulties for the continued operation of Trident, particularly as the nuclear warheads must travel on a regular basis up and down the country between Faslane and the Burghfield atom bomb factory in Berkshire. The River Clyde and Loch Long, which lead up to Faslane and Coulport, are home to sailing clubs, fishing vessels, pleasure boats and commercial traffic in addition to nuclear submarines and other naval ships.

The constitutional question

Could Scottish opposition to Trident be the trigger that leads Scotland to withdraw from the UK? That may seem an unlikely scenario given that Scottish voters so recently rejected the independence option in the referendum of 2014. In *Survival*, the journal of the International Institute for Strategic Studies, however, William Walker poses this as a very serious question.[193] 'The nuclear weapon system designed to guarantee the UK's survival could hasten its political demise,' he says. He bases his argument on the fact that Trident now symbolises for a growing number of people in Scotland the domination which is imposed on them from London.

Scotland's legal obligations

Scotland has always maintained its own legal system, separate from England and Wales. In the Scotland Act of 1998, giving Scottish devolved institutions the powers of government they now have, it is specifically stated that the actions of those institutions 'must be compatible with international obligations'.[194]

A number of high-profile court cases in Scotland have resulted in the acquittal of peace protesters on the legal grounds that they were acting in accordance with international law to stop international crimes being committed at Faslane. In response, Scotland's highest judge, the Lord Advocate, ruled that Trident was not breaking international law and instructed the lower courts in Scotland to reject that legal argument.

This continues to be a highly contentious legal issue in Scotland. In 2011, two former World Court justices from the Hague came to Scotland to explain the 1996 Advisory Opinion (see Chapter 12) and its relevance to Scottish law.[195] The important point to be made in relation to Trident and the UK as a whole is that the legal interpretation of international law in Scotland does not necessarily mirror the interpretation made by high court judges or the Supreme Court in London.

Since Scotland is under a legal obligation to comply with international law- and must interpret that law through its own legal system – it is perfectly possible for Trident to be ruled illegal in Scotland according to the principles of international law as laid out in Chapter 12. This would have a significant effect on the UK's ability to maintain Trident in Scotland, even without Scotland becoming an independent state.

Nowhere else to go

When the Clyde was chosen as the base for Polaris, and then Trident, it was not because the location was suitably far away from London and in the event of war would only affect the Scots. In fact, due to the stringent safety requirements for the handling and storage of nuclear warheads, the main factor in choosing a location was the proximity to a large enough area for storage that could be kept highly secure.[196]

The only two alternative locations that have existing facilities for handling submarines are Devonport and Barrow. These are both surrounded by build-up urban areas, however, and do not have the necessary land available for the safe storage of nuclear weapons.

Two other possible sites that were originally considered for Polaris but ruled out were Milford Haven in Wales and Falmouth in Cornwall. These again have similar drawbacks today. Apart from needing to be kept away from houses and public roads, the warheads need to be kept away from each other, not only to prevent one accident triggering others but also to lessen the chance of a direct nuclear attack destroying the whole arsenal. For this reason, the nuclear arms depot at Coulport takes up 304 hectares of land, approximately 15km x 2 km, with a perimeter that is 30 km long.[197]

Detailed study of the possible alternative locations for Trident indicate that apart from the enormous expense involved, which has not been calculated, there is no other UK location outside of Scotland that would meet existing safety standards laid down by the Office of Nuclear Regulation and the Defence Nuclear Safety Regulator.[198] These safety standards could be relaxed, or the submarines could be based in France or the USA. Apart from that, Faslane is the only option for retaining Trident.

Summary

What does it mean for the UK that 58 out of 59 Scottish MPs in Westminster oppose Trident renewal, together with 97 out of 115 MSPs in Holyrood?

Trident is based in Scotland, and yet an overwhelming majority of Scots appear to be opposed to it.

Because of the dangers of storing the nuclear warheads too close to each other, a large amount of land is needed that can be kept secure allowing easy access to the submarines. Alternative deep water ports in England and Wales have all been rejected as possible sites for Trident because of this requirement.

Leaving Trident in Scotland against such strong opposition carries other risks for the UK government. By further antagonising Scottish opinion over the Trident issue, the government may yet be faced with calls for another referendum and the break-up of the UK – the very thing which Trident is supposed to prevent.

Short of another referendum, there are many other tactics which may be used in Scotland in the coming months and years to obstruct or make impossible to continued deployment of Trident in Scotland. Among other things, the Scotland Act of 1998 requires the Scottish authorities to abide by international law. In a situation where the UK government may *not* be abiding by international law in its continued deployment – and renewal – of Trident, where does that leave the Scottish government?

Scotland may not have a say in the 'reserved' issue of Trident as a defence matter. But as a country with its own legal system and obligations to follow the dictates of international law, it may yet have an important – and insurmountable – say in what happens next with Trident.

PART FIVE

We are Doing All We Can to Disarm

CHAPTER 17

Is the UK Committed to 'Multilateral' Disarmament?

WHEN PRESSED, ALMOST every politician who supports Trident will say that of course they are in favour of nuclear disarmament, who isn't? They too want to see a world that is eventually free of nuclear weapons. As we have seen in Chapter 12, this is not just an aspiration but a legal obligation. But getting rid of our own nuclear weapons 'unilaterally' is not, they say, the way to achieve this. Rather, what they will invariably say is that they are for 'multilateral' nuclear disarmament and that the UK government has always been fully committed to this approach.

> As a responsible Nuclear Weapons State we are committed to the long-term goal of a world without nuclear weapons and we recognise our obligations under all three of the pillars of the NPT. We will work with our international partners to tackle proliferation and to make progress on multilateral disarmament... We will continue to press for key steps towards multilateral disarmament, including the entry into force of the Comprehensive Nuclear Test Ban Treaty and successful negotiations on a Fissile Material Cut-Off Treaty in the Conference on Disarmament.[199]

Sir Jeremy Greenstock was UK ambassador to the United Nations from 1998–2003, during which time he was in the unenviable position of trying to secure UN Security Council support for the invasion of Iraq. His book about the Iraq War was subsequently blocked from publication by the Foreign Office. While his views on the Iraq War are still somewhat controversial, his position on Trident is quite clear. In his defence of the government's 'step-by-step' approach to nuclear disarmament, Sir Jeremy insists that the UK has done all it can – and more than other nuclear weapon states – to steer the process of multilateral disarmament towards the eventual elimination of nuclear weapons as obligated by the Non-Proliferation Treaty.[200]

Disarmament and Arms Control

It is certainly the case that the UK has played a role in nuclear weapons negotiations that have taken place internationally – and a key role in some of them, for instance in the formulation of the NPT itself. But overall, what is the UK's record on multilateral disarmament? And just how serious is the UK about achieving nuclear disarmament through multilateral negotiations?

First of all, we need to distinguish between what is known as 'disarmament' and what is euphemistically called, 'arms control'. Disarmament involves the destruction of weapons leading to an overall reduction in weapons and eventually their elimination. Examples of disarmament treaties in the nuclear field include the INF Treaty of 1987, which got rid of a whole class of nuclear weapons in Europe, and the START and NewSTART treaties, which reduced the numbers of strategic nuclear weapons held by the two superpowers by up to 50% in each case.

The Landmines Treaty, the Biological Weapons Convention and other such treaties have also led to the near complete elimination of certain types of weapons. These are therefore disarmament treaties.

By contrast, arms control treaties have curtailed certain activities or even put a lid on certain activities but without leading directly or indirectly to a reduction in the numbers of weapons involved. Examples of this are the Non-Proliferation Treaty, which seeks to prevent other states from obtaining nuclear weapons but did not curtail existing nuclear weapons states from continuing to increase their nuclear stockpiles. Another example is the Partial Test Ban Treaty, which prohibited nuclear testing in the atmosphere but did not stop testing altogether (which continued underground). Nor did it stop the nuclear weapons states from continuing to increase their nuclear stockpiles.

In terms of nuclear disarmament, as opposed to arms control, the *only* multilateral treaties that have led to actual disarmament, that is, a decrease in the numbers of nuclear weapons, have been between the US and the Soviet Union. None have involved the UK, and as we shall see in the next chapter, all the reductions in the UK's nuclear arsenal which have taken place since the height of the Cold War have been the result of unilateral action on the part of the UK government, not as a result of multilateral negotiations.

In support of its claim that the UK is working to 'make progress on multilateral disarmament', the NSS/SDSR cites 1) its work with Norway on verification; 2) its work to bring into force the CBTB; 3) its work towards a Fissile Material Cut-Off Treaty. These are all useful and important multilateral developments but none of them involve disarmament as such but are instead all examples of arms control.

Progress on disarmament verification

The UK has been working with Norway to advance verification technologies that can monitor compliance with disarmament and arms control treaties and obligations. Verification of nuclear testing is comparatively straightforward, since seismological equipment for monitoring earthquakes is now installed in key locations around the globe and these sites are linked up to each other in an effort to provide better warning of earthquakes and tsunamis. Nuclear tests, even underground and underwater ones, are large enough to register as small 'earthquakes' on seismological equipment and therefore it is virtually impossible for any country to conduct a nuclear test without it being picked up by such equipment.

Satellite imagery, including infrared photography which picks up signs of intense heat, is also able now to effectively monitor above ground nuclear explosions taking place anywhere in the world. Satellite monitoring has also been used to demonstrate that disarmament agreements have been kept, for instance allowing the Soviets to see for themselves the destroyed, chopped up US long-range bombers spread out on the ground in compliance with the START treaty.

The UK–Norway Initiative is a collaboration between experts from Norway and the UK to investigate technical and procedural challenges associated with verification of nuclear warhead dismantling.201 Already there are many well-established procedures in place for weapons inspectors to verify that nuclear materials from nuclear power stations are not being diverted to weapons use, for instance. Further steps in building confidence that verification of nuclear disarmament measures is possible and practically feasible are important. But these are only a small part of an actual disarmament process and do not constitute disarmament itself.

A Comprehensive Test Ban Treaty (CTBT)

The Soviet Union unilaterally stopped their nuclear testing, underground as well as in the atmosphere, in 1991. The US followed suit in 1992 and France and China in 1996. Since UK underground testing was dependent on US facilities for nuclear testing in Nevada, these also stopped when US testing stopped. The last UK test was therefore in November 1991.

The Comprehensive Test Ban Treaty was designed to consolidate these unilateral decisions into a legally binding treaty that would also prevent other countries from conducting nuclear tests. Negotiations on the CTBT began in 1993 and were concluded in 1996. At the time of publication, 183 countries have signed the CTBT, but it has not entered into force because three countries with nuclear weapons have not yet signed it (India, Pakistan and North Korea) and are continuing with their nuclear tests. Three other countries with nuclear weapons have signed but not ratified the CTBT: the US, China and Israel. As long as the US and China do not ratify the Treaty, it cannot enter into force according to the terms of the treaty.

The UK has signed and ratified the CTBT. By remaining part of the nuclear club (the 'N5'), successive UK governments have claimed they are in a better position to eventually persuade the US and China to ratify the treaty and allow it to enter into force. There is no evidence, however, that the UK has made any progress on this front in the last 20 years, since the US and China are still refusing to ratify.

The Fissile Material Cut-Off Treaty (FMCT)

The UK government is very proud of its role in promoting the Fissile Material Cut-Off Treaty and working towards an agreement that would get this treaty onto the books and into force. The FMCT is a treaty that would prohibit any further production of nuclear weapons-grade fissile material (enriched uranium and plutonium) and thus make it less likely that countries which do not already have weapons-grade fissile material would be able to build nuclear weapons.

But as the name suggests, it is a 'cut-off' treaty, stopping production of fissile material where it is at the moment. Thus it is an arms control rather than a disarmament measure as defined above. Countries which already have weapons-grade fissile material, like the UK, would not be required under this treaty to reduce or eliminate their existing stocks.

Like the Partial Test Ban Treaty and the Comprehensive Test Ban Treaty, the FMCT would help to reduce the future production of nuclear weapons from those countries which do not have any. But in fact, the five declared nuclear weapons states (N5) have more than enough fissile material to meet their requirements for a very long time. As the UK and other NWS decommission and dismantle old, unstable warheads from the 1950s, they merely recycle their fissile material into newer warheads. Even then they have more fissile material left over than they need. So a FMCT in fact does nothing at all to reduce or even to incentivise the N5 to reduce their nuclear stockpiles still further. Indeed, the UK reputedly has a stockpile of 140 tonnes of Plutonium, enough to make 20,000 Nagasaki sized bombs.[202]

The FMCT, like the CTBT, are examples of arms control initiatives that favour the N5 and allow them to continue modernising and upgrading their nuclear weapons while making it seem as if they are working towards disarmament. The UK's role in this game is central.

Conference on Disarmament

The UK's preferred 'chamber' for multilateral negotiations on nuclear disarmament is the UN Conference on Disarmament.[203] This is a forum that was established by the international community in 1979 for multilateral negotiations on disarmament issues. The Chemical Weapons Convention, signed in 1993, was successfully negotiated in this forum and other negotiations have been initiated in this forum, including the FMCT and the CTBT. Currently the conference is made up of 65 countries, including the UK, and it operates on the basis of consensus, meaning that any one of the 65 countries can veto a decision.

Since 1997, the CD has been deadlocked with vetoes used not just to prevent a programme of work being agreed but even to prevent agendas from being set, meaning for much of that time, the Conference on Disarmament has not even been able to agree on what they are going to talk about, let alone on any matters of substance. This stalemate has made the CD the laughing stock of the international community. Sixty-five countries have been sitting around a table in Geneva, week after week, year after year, giving speeches to each other but accomplishing absolutely nothing.[204] And this is the forum through which the UK claims it is working towards multilateral nuclear disarmament.

There are other multilateral forums available for discussing nuclear disarmament, including the UN First Committee, which deals with disarmament affairs, the UN General Assembly, which votes every year on a raft of resolutions from the First Committee, and the UN Security Council, which also has its share of discussions and resolutions relating to matters of nuclear disarmament.

Where has the UK stood in relation to these multilateral discussions?

UK voting record in the UN General Assembly

It is difficult to conclude that the UK has taken multilateral disarmament seriously when it has voted against nearly every initiative or proposal put forward for multilateral disarmament in the United Nations General Assembly. This voting behaviour goes back not just years, but decades. Sometimes it has been only the US and the UK who have voted against disarmament measures put forward by other countries. Sometimes they have been joined by most or all of the other nuclear weapons states, and sometimes by other NATO allies and/or other countries which for whatever reason have opposed particular proposals.

As an example of the UK's position on multilateral nuclear disarmament at the UN, it issued, together with the other four NWS, the following statement in response to the recent vote in December 2015 on 'taking forward multilateral nuclear disarmament' in the UN General Assembly, which all five nuclear weapons states voted against:

> This resolution attempts to promote nuclear disarmament whilst ignoring security considerations. We do not believe that such an approach can effectively lead to concrete progress. Our five States, like many others present here, are concerned with this divisive approach, which in no way brings the international community closer to nuclear disarmament.[205]

Apart from voting in favour of resolutions which call on other countries to support the CTBT or the FMCT, the only recent multilateral disarmament resolution in the UN General Assembly on which the UK voted 'yes' was a resolution in 2011 which, among other things, congratulated the UK for announcing how many warheads were in its nuclear stockpile.[206]

The Open Ended Working Group and Oslo Process

In an effort to break the deadlock in the Conference on Disarmament and the to address the lack of progress on promises made in the NPT, the UN agreed in 2012 to set up an 'Open Ended Working Group on Taking Forward Multilateral Nuclear Disarmament Negotiations' (OEWG). The UK voted against the setting up of this group and did not take part in any of its deliberations.

In a joint statement by the UK, US and France, the UK made clear it was not only opposed to the establishment of the OEWG, but to 'any outcome it may produce.'[207] This seems a rather extraordinary position for a country claiming to be working for multilateral disarmament.

In 2013, an international conference was held in Oslo on the 'humanitarian impacts of nuclear weapons'. Again the UK, along with other N5 countries, refused to take part, stating that:

> The UK is concerned that the Oslo Conference will be an unhelpful

> diversion from the pursuit of progress on multilateral nuclear disarmament through [the] existing fora and that it represents a potential challenge to the current consensus-based step-by-step approach to multilateral nuclear disarmament. The UK is concerned too that some states and NGOs may seek to use the Conference as a vehicle to push for ambitious disarmament measures that the UK does not support, that cannot succeed, and that may risk undermining the consensus-based step-by-step approach.[208]

The UK continued its opposition to what became the 'humanitarian initiative' coming out of the Oslo conference, boycotting a follow-up conference in Nayarit, Mexico, in 2014. The UK (along with the US) did attend the third and final international conference on humanitarian impacts, held in Vienna in December 2014.

However, the statement issued by the UK delegate to the conference reiterated the UK's position on nuclear disarmament, stating that the UK would retain its nuclear weapons 'for as long as it is necessary', and declaring that a treaty banning all nuclear weapons would 'jeopardise strategic stability.'209 When several proposals emanating from the Vienna conference made their way to the UN General Assembly in October and December 2015, the UK once again voted against all of them.

2015 NPT *Review Conference*

The NPT comes up for 'review' every five years. Intense deliberations take place over a period of three or four weeks and normally there is a final report outlining any areas of progress made and steps to be taken over the next five years. This must be agreed by consensus of all 189 countries who are parties to the treaty, so if just one country is not in agreement with the text, it cannot be adopted. In 2015, the final outcome document was rejected by three countries, meaning that the whole four weeks of negotiations among 189 countries came to nothing.

The three countries who threw out the final text of the 2015 NPT Review Conference were the US, Canada and the UK. Why did they do that? It was a last minute intervention by Israel, which is not a party to the NPT, which convinced the three countries to veto the final outcome. This was because the final text included a commitment to hold a conference in 2016 on the setting up of a nuclear-free zone for the Middle East.[210]

Setting up a nuclear-free zone for the Middle East was actually a commitment which all members of the NPT agreed to 20 years ago in 1995.

Successive UK governments have insisted that this was one of their primary objectives to achieve on the nuclear non-proliferation front. While Israel has always declared itself opposed to setting up such a zone, the 1995 'indefinite extension' of the NPT would not have been possible without this commitment on behalf of the N5.[211]

Nevertheless, despite its commitments to a NFZ for the Middle East as agreed in 1995, despite its claim in successive reports to parliament that it was pursuing this aim, and despite all the effort that went into the 2015 NPT review conference, including many other positive steps that will not now be implemented, the UK government chose to block the final report in order to protect Israel from a commitment to hold this conference.

Summary

Successive UK governments have insisted that their preferred route to nuclear disarmament is through 'multilateral' negotiations rather than through 'unilateral' action. The UK record in the many multilateral platforms that have sought to achieve nuclear disarmament is nevertheless worse than disappointing.

The UK has shown not only by its determination to press ahead with Trident renewal, but also by its behaviour at the UN, that it has no real commitment to multilateral nuclear disarmament at all. Instead, together with the other nuclear weapons states, it presses ahead with nuclear weapons as if they will be with us forever and does only the barest minimum to deflect criticism of this 'nuclear weapons forever' position.

Even the initiatives which the UK government chooses to highlight as evidence of its serious commitment to multilateral disarmament belie its real intentions. The three programmes normally highlighted are the UK's involvement with Norway in disarmament verification, efforts to bring the comprehension Test Ban Treaty into force and progress towards a Fissile Material Cut-Off Treaty.

All three of these initiatives are 'arms control' rather than 'disarmament' initiatives. Unlike the INF treaty, START or the NewSTART Treaty, these initiatives do not involve destruction or disarmament of a single nuclear warhead. What's more, all three are targeted specifically at other states, rather than at the UK or other existing NWS.

The UK has never offered or agreed to any independent verification of its own warhead dismantling programme. We can only take the government at its word that it has dismantled many as 300 outdated warheads. So while it is to be applauded that the UK is working with Norway on systems of disarmament verification, an easy first step which has yet to be taken would be to allow independent verification of the UK's own disarmament programme.

The CTBT prohibits all nuclear testing that involves actual nuclear explosions, underground as well as above ground. Without such tests it is virtually impossible to design and develop new types of nuclear weapon. However, with the aid of sophisticated computer-simulated tests which do not involve an actual nuclear explosion, the US has been able to design and develop new types of nuclear weapon without violating the CTBT. So far, only the US has mastered this technology (and given the UK access to it), giving these two countries an unfair advantage over other NWS.

The FMCT would stop countries from producing any more fissile material. But the UK already has more than enough fissile material to make as many nuclear weapons as it could possibly want in the coming decades. So, again, this is aimed at countries which do not already have the stocks of fissile material which the older nuclear powers already have.

The UK has voted against, blocked or boycotted virtually every other multilateral nuclear disarmament initiative – and there have been many. At the 2015 NPT Review Conference, the UK shamefully blocked, together with the US and Canada, the entire outcome of four week's work by 189 countries to make progress on a whole range of nuclear weapons issues.

CHAPTER 18

Hasn't the UK Already Disarmed to the Minimum?

DES BROWNE IS proud of the fact that under the last Labour government, the UK's stockpile of nuclear weapons was reduced to less than half of what it had been during the Cold War. Des considers this proof that the UK is serious about disarmament and has taken bold steps towards the final goal of zero nuclear weapons.[212]

At its peak in the late 70s and early 80s, the UK had approximately 500 nuclear warheads of its own, plus another 387 US warheads assigned to British forces in Germany. On top of this there were also US nuclear warheads stationed at bases in the UK but assigned to US forces. According to the latest reports, the UK now has 215 or so warheads in total and this is to be reduced down to 180 by the mid-2020s. All the US nuclear weapons assigned to British forces in Germany have been removed, together with all US nuclear weapons stationed in the UK.

The Intermediate Nuclear Forces (INF) Treaty between the US and the Soviet Union in 1987 was the first (and so far, the only) multilateral agreement that removed an entire class of nuclear weapons from the inventories of the countries involved. By the early 1990s, all of the so-called 'battlefield' nuclear weapons were withdrawn from both sides in central Europe, including those owned by the US but operated by other countries, such as the British Army of the Rhine (BAOR) in (West) Germany. This treaty left the UK with a sizable stockpile of its own battlefield weapons, which the Blair government decided unilaterally to remove from service.

Battlefield nuclear weapons

One of Britain's home-grown nuclear weapons was called the WE-177 and came in several variants. One of these was the WE-177A, a nuclear depth charge designed to be dropped by Sea King helicopters flying over Soviet nuclear submarines. Former Royal Navy Commander Rob Green, who was responsible for a Sea King helicopter crew training to drop the WE-177A, described it as a 'suicide mission', since the nuclear explosion below the sea would assuredly destroy the helicopter above it before the crew would be able to get out of range.[213]

It is of course to be lauded that the British government took the decision to withdraw these weapons from service. However, we must be under no illusion that this was a form of 'multilateral' disarmament since no negotiations took place with any other state. The weapons were simply withdrawn from service because they were no longer seen as useful or appropriate. The real question is how they could ever have been considered useful or appropriate in the first place.

From Polaris to Trident

The replacement of Polaris with Trident in the 1990s also involved an overall reduction in the total number of warheads in the UK stockpile. Each Polaris 'Resolution' class submarine was designed to carry 16 missiles and each missile could deliver three nuclear warheads, making a total of 196 warheads for four submarines. Later, the Chevaline programme reduced the number of warheads on each missile to two, but with the addition of numerous decoys that were designed to confuse the Soviet missile defences, making it more likely that the two real warheads would get through to their target.

When Trident was first proposed as a replacement for Polaris, it was to have 16 missiles on each sub, as before, but each missile could hold up to 12 warheads, which would have been a massive increase in warheads. However this was then scaled back several times until Trident is now left with 40 warheads per sub, or 160 in total. This is to be reduced still further to 120 warheads in total by the 2020s.

The Polaris A3 warheads had a destructive capacity of approximately 200 KT each (or 12 times the size of the Hiroshima bomb) while Trident D5 warheads are believed to have a maximum yield of 100 KT (or six times the size of the Hiroshima bomb).[214]

So, in terms of destructive capacity as well as numbers of warheads, Trident would appear at first glance to be a *reduction* of nearly 50% in terms of sheer destructive capacity from the original Polaris. But everyone who knows about these things knows very well that this is not the whole story. In fact, Trident is hugely more powerful and more dangerous than Polaris.

First of all, Polaris missiles had a range of 2,500 nautical miles (4,630 km), which meant that to reach Moscow, for instance, Polaris submarines had to stay within a certain portion of the North Atlantic to be within range. That in turn made them more vulnerable to detection and possible attack by the Soviets. Trident missiles have a potential range of more than 7,400 km (depending on payload), or nearly double the range of the Polaris missiles, giving them much greater freedom to roam the seas further away from the UK and further away from Soviet submarine detection vessels. Trident submarines can also travel faster, at greater depths, and much more quietly than their Polaris equivalents, making them much more difficult to track down and destroy.

An important measure in the development of nuclear weapon technology is what is called 'circular error probable', or CEP. This measures the distance within which the warhead is likely to reach its intended target. As we have already discussed in Chapter 1, Trident missiles, with a reputed CEP of only 300 feet,[215] were the first class of nuclear weapon which were powerful enough and accurate enough, even after being launched from a random location at sea, to be able to destroy a 'hardened' target like an underground command bunker or an ICBM missile silo, both likely to be buried under many feet of reinforced concrete.

Polaris missiles had a CEP of 1,800 feet, which was not sufficient for this level of precision targeting. Thus the switch from Polaris to Trident, seemingly involving a unilateral reduction of UK warheads and of warhead destructive power, actually involved a significant increase in terms of nuclear weapons technology.

The reduction from 160 to 120 'operational' warheads announced in 2015 appears to be a slight of hand more than anything else. Out of a total reported number of nuclear warheads, estimated now to be 215, only a certain number are considered 'operational' or 'deployed'. Traditionally, this was the number assumed to be fitted on missiles and loaded on submarines, ready to be fired, with the remainder as 'spares' sitting in storage at the Coulport nuclear weapons depot in Scotland.

In 2015, this number was announced to be only 120 after being reported for several years as 160. Does that mean that the UK dismantled and put into cold storage 40 nuclear warheads in 2015? Or does it simply mean that because one submarine (the *Vanguard*) is currently out of action and undergoing major repairs and an overhaul, the warheads assigned to that submarine are no longer considered 'operational'? As far as anyone is able to ascertain, it is the latter.

Minimum needed for deterrence

In 1988, then-Prime Minister Margaret Thatcher announced that the 'minimum credible deterrent' needed to keep Britain safe from nuclear attack was 512 nuclear weapons, at sea and ready to fire at a moment's notice. In 1995, that number was reduced to 300. In 1998 it was reduced still further to 200 and in 2006 it was reduced to 160. In 2015, it was announced in the Strategic Defence Review that the minimum deterrence needed to protect the UK was 120 nuclear warheads on continuous at-sea patrol.[216]

The truth is there is no way to define what constitutes a 'minimum' deterrent and no calculation that will provide us with one. The UK at one time considered their contribution to NATO to be able to destroy 40% of the people and infrastructure of Moscow, the so-called 'Moscow criterion'. To do that would theoretically require one megatonne of nuclear power, but there is no reason to think that 40% destruction is any more of a deterrent than 30% or indeed 20%.[217]

At present, we are told that Trident missiles have been 'de-targeted' and are not pointing at anyone. In order for them to be fired, an agreement would have to be made as to what to target and instructions given to the submarine to set up the targeting. This would apparently take only a matter of minutes.[218] But a system that is now designed to 'deter' an unknown adversary from an unknown act of aggression cannot also be defined in terms of a 'minimum' deterrent. What if the country in question were North Korea and all it took was a small nuclear warhead to 'deter' such a small country from taking action against us? What, on the other hand, if the country in question were China? Their leaders might well calculate that they could afford to lose a certain proportion of their very large population and still 'survive' as a nation.

Replacing or upgrading

One of the commitments given by Tony Blair at the time of the 'initial gate' decision on Trident renewal in 2007 was that this would not involve any 'upgrade or expansion' of the current Trident systems.[219] Since then, the government has been at pains to stress that it is not a modernisation programme but merely a 'replacement' of old stock that will soon reach its natural 'sell-by' date.

As we have just seen, the replacement of Polaris with the current Trident system involved a considerable increase in terms of technical advancement. There are no plans to replace Trident warheads before 2019, so we do not know what qualitative or quantitative changes may be made there.

The upgrading of the D5 missiles for Trident has already been done, through the life extension 'D5LE' programme. Among other things, this has involved changes to the Arming, Fusing and Firing (AF&F) mechanism which enables Trident missiles to more reliably detonate as a 'groundburst' explosion (see Chapter 2). This increases the ability of Trident to be used as a first strike weapon against Russian hardened missile silos and underground command bunkers. This kind of technical improvement increases the risk of launch-on-warning and therefore must count as an escalation in the nuclear arms race.[220]

What about the submarines? The new submarines are not just re-built Vanguard-class submarines but a new *class* of submarine. This implies a whole range of new features that will make the successor class submarines bigger, better, faster, quieter and more deadly than their Vanguard predecessors. Since there are some design flaws in the current Vanguard class (see Chapter 13) these would presumably be fixed. There are also plans for a new advanced design nuclear reactor to provide propulsion for much longer patrols at sea.

The most important changes, however, will be related to the ability of the submarines to avoid detection and evade threats. Continuing advances in anti-submarine warfare mean that current Vanguard submarines cannot be guaranteed to remain hidden and safe from attack. Despite the fact that HMS *Vanguard* collided with *Le Triomphant* in open seas (see Chapter 13), these submarines may not be as 'undetectable' as they are portrayed.

Further advances in underwater drones and new forms of sonar detection make it almost inevitable that the new Successor submarines will be obsolete before they even enter the water in the 2030s. The whole concept of an undetectable underwater platform providing an absolute guarantee of being able to strike back at any aggressor who threatens the UK may soon be called into question.

In the meantime, whatever advances are included in the development of the new Successor submarines to try to evade detection, for instance with the use of 'stealth' technologies and quieter propulsion, these are improvements on Vanguard class submarines. This once again constitutes 'upgrading and expansion' of existing capabilities even if not technically an 'increase' in destructive capabilities as such.

Summary

The UK has reduced its total stockpile of nuclear weapons from a peak of 520 in 1983 to the present number of around 215. Most of the 300 or so warheads that have been withdrawn from service were obsolete, unusable weapons designed for use on the battlefield. It is good that these weapons have been withdrawn, but does it signal an intention on the part of the UK to continue reducing the nuclear stockpile until it reaches zero?

The reduction of warheads and of warhead yield resulting from the transition from Polaris to Trident does not represent a real reduction in nuclear firepower but instead a substantial *increase* in the capability of UK nuclear weaponry to attack and destroy military targets in Russia or elsewhere. When the UK government talks of having reduced the nuclear stockpile to the 'minimum' needed for deterrence, this is no way to determine what that minimum actually is.

CHAPTER 19

Would Disarmament by the UK Have Any Effect?

EVEN WERE THE UK to eliminate its nuclear arsenal, it is claimed that this would have no effect on the overall 'balance of terror' posed by nuclear weapons, since the US and Russia between them hold 99% of the world's nuclear weapons stockpile. Unilateral action by the UK would not influence the US or other nuclear weapons states to follow suit, but on the contrary would mean the UK losing whatever influence it does have with those other nuclear weapons states, leaving the world in a more dangerous place, not a less dangerous place. Only when the US and Russia have brought their levels of nuclear weapons down to levels similar to UK, France and China is there any point in the UK being part of multilateral negotiations to reduce nuclear arsenals still further.

This is the argument put forward by the government when they have, on those rare occasions, admitted that there is no current or likely future need for Trident and they are under international obligation to eliminate the UK's nuclear weapons. 'There would be no point' is the plea.

It is very true that the US and Russia hold between them the vast majority of nuclear weapons. The UK, with a mere 215 nuclear warheads, is small fry compared to the tens of thousands of nuclear warheads held by US and Russia. Furthermore, it is entirely possible that any further unilateral action by the UK to disarm might have no effect at all on the positions of the other N5 countries. The threat posed to the world by nuclear weapons would continue to hang over us, even if or when the UK removes all its weapons. So would there be any point in doing so?

Clarifying the question

We need to be clear what is at issue here. It is a rather weak argument, on its own, to suggest that Britain giving up its nuclear weapons would have little or no effect on other states giving up theirs. So what? If you are in favour of nuclear weapons, it is presumably because you believe they serve some useful purpose to the UK, in which case you don't want to give them up regardless of whether that has any effect on other countries. If you are opposed to nuclear weapons, it is presumably because you are not convinced they serve any useful purpose and believe we would be better off without them. In that case you are also uninterested in the effect that giving them up may or may not have on other countries.

The impact of giving up the UK's nuclear weapons is therefore rather peripheral to whether or not anyone is for or against giving them up. Surely we should decide which is the right course of action for the UK, regardless of what other countries may or may not do in response? Nevertheless it is an argument often put forward by government, the main effect of which is to say, 'we are not the culprits here, it is the Americans and the Russians you should be targeting for more disarmament, not the UK'.

There is indeed at least one good reason to take the view of other countries into account on this particular issue, and that is because nuclear deterrence is all about *perceptions* and is therefore at least as much about what other countries think as it is about what the UK actually does. Deterrence theory is primarily about what Russia or other potential adversaries think, but since, as we have seen, Trident is assigned to NATO and is very much tied into the US nuclear posture, it is also intricately tied into what the US and other NATO countries think and do.

For instance, if the US suddenly decided to give up its nuclear weapons, where would that leave the UK? Even if France decided to give up its nuclear weapons at this stage, it would have profound implications on the 'credibility' of UK deterrence theory, since it would imply that France had calculated that nuclear weapons were no longer needed and/or no longer functioning as a 'deterrent'. How could the UK pretend that its own nuclear weapons were still needed and acting 'every minute of every day' as a deterrent if its closest neighbour had decided otherwise? The same applies in reverse.

What influence does the UK have on the world stage?

We looked in Chapter 11 at the question of whether possession of nuclear weapons gives the UK a 'seat at the top table' that it would not otherwise have. There is a contradiction between thinking that Britain would lose its influence in the world if it gave up nuclear weapons and thinking that giving up its nuclear weapons would have no influence on any other country. Does Britain have influence in the world or doesn't it?

Apart from being one of the five permanent members of the UN Security

Council, the UK is also a key player in NATO, the G8, the OECD, the WTO, the IMF, the European Union, the OSCE, UNESCO, the Council of Europe and, of course, the British Commonwealth. The UK has the fifth largest economy in terms of GDP and London is often considered to be the financial capital of the world.[221] The UK ranks fifth in terms of its military firepower as well as in terms of its military spending, and would probably remain very near the top of those two tables even if Trident were not included.[222]

When it comes to the 'special relationship' with the US, this is more of a two-way street than most people imagine. We cannot know what might have happened if Prime Minister Tony Blair had refused to go along with President Bush's Iraq War plans, or indeed what would have happened if Tony Blair had not only refused but actively sought to talk Bush and his administration out of the whole idea. What we do know is that Bush was reluctant to take the USA into the Iraq War without the active support of at least one key ally.

When, in 2013, the Westminster parliament voted against air strikes to bring down President Assad in Syria, the US also cancelled its own plans for air strikes in Syria at that time.[223] This was a hugely significant indication of the influence which the UK *can* have on US foreign policy.

During WWII, the influence which Churchill had on the thinking of President Roosevelt was quite evident when it came to joint war planning as well as in meetings of the 'Big Three' (including Stalin) which took place throughout the war. Although the Suez Crisis and other incidents may have soured relations with the Americans from time to time, Margaret Thatcher was highly regarded by the Reagan administration in the 1980s and Tony Blair arguably had influence on the Bush administration during the 2000s.

It was Margaret Thatcher who pushed President Reagan to put intermediate nuclear forces in Europe. It was Thatcher who made the US bombing of Libya in 1986 possible when no other country would let the US use their airspace. And it was Thatcher who introduced Mikhail Gorbachev to Reagan as 'the man we can do business with'.

British influence inside the 'N5' club of nuclear weapons states

Despite differences of opinion on many other matters, the interests of the five nuclear weapons states coincide perfectly when it comes to nuclear weapons. It seems to be in their collective self-interest to manage the expectations of other countries so as to keep the hope of nuclear disarmament alive while at the same time dampen any sense that this will happen any time soon. The 'N5' meet regularly to review the commitments they have made to successive

NPT review meetings, and these meetings are always described as 'cordial', despite all the hard talk about Ukraine and the imposition of sanctions against Russia by US, UK and France.

The N5 regularly vote together at the UN when it comes to voting *against* nuclear disarmament proposals. They often issue joint statements in support of their position as the official nuclear weapons states, as we have seen in Chapter 17. The key stumbling block preventing further progress in multilateral nuclear disarmament is the belief, or the claim, that the security conditions 'are not right' for disarmament at the moment. Another is the claim that 'only a step by step approach' can ensure there is sufficient trust among the NWS for disarmament to take place.

The most pernicious of reasons for the lack of progress is that further disarmament will 'destabilise' international relations and be bad for world. In other words, the NWS want to carry on maintaining their monopoly of nuclear weapons and have no real intention of giving them up. The UK's influence on the other N5 NWS is clear when we look at the language used to justify this continuing lack of progress.

What are the possible implications of cancelling Trident?

So what would happen internationally if the UK decided to cancel Trident renewal and renounce its possession of nuclear weapons? We cannot know the future, of course, but we can postulate what might be some of the reactions from the other N5 NWS, from the other non-N5 NWS (especially India, Pakistan and Israel), from the non-nuclear states who nonetheless come under the nuclear 'umbrella' of NATO and from the other non-nuclear weapon states.

The N5, as the world's premier nuclear 'club', would be devastated to have one of their number break ranks and renounce their nuclear weapons. Officially they would undoubtedly say that they 'fully accept the sovereign will of the British people' and might even try to downplay its implications, saying that Britain, 'of course, has a right to do this in order to save money at a time of austerity', and that this 'in no way reduces the resolve of the other four NWS to continue their efforts to maintain international peace and security through nuclear deterrence' and so on.

Privately, the other NWS would almost certainly be worried what impact this might have on their own public opinions and elected assemblies. After all, if Britain has decided it no longer 'needs' nuclear weapons, why should France 'need' them? Public opinion in the US would be particularly affected by a British decision like this, for all the reasons mentioned above. No doubt some in Congress would call for the US to increase its nuclear weapons arsenal to make up the difference for the loss of UK nuclear weapons and some would no doubt be calling for sanctions against the UK for 'abandoning' its commitments to the US and to NATO, leaving NATO 'exposed', shifting even more of the nuclear 'burden' on to US taxpayers...

There might even be calls in the US Congress for the US to pull out of Europe and leave them to their 'fate' if they are not willing to pull their weight in NATO. We have heard all of this before during crucial periods of the Cold War and even as recently as last year when President Obama castigated Europeans for not spending enough on defence. This kind of talk could also, however, lead to calls for a further *reduction* in the US arsenal and a cutting of the huge expenditure currently being used to upgrade every aspect of the US nuclear arsenal. If the UK is pulling out of the nuclear business, why should the US continue carrying such a heavy burden for the NATO nuclear 'umbrella'?

Once one country decides to give up its nuclear weapons and people notice that it is not suddenly invaded by the Russians as a result, all kinds of questions might start to surface as to why other NWS need to hold on to theirs. The spell would be broken. This could lead to renewed calls for the US and the Russians to go back to the negotiating table and make some progress in further reducing their arsenals. China in particular, which has a much smaller nuclear arsenal than the US or Russia, might be tempted to join Britain in renouncing its nuclear weapons. There is no guarantee that this would happen, of course, but China has consistently been the one member of the N5 club with the least vested interest in the status quo and thus most likely to 'break out' of the club if the UK does not do so first.

India and Pakistan, as former British colonies and members of the British Commonwealth, both have hugely important ties with the UK, not least because there are nearly 2.5 million people of Indian or Pakistani origin living in the UK. The UK has had very little leverage on the governments of India and Pakistan when it comes to nuclear weapons precisely because the UK has always insisted on its own right to have them. On what grounds could the UK tell India or Pakistan that they should not have them as well?

Renouncing Trident in and of itself might not have that big an impact on countries like India and Pakistan, but if it were coupled with a newly energised zeal for promoting a nuclear-free world and encouraging other countries to also disarm, it could have a much larger effect.

One of the stumbling blocks to a more comprehensive peace in the Middle East has been that Israel maintains nuclear weapons and continues to block any progress towards a nuclear-weapons-free zone for the Middle East. The UK has long worked for this, but again, has had little sway with

Israel so long as it has insisted that nuclear weapons are 'essential' for its own national security.

We looked at the NATO question in more detail in Chapter 9, but here it is worth noting that NATO is already hugely divided internally on the issue of nuclear weapons. Were Britain to renounce nuclear weapons, this would be likely to bring the issue out into the open and almost certainly encourage further questioning of NATO's reliance on nuclear weapons. Public opinion in countries like Belgium, Germany and the Netherlands is already very divided on nuclear weapons. A cancellation of Trident by the UK could easily push the governments of those three countries to review their continued deployment of the B-61 nuclear bombs as part of their NATO nuclear-sharing arrangements.

By far the biggest impact of any decision by the UK to end its dependency on nuclear weapons would be felt in the 150 or more non-nuclear, non-NATO countries which have been demanding for years that the NWS disarm. It is hard to imagine the scale of the shock, disbelief and then utter jubilation that might follow such a decision. It could be as significant as South Africa giving up apartheid or the Berlin Wall coming down in terms of global impact.

Even if the impact of UK disarmament on the US and other NWS was minimal and muted, the impact on the rest of the world would be such that the US and other NWS could hardly be unaffected by it. There is already a large global movement calling for the total elimination of nuclear weapons. This boost to their campaign would send shock-waves through the capitals of the NWS and enormously boost the indigenous anti-nuclear movements in countries like the US.

Who but the UK can take the lead?

Sooner or later, one of the nuclear weapons states has to be the first to go non-nuclear. It could be the UK, it could be China – it could even be the US. The rationale for maintaining nuclear weapons grows weaker and weaker every day, while the threat they pose and the risk that one will go off by accident or by design grows stronger. With 121 countries committed to 'filling the legal gap', 139 calling for a treaty to ban them and 151 countries already inside nuclear-free zones, governments and civil society around the world are working very closely together to make a nuclear-free world a reality.

Summary

What might be the impact internationally, if the UK gave up Trident? Would it be 'dangerous and destabilising' or would it have no effect at all? While it is impossible to know for certain, it is likely that the impact would be significant and mostly positive.

The US and France might well react negatively and even lash out with some kind of punitive response were the UK to exit the nuclear club. This is because a UK exit would immediately put them under new and powerful pressure to do likewise. It would undermine their existing rationale for needing nuclear weapons themselves.

Other NATO countries would almost certainly welcome a UK exit and it could well create a new momentum for a radical renewal of NATO's nuclear posture. It would likely lead to renewed calls in Belgium, Netherlands and Germany for an end to deployment of US nuclear weapons in those countries. Some would no doubt interpret this as 'de-stabilising' to the NATO alliance. For others it would be a welcome step forward.

In the rest of the world, a UK decision to renounce nuclear weapons would almost certainly be received with nothing short of jubilation. While it may matter more to UK politicians what the US government thinks than what assorted third world governments think, there can be little doubt that the UK's stature among the vast majority of the world's countries would soar.

For more than 50 years, the 'big five' nuclear weapons states have maintained an iron grip on their nuclear status and refused to let go of it. For the UK, or any of the other NWS, to take the first step towards total elimination of its nuclear weapons would be electrifying and create a whole new international environment for further steps toward nuclear disarmament.

PART SIX

The Bomb is Here to Stay

CHAPTER 20

'But You Can't Uninvent the Bomb'

SINCE WE CANNOT 'uninvent' nuclear weapons – put the genie back in the bottle, so to speak – they are with us forever. The best we can hope for is to manage them safely and responsibly and hope they are never used. This is the final argument of those who grow impatient with the whole issue of disarmament and creating a nuclear-free world. 'It's simply not possible,' they retort.

It is undeniably true that nuclear weapons cannot be 'uninvented'. The knowledge of how to make them is not only out there, it is in the public domain and freely available on the internet. Even if all nuclear weapons were dismantled and the world was declared nuclear-free, what's to stop any country at any time from building new ones?

Here is where we must get practical as well as philosophical. Yes, it will always remain possible for someone to build a nuclear weapon no matter what steps are taken to achieve global nuclear disarmament. But, first of all, is that an argument for the UK to continue indefinitely holding on to its own nuclear weapons? As we have seen in Chapter 3, having nuclear weapons may or may not 'deter' someone else from attacking the UK with nuclear weapons, but if they are determined to do so, having nuclear weapons cannot stop them. In fact, however improbable it is that nuclear weapons have deterred other countries from attacking the UK up to this point, the reality is that if the world abolished nuclear weapons and some regime somewhere was determined to defy the international community and build them anyway, how likely is it that such a regime would be deterred from using them?

The UK's possession of nuclear weapons does not prevent another country from obtaining their own nuclear weapons, nor is it likely to deter them from using them against the UK if that is what they intend. Either way, the fact that you can't uninvent nuclear weapons or prevent other countries from obtaining them is not an argument for the UK to hold on to its own nuclear weapons. Surely it is in fact *less* likely that a rogue regime would want to have their own nuclear weapons *or* want to target them at the UK if the UK itself did not have any?

The case of poison gas

You cannot uninvent poison gas, or other chemical or biological weapons, either. It is far easier for any country to make their own chemical weapons than it is for them to make their own nuclear weapons, as we shall see below. Yet poison gas was not used in WWII, even though both sides had vast stockpiles of it. All chemical weapons have now been banned by international treaty and although they were allegedly being used in Syria, those weapons have now been removed under the terms of the Chemical Weapons Convention. The UK once maintained stockpiles of chemical weapons and continued to develop new ones right up to the time of the Convention, but has now destroyed the stockpile and ceased to develop chemical weapons (as far as we know).

The truth is that even if something has been invented and cannot be uninvented, that does not mean we have to live with it. Even in the nuclear weapons field, many different types of weapon and delivery system have been tried and even deployed in the field before being withdrawn as unworkable, too dangerous, outmoded or just plain crazy. These have included deployment of nuclear warheads to be fired from the back of a jeep, nuclear 'demolitions' bombs strapped onto the back of a soldier to be hand-placed in the battlefield and nuclear depth-bombs dropped from ships and helicopters. The biggest H-bombs of the Cold War era have all been dismantled by now for the same reasons.

Ward Wilson, in his book *Five Myths about Nuclear Weapons*, describes all sorts of weapons systems and other technologies which have become obsolete and long-since abandoned.[224] Why should nuclear weapons not share the same fate as these?

Most countries do not have nuclear weapons

Out of 193 member states of the United Nations at present, only nine are known to have nuclear weapons. That means 184 countries do not. Twenty-nine of those countries come under the NATO or other nuclear 'umbrella' relationships with the US, but still they do not have nuclear weapons of their own, as the UK insists it must. Many of those 29 are among the 59 who, according to the IAEA have the *capacity* to build nuclear weapons at the present time. Twenty-nine countries have started nuclear weapons programmes and then abandoned them. South Africa built several nuclear weapons before dismantling them and abandoning their nuclear weapons programme. Thirty-one countries have civil nuclear power stations from which they could, if they wished, obtain weapons-grade plutonium. Another 46 countries have uranium deposits from which they could, theoretically, obtain weapons-grade uranium.

So what are the reasons that so few countries in fact have chosen to build and possess nuclear weapons? One reason is the expense. As we have seen, it costs roughly 5% of the UK's defence budget to maintain Trident. That is with the UK already having the fifth highest defence budget in the world, and getting a bargain rate from the US for the missiles and many of the components of the warheads themselves. France, without those extra sweeteners from the US, spends nearly 25% of its defence budget on nuclear weapons. The US spends nearly 10% of its massive $500 billion defence budget on nuclear weapons and altogether plans to spend up to $1 trillion on nuclear weapons development and modernisation over the next 30 years.

These figures do not take into account the years of research and development that have gone into nuclear weapons technology up to now and the enormous costs involved with that. Not many countries have that kind of money to spend on nuclear weapons, or if they did, might choose to spend it on other priorities. Some historians have argued that it was the cost of keeping up with the US in the nuclear arms race that 'broke' the Soviet bank account and caused the collapse of the Soviet Union.[225]

There are many other reasons why the vast majority of countries have chosen not to develop their own nuclear weapons capacity, including all the reasons covered in other chapters of this book – legal, moral, practical, utilitarian and security reasons. Most of all, there is a large and growing consensus throughout the world that nuclear weapons make the world less safe and not more so. Why would anyone choose to develop a weapon that is going to make them less safe?

Tony Blair, in his memoirs, said that if Britain didn't already have nuclear weapons, we wouldn't choose now to acquire them. But then he went on to say that since we *do* have them, we don't want to now get rid of them.226 For all the reasons we have been looking at in this book, most countries by now realise that the tide has turned on nuclear weapons. They are a weapon of the past, not of the future. But if progress on disarmament is not achieved, will countries such as South Korea, Japan, Egypt and others remain so convinced?

Verifying disarmament

Fortunately for those who want to see a global ban on nuclear weapons, the process for ensuring that countries comply with such a ban is far more straightforward than for, say, chemical weapons or landmines. Because nuclear explosions are so massive, they are very hard to hide. While it is conceivable to produce nuclear weapons without ever testing one, and Israel may have managed to do that, although they probably tested their first weapon jointly with South Africa, most countries that would want to produce a nuclear weapon would want to test it out, not only to see if it works but also to show to the world that they have one.

There is no place left on earth, under the earth or even under the sea, where a nuclear explosion would not be detected by infrared satellite imaging and/or by seismic equipment used for detected earthquakes. So it is literally impossible for a country to test a nuclear weapon without it being known. This is not something that can be said for any other type of weapon system.

To produce a working nuclear weapon also requires a delivery system of some kind – airplane, missile, mobile bomb launcher, whatever. While there may be some rather crude delivery systems available for detonating a nuclear device *in situ* wherever that may be, in most cases delivering a nuclear weapon requires very sophisticated missile technology, which as we have seen, the UK itself does not even have. Heavy bomber aircraft for delivering nuclear weapons also require a level of sophistication which most countries do not have. Once again, testing of medium or long-range missiles or aircraft is very hard to do in the modern world without detection.

By far the biggest challenge of building a nuclear weapon is not the design, which can be obtained from the internet, but obtaining the raw materials for making the bomb: either highly-enriched uranium or plutonium. The enrichment of uranium is a vastly expensive and complicated process which requires sophisticated and high precision equipment.

Plutonium can be created (it does not exist naturally) in certain designs of nuclear power station, but since civil nuclear power stations can be monitored by the IAEA it is difficult to produce plutonium undetected without withdrawing from the IAEA and sounding a warning bell to the international community as was the case with Iran.

The recent deal reached between Iran and a group of countries trying to prevent it from building a nuclear weapon is a good example of how difficult it is for any country to produce nuclear weapons without being noticed. Of course any country can choose to go ahead anyway, but there may be global consequences for doing so.

The UK government is rightly proud of the work they have been doing with Norway to further the verification procedures needed to ensure that no country can develop nuclear weapons unnoticed. This same technology can be used to ensure that all countries disarm their existing nuclear weapons.

In the 1980s, following the INF Treaty which abolished all intermediate-range nuclear weapons in Europe, Russian inspectors were invited onto to US bases to verify withdrawal and dismantling of nuclear weapons systems and US inspectors were invited onto Soviet bases to verify the same thing on the other side. In the case of the START Treaty which required destruction of a certain number of existing long-range nuclear bombers on both sides, the US and Russia both chopped up planes into pieces and left them spread out on the ground until satellite reconnaissance from the other side could verify that they had been destroyed.

Summary

While it is not possible to 'uninvent' anything, it is certainly possible to get rid of things we no longer want or need, including obsolete weapons systems like Trident. All that is needed is the political will and ways can be found to verify disarmament moves and to monitor compliance.

The reality is that most countries do not have nuclear weapons. Some have the capability to produce nuclear weapons and have chosen not to. Others have developed them or begun developing them and then decided to abandon their nuclear programmes.

Because nuclear weapons are so massive in their destructive power and require such sophisticated and expensive facilities to manufacture, their elimination is much easier than any other weapon to monitor and verify.

There will always be the possibility that an advanced industrialised country could at some point in the future manufacture nuclear weapons if they chose to. Current monitoring and verification technologies mean that it will be much more difficult for them to do so without the rest of the world finding out about it. In a world in which nuclear weapons are not acceptable under any circumstances the norm will be established in which it is less likely that any country will choose to manufacture them once they have been eliminated.

CHAPTER 21

Would Opposition to Trident Make Labour 'Unelectable'?

THE ELECTION OF Jeremy Corbyn as leader of the Labour Party and his commitment to undertake a review of Labour Party policy on Trident has drawn many commentators both inside and outside of the Labour Party to suggest that if Labour went anti-Trident, they would be 'unelectable'. Comparisons are usually made to the 1983 general election, when Labour had an anti-nuclear weapons policy and suffered its largest electoral defeat in post-war history. But did Labour lose the 1983 election because of its anti-nuclear position and even if it did, does that mean it could not win an election in 2020 with such a position?

Britain's possession of nuclear weapons has long been a bone of contention within the Labour Party. Initially, the post-war Labour Prime Minister, Clement Atlee, joined with US President Truman and the Canadian Prime Minister MacKenzie King in calling for the complete elimination of nuclear weapons and the placing of all nuclear information and technology in the hands of the United Nations.[227] Privately, Atlee not long afterwards gave the go-ahead for the UK to unilaterally build its own nuclear bomb.[228]

This development of a UK nuclear weapon was kept secret from parliament and from the British people until Winston Churchill and the Conservatives returned to power in October 1951. By this time more than £100 million had been spent secretly developing a British atom bomb and the UK's first nuclear test was about to take place.[229] The enormous costs involved in developing the bomb, at a time of national austerity and deeply unpopular spending cuts to the newly-created National Health Service, led to heated disputes at the 1952 Labour Party conference and a strengthening of support for the left-wing 'Bevanite' faction led by the former Health Minister and anti-nuclear campaigner Aneurin Bevan.

By 1960, growing public concerns about atmospheric nuclear testing, the development of larger and larger hydrogen bombs and the increasing tensions of the Cold War led to a decisive vote at Labour Party conference for the party to get rid of the UK's nuclear weapons and to lead the way to global nuclear disarmament. The Labour Party won the 1964 general election with a clear mandate to disarm, but almost immediately the new Prime Minister, Harold Wilson, began discussing the idea of a 'multilateral nuclear force' consisting of the UK, France and Germany as a solution to the UK abandoning its own independent nuclear force.

By 1964, the UK was already committed to building four Polaris submarines and buying Polaris missiles from the US. Harold Wilson continued on with this programme, despite the Labour Party's policy on disarmament and the manifesto commitment made at the general election.

During the 1970s, successive Labour governments would once again embark on a secret programme to upgrade the Polaris missiles with 'Chevaline' at a cost of over £1 billion, without informing parliament or the British public.[230] When the Labour Party was swept out of power by Margaret Thatcher in 1979, this once again led to recriminations and divisions at the subsequent Labour Party conference in 1980.

As it did two decades earlier, the 1980 Labour conference voted a second time in favour of a clear and unequivocal commitment to nuclear disarmament. This was one, but by no means the only, factor which led to an irrevocable split within the Labour Party and the creation of a new political party, the Social Democratic Party (SDP), in 1982.[231]

The 1983 General Election

There is one very clear reason why Labour lost the 1983 general election with its worst ever post-war electoral result. Four prominent former government ministers and leading figures in the Labour Party defected to form a separate political party (the SDP), taking with them 29 Labour MPs, the infrastructure and support of those MPs' constituency labour parties and millions of Labour voters whose allegiance was to their local MP and their local Constituency Labour Party.

The total number of people who voted Conservative actually *fell* by about 685,000 from 1979 to 1983 while to total number of people voting against the Conservatives (ie for Labour plus Liberals or Liberal-SDP alliance) *increased* by about 400,000. In terms of the total electorate registered and eligible to vote, almost as many people did not vote at all (27.3% of all eligible voters) as voted Conservative (30.9% of all eligible voters) in 1983.

The overall figures, however, do not give the full picture of what went on in the 1983 election. In any election where a first-past-the-post electoral system is combined with more than two main parties on the ballot, what tends to happen is that a smaller party takes votes away from one of the two larger parties, leaving the other larger party to win the seat, even if it is with fewer votes than they have received on previous occasions when they lost.

In 1983 what happened, in constituency after constituency, is that the SDP took votes away from the Labour candidate, leaving the Conservative candidate to win the seat, even though the Conservative candidate may have received fewer votes than they had received at the 1979 election. Remember, 685,000 *fewer* people voted Conservative in 1983 than in 1979, and yet they gained an additional 38 seats in what was considered to be a 'landslide' victory.

For the purposes of the election the SDP, which had broken away from the Labour Party, joined forces with the Liberal Party to form the SDP-Liberal Alliance. The SDP was more pro-nuclear than the Liberals, who were historically opposed to nuclear weapons. There was a certain amount of division among the ranks of the Liberal Party when the joint Alliance policy on disarmament and defence was agreed as a basis for the 1983 election manifesto. The manifesto sought to distance the Alliance from Labour's 'unilateral' position and was very pro-NATO and NATO's existing nuclear weapons policy. On the issue of deployment of US cruise missiles in Britain, the manifesto was equivocal, leaving it up to an Alliance government to decide 'whether or not to oppose the deployment'.[232]

On the issue of replacing Polaris with Trident, however, the Alliance manifesto was crystal clear: 'Trident should be cancelled to avoid a new and provocative contribution to the nuclear arms race and demonstrate our commitment to arms control'.[233] This was the position on which they fought the 1983 election and in some respects it was more 'unilateralist' than the Labour position.

Despite the 1980 conference commitment to nuclear disarmament and all the controversy surrounding Michael Foot and the Labour Party position on the issue, the Labour Party's 1983 election manifesto was drafted to be as acceptable as possible to the right-wing of the party and it was hoped, to the electorate. The Labour manifesto thus committed the party to 'the inclusion of Polaris in negotiations over disarmament'[234] and included other references to multilateralism as well as a commitment to cancel Cruise and not building Trident.

Thus, whether people voted Labour or SDP, they were voting against Trident. People who voted for parties with an anti-Trident position in 1983 outnumbered people who voted for parties with a pro-Trident position by at least three million.

The 2015 General Election

There are some interesting parallels between the 1983 and the 2015 general elections. Once again, a large number of people did not vote at all. In this case, 33.9% of all registered voters did not vote, while only 23.8% of registered voters voted Conservative, with 19.9% voting Labour and 22.4% voting for other parties.

As in 1983, the Conservatives won many more seats than their total vote would indicate. Overall, they increased their share of the vote by just 0.8% over the previous election, from 36.1% in 2010 to 36.9% in 2015. Labour, on the other hand, increased its share of the vote by 1.4% over the previous election, from 29.0% in 2010 to 30.4% in 2015.

As in 1983, what happened in 2015 in a large number of constituencies was that people voted for other parties rather than for Labour (or the LibDems), leaving the Conservatives with more overall votes and winning the seat. In this case, however, it was not a break-away party like the SDP but the SNP, Greens and other smaller left-wing parties who took votes away from Labour and left the Conservatives with the most number of votes. The Conservatives ended up with a working majority of just 12 seats in parliament. If just six of these had been won by the Labour Party instead, we would not now have a majority Conservative government.[235] The following table shows ten seats where the Conservative won by very slim margins that were smaller than the total Green vote in that constituency. If Labour had been able to attract the Green vote, or had had an electoral pact with the Greens, they could probably have won those seats.

Table 1: Labour seats lost to the Green or Plaid Cymru vote

Constituency	*Conservative majority*	*Green/Plaid Cymru vote*
Bedford	1,097	1,412 (G)
Brighton Kemptown	690	3,187 (G)
Bury North	378	1,141 (G)
Croydon Central	165	1,454 (G)
Derby North	41	1,618 (G)
Gower	27	1,161 (G)
Morley and Outwood	422	1,264 (G)
Plymouth Sutton	523	3,401 (G)
Telford	730	930 (G)
Weaver Vale	806	1,183 (G)

Cardiff North	2,137	2,301 (PC)
Vale of Clwyd	237	2,486 (PC)

As was the case in Scotland, Labour mainly lost votes to parties that were *more* left-wing and not *less* left-wing than itself at the 2015 election. The SNP, Greens, Plaid Cymru and other smaller parties which took votes away from Labour were all anti-Trident, anti-austerity, anti-war parties that attracted Labour voters fed up with a Labour party that was not providing more of an alternative to the Conservative-LibDem coalition government.

Labour lost 40 seats to the SNP in Scotland. Since 55.3% of Scots had voted 'no' on the independence referendum just six months prior to the 2015 general election, it does not make sense to conclude that they voted SNP in the general election in order to further the cause of Scottish independence per se (see also Chapter 16). It is much more likely that large numbers of Scottish voters were incensed that the Labour Party so closely aligned itself with the coalition government not only on the referendum issue, but also on many other issues of particular concern to Scots, including the renewal of Trident and the austerity cuts.

The Liberal Democrats, meanwhile, lost a total of 49 seats. The nine lost in Scotland to the SNP and the 12 lost to Labour in England can easily be explained by the fact that the Liberal Democrats, even more than Labour, were associated with the Conservative agenda on austerity, Trident and many other issues which LibDems had previously fought against. The remaining 26 seats went to the Conservatives for the same reason so many Labour seats went to the Conservatives in 1983. Large numbers of LibDem voters, dissatisfied with their party's alignment with the Conservatives, voted in 2015 for the Labour party, Greens or other small parties. But with Labour having no chance of winning many of the seats that are traditionally two-way races between LibDems and Conservatives, the Conservatives once again ended up with the most number of votes and taking the seat.

Table 2: LibDem seats lost to the Green vote

Constituency	*Conservative majority*	*Green vote*
Bath	3,833	5,634
Eastbourne	733	1,351
Lewes	1,083	2,784
St Ives	2,469	3,051
Twickenham	2,017	2,463

Table 3: LibDem seats lost to the Labour vote

Constituency	*Conservative majority*	*Labour vote*
Berwick on Tweed	4,914	6,042
Brecon and Radnor	5,102	5,904
Cheadle	6,453	8,673
Colchester	5,575	7,852
Hazel Grove	6,552	7,584
Kingston and Surbiton	2,834	8,574
Portsmouth South	5,241	8,184
Sutton and Cheam	3,921	5,546
Thornbury & Yate	1,495	3,775
Torbay	3,286	4,166

The final factor of crucial importance to understanding the 2015 election, as well as many other elections, is how voter turn-out affects the results at constituency level. The total turn-out in the 2015 election was 66.1%, one percentage point higher than in 2010. But this figure disguises quite large variations from constituency to constituency. In 181 constituencies, the turnout was above 70% and as high as 81% (in Renfrewshire East), while in 100 other constituencies, the turnout was below 60% and as low as 46% (in Manchester Central).

The size of the electorate also varies from constituency to constituency, but assuming an average size of around 70,000 electors in a constituency, the difference between a 60% turnout and a 70% turnout is about 7,000 votes. Since nearly all the constituencies which changed hands, outside of Scotland, did so with majorities of considerably less than 7,000, we must assume that the people who chose not to vote – or what we might call the Russell Brand factor – are at least as important to the outcome in many constituencies as those who did actually cast a vote.

Apart from Scotland, virtually all the seats with a turnout of more than 70% were traditionally Conservative seats. Apart from Northern Ireland, virtually all the constituencies with turnout below 60% were ones where traditionally Labour has been the strongest party. In other words, it appears that in the 2015 election, Conservatives were more successful in getting their traditional 'core' voters to the ballot box than Labour was at getting its traditional 'core' voters to the ballot box. When as many as 7,000 votes are at stake in a single constituency and where one party may win with a majority much smaller than 7,000 votes, getting out the vote really matters.

If more Labour voters had bothered to vote in Blackpool North, for instance, where turnout was only 63%, they almost certainly could have taken that seat from the Conservatives, since the Conservative majority was 3,340. A turnout of 73% instead of 63% would have brought out at least double that number of additional voters.

This pattern is repeated in at least 55 marginal seats across England and Wales, where the Conservative majority is very small relative to the lower than average turnout. Not all those non-voters would have necessarily voted Labour, of course, but the overall election result might have looked quite different if that many seats had changed hands from Conservative to Labour, in addition to the seats which could have stayed Labour or LibDem as described above.[236]

Could Labour win under Jeremy Corbyn?

It is undeniably the case that Tony Blair won three successive elections on a more right-wing, pro-nuclear agenda. What is unknowable is whether, after nearly 20 years of Thatcherism, the UK would have elected a Labour government in 1997 no matter how right-wing or left-wing it had been. What is clear from analysing the results of the 2015 election is that a more left-wing Labour party probably would have had a better chance of winning that election than the party which went into the election standing for

> A strong economic foundation; Higher living standards for working families; An NHS with the time to care; Controls on immigration; A country where the next generation can do better than the last; Homes to buy and action on rent.[237]

A week is a long time in politics and the next general election, due in 2020, is at the time of writing a very long way off. Many things can happen between now and then and it is impossible to predict what the political landscape might look like then. Nevertheless, it is fair to say that a Labour Party which is able to get its core voters out to vote on polling day and which stands for a clear alternative to the Conservatives has just as much chance of winning an election as one which tries to reach out to the elusive 'middle ground' and gain votes from those who would have previously voted Conservative.

Opinion polls are notoriously difficult to assess on an issue like Trident, because the results depend very much on who is asking the question, how exactly the question is framed, and within what context the question and the polling itself takes place. Nevertheless, there is every reason to believe that public opinion, when it is adequately informed about the issues involved, will tend to come down in favour of abolishing all nuclear weapons, including Britain's.

If there is a proper debate about Trident in the country at large, and if there is then a proper debate about Trident within Constituency Labour Parties and the trade union movement, there can be few who doubt that the result will be a Labour policy opposing the renewal of Trident. If that policy were then to be properly debated within the Parliamentary Labour Party and within parliament itself, it could well lead, if not now then certainly in the near future, to a decision to cancel Trident.

Summary

The Labour Party suffered its worst electoral defeat at the 1983 General Election, and it had a strongly anti-nuclear policy at that time. It also had a strongly worded anti-nuclear manifesto for the 1964 election, and it won that one.

Labour abandoned its anti-nuclear position at other general elections and still lost (in 1979, 1988 and 1992), so it is difficult to argue that the party's position on nuclear weapons has at any point been decisive in winning or losing elections.

The Labour Party lost the 1983 election because a large selection of the party defected to a new political party – the SDP – and took their constituencies with them. While the SDP was less committal on some nuclear issues, like the introduction of US Cruise Missiles to Britain, the SDP manifesto made clear they were opposed to replacement of Polaris with Trident and were committed to eliminating Polaris through disarmament negotiations.

In 2015, the Labour Party lost a large number of seats to the anti-Trident SNP vote in Scotland. In England, it was mostly the collapse of the Lib Dem vote which gave the conservatives a clear parliamentary majority. But in England and Wales as well as in Scotland, it was the anti-Trident and anti-austerity votes that went to the Green Party, Plaid Cymru and other smaller parties to the left which cost Labour the election.

On the basis of the 2015 election alone, it is likely that a more left – wing and anti-Trident Labour Party could have done better at the polls than the party as it stood at that time actually did. No one can predict what the political landscape will look like by 2020, but there is no basis for the belief that an anti-Trident position means the Labour Party cannot win a general election.

CHAPTER 22

Can Nuclear Weapons be Morally Acceptable?

SIR MICHAEL QUINLAN was a key architect of Britain's nuclear deterrence policy and also a devout member of the Roman Catholic Church. He claimed no contradiction between his work and his Christian faith. Quinlan defended nuclear deterrence on moral grounds, insisting that nuclear weapons, nuclear deterrence and indeed nuclear war could be justified according to the 'just war' criteria of the Roman Catholic Church. The Church of England's General Synod, in February, 1983, appeared to agree with Quinlan when they took the position that nuclear weapons were necessary to the defence of the realm:

> It is the duty of Her Majesty's Government and her allies to maintain adequate forces to guard against nuclear blackmail and deter nuclear and non-nuclear aggressors.

Paul Schulte is a Senior Fellow at the UK Defence Academy as well as chair of the Council on Christian Approaches to Disarmament and Defence. He has served in various capacities in the Ministry of Defence and written extensively on defence and security matters. According to Paul,[238] the UK has a 'moral obligation' to have its own nuclear weapons, because we are otherwise unfairly expecting someone else, ie the US, to carry the moral burden of providing that nuclear protection on our behalf.

This argument has been discussed in Chapter 9, but Paul Schulte takes it one step further by claiming that we have a moral duty, not only to share in the protection we may get from nuclear weapons, but to share in the opprobrium and guilt of having them and potentially of using them. If the US is going to carry the can, as it were, of having and potentially using nuclear weapons, it is not right that we in the UK should wash our hands of it and pretend we do not share in the responsibility for that.

Lesser of two evils

During the Cold War period, support for nuclear weapons was based largely on the presumption that these weapons were all that was saving the UK from being overrun by an evil, 'totalitarian' regime as bad, if not worse, than Hitler's Nazism. That belief was supplemented, especially among Christians, with the threat which 'godless communism' posed to Christianity. 'Better dead than red' was the battle cry for those who rejected the moral arguments for doing away with nuclear weapons.

Even for those who fear or despise Putin and claim we are in a new Cold War with Russia now, the same arguments about godless communism no longer apply. What then, are the moral and/or theological arguments in favour of retaining nuclear weapons in an age where the threat of Communism is no longer relevant and where Russia's prosperity depends on trading relationships with the international community? There are, of course, those moral crusaders who have transferred their fear and loathing from communism to Islamist extremism and describe the world today as a battle for the soul of humanity between Christianity and Islam.

That argument is not relevant with respect to Russia, but could perhaps be used in relation to a possible nuclear threat from Iran, Pakistan or some new form of nuclear-armed Islamic extremist threat to the West. However, even during the crusades against Islam in the 11th century, Christians were expected to follow the rules of just war and to be bound by them.

Just War Theory

In order for a war to be 'just', according to St Augustine of Hippo in the fourth century AD, certain conditions must be met, and these fell into two categories: first, the conditions for *going* to war ('jus ad bellum') and second, the conditions for *waging* war ('jus in bello'). Thomas Aquinas further elaborated on these in the 13th century and they have continued to be refined ever since. While the complete list of just war criteria can vary according to who is compiling it, the most common criteria include the following:

Jus ad bellum:

- Just cause – the reason for going to war must itself be just.
- Competent authority – only a properly constituted authority (ie government) can wage war justly.
- Probability of success – there must be a reasonable chance of winning the war.

- Last resort – all other means short of war must have been tried first.
- Proportionality – the benefits of winning the war must outweigh the expected costs of waging it.

Jus in bello:
- Distinction – acts of war must be targeted at all times at combatants and not at non-combatants.
- Proportionality – any harm to civilians must be proportionate to the military advantage to be gained.
- Military necessity – war must be conducted, and targets of attack chosen, solely to achieve victory.
- Fair treatment of prisoners of war – No torture or mistreatment.
- No means *malum in se* – No inherently 'evil' or inhumane weapons to be used.

Sir Michael Quinlan believed that these criteria could be met, even in the case of a nuclear war.[239] However, few theologians today would agree with him. In 1982, a Working Party of the Church of England, under the chair of John Baker, Bishop of Salisbury, produced a detailed and comprehensive examination of Britain's nuclear weapons policy as seen from a moral perspective. This was entitled *The Church and the Bomb: Nuclear weapons and Christian conscience*[240] and it was a significant contribution to the debate at that time. The report called for the UK's renunciation of its 'independent nuclear deterrent', cancellation of (the original) Trident and a phased withdrawal of all nuclear weapons.[241]

> It is in our view proven beyond reasonable doubt that the Just War theory, as this has developed in Western civilisation and within the Christian Church, rules out the use of nuclear weapons…[242]

As we have already seen in Chapter 12, the legal requirements for waging war are based largely on the distinction between combatants and non-combatants, the latter being protected under a whole raft of international conventions and protocols from the indiscriminate and disproportionate effects of warfare.

When it comes to nuclear war, these distinctions become quite difficult to sustain, since even the smallest nuclear weapons are extremely powerful. Even if these are targeted at a purely military target, it is hard to imagine that civilian populations would not be severely affected. This is especially the case because of the uniquely harmful properties of ionising radiation and the fact that radioactive fallout can travel considerable distances before coming down to contaminate people who have nothing to do with the fighting or may even be in a neutral third country which has specifically chosen to stay out of the fight.

The reality is that the vast majority of nuclear weapons in the world, including as far as we know most if not all of the UK's stockpile of nuclear weapons, are *not* minimum yield, 'small' nuclear weapons but in fact weapons many times more powerful than those dropped on Hiroshima and Nagasaki.

To what extent can weapons capable of destroying a medium to large size city be considered 'proportionate' or 'discriminate'?

Retaliation

In terms of the actual use of the UK's nuclear weapons, we described in Chapter 1 the two situations in which they might conceivably be used:

1. In a first strike against a nuclear weapon state, either threatening to invade or in the process of invading the UK or one of its allies.
2. In a second, or retaliatory, strike after the UK has been hit by one or more nuclear weapons.

In the second of these two situations, where the 'deterrent' has failed and the UK has already been hit by nuclear weapons, would it be morally right to retaliate?

We live in a society which uses punishment to change behaviour. We punish children for doing something wrong and we punish criminals for doing something wrong. Surely, we also punish a country for launching weapons of mass destruction against us.

There are, however, legal as well as moral restrictions on the forms of punishment we use. It is no longer legal to inflict corporal punishment on children, nor to inflict capital punishment on convicted criminals. Punishment, like war, is required to be proportionate and discriminating. In particular, 'collective punishment' of a whole community for the sins of one or a few of them, as condoned in the days of the Old Testament, is now considered illegal and immoral, since it does not discriminate between those who are perpetrators and those who are innocent.

It is children, elderly, sick and disabled people who often suffer the most from collective forms of punishment. These are probably the least culpable for whatever the punishment is in response to. Dropping nuclear weapons on another country as an act of retaliation is therefore a disproportionate and indiscriminate form of collective punishment at best. At worst, it is nothing other than an act of revenge – a lashing out in anger against someone (or in this case a very large number of people) to compensate for a loss or tragedy for which those particular people may not even be directly responsible. Can that ever be morally acceptable?

First strike

When it comes to a first strike with nuclear weapons, under what conditions might this be considered morally acceptable? Let us make the assumption that this is genuinely in the interests of self-defence. The UK is being invaded and in order to stop the invading army from gaining a foothold, the UK bombs them with nuclear weapons.

Let us make the further assumption that in this scenario all diplomatic efforts have failed, that every precaution has been made to target the invading army in such a way as to minimise civilian casualties, that the yield is 'small' and will mostly kill troops and destroy their tanks and other vehicles or ships. Are the conditions of just war sufficiently met to allow for a moral justification for the use of nuclear weapons, at least under these very limited circumstances and within the boundaries of just war theory?

To be the first to use a nuclear weapon in a world which has so far avoided any use of nuclear weapons since the first bombs were dropped in 1945 would be a big step. It is hard to imagine that it would be met with anything other than horror and opprobrium from every corner of the world. It is also hard to imagine the scenario above matching any kind of real life situation, since an invading army would by definition be very near, or already on, the territory of the UK or one of its allies. Thus bombing them with nuclear weapons would mean, in effect, dropping nuclear bombs on the UK or one of its allies. The use of a 'small' nuclear weapon which would be able to minimize destruction beyond the military target itself is likely to be ineffectual. Such a scenario would then lead to more such bombs being dropped, moving us all into a full-scale nuclear war scenario. This is very different to any such situation which tries to stay within the limits of just war theory.

Inhumane weapons

In any conceivable scenario in which we might be tempted to claim that it could fit within the criteria for a just war, we must finally look at the last of these criteria, the injunction against use of weapons that are in themselves inherently evil or inhumane. Weapons which 'unnecessarily aggravate the sufferings of disabled men, or render their death inevitable' fall under this category. That was the basis on which the exploding bullet was outlawed in 1868,[243] the dum-dum bullet in 1899[244] and asphyxiating, poisonous and other gases in 1925.[245]

Nuclear weapons, as we have seen, have the unique property of releasing large quantities of highly dangerous radiation, not only into the immediate surroundings but also high up into the atmosphere where it can be carried for thousands of miles. The effects of radiation also vary, but even at relatively low levels can cause sterility, long-terms cancers and leukaemia as well as birth defects in subsequent generations. At higher levels it destroys cells and internal organs, damages blood and bone marrow and causes other debilitating diseases that lead to death over a matter of days, weeks or months.

It is hard to see how a weapon like this can be considered 'humane' even when used only on combatants, since it would inevitably cause unnecessary and prolonged suffering not only to the soldiers themselves but to their progeny as well.

Just war revisited

Just as some lawyers will continue to argue that the use of nuclear weapons can be legal under international law, some Christian theologians will continue to argue that the use of nuclear weapons can be morally justified in terms of just war theory. The reality, however, is that the nature of nuclear weapons makes a mockery of both these arguments.

In a statement to the Vienna Conference on the Humanitarian Impacts of Nuclear Weapons, Pope Francis declared that

> the provisional justification [the church] once gave for possession of nuclear weapons for the sake of 'deterrence' during the Cold War is no longer valid... Now is the time to affirm not only the immorality of the use of nuclear weapons, but the immorality of their possession, thereby clearing the road to nuclear abolition.[246]

Other faiths

Other religions too have spoken out on the morality of nuclear weapons. They all contain injunctions against killing and especially against the indiscriminate killing of women, children or other unarmed non-combatants.

In the Quran, for instance, it is clear that there are 'limits' to fighting and killing, even in the case of jihad: 'Fight in the cause of God those who fight you, but do not transgress limits; for God loveth not transgressors.'[247] These limits, according to Islamic scholars, include protecting the innocent: 'Do not kill women, children, the old, or the infirm; do not cut down fruit-bearing trees; do not destroy any town...'[248] The limits also forbid aggression and suggest that violence is only acceptable when it is in response to violence: 'Fight in the way of God against those who fight against you, but begin not hostilities. Lo! God loveth not aggressors.'[249] and 'if the enemies incline towards peace, do you also incline towards peace.'[250]

In Judaism, war is only permitted in self-defence and only after every effort has been made to make peace. There are many rabbinic and other traditions in Judaism which severely restrict what is allowed to take place in war, including an unusual requirement in the Talmud explicitly prohibiting the waging of war that involves killing more than one-sixth of the population in the process.[251] The protection of non-combatants and prisoners is also of paramount concern:

> The soldier shall make use of his weaponry and power only for the fulfilment of the mission and solely to the extent required; he will maintain his humanity even in combat. The soldier shall not employ his weaponry and power in order to harm non-combatants or prisoners of war, and shall do all he can to avoid harming their lives, body, honour and property.[252]

In Eastern religions,[253] there is a much stronger emphasis on nonviolence and non-killing in general. Interestingly, there are some ancient texts which expressly forbid the use of weapons of mass destruction. For example, in the Ramayana (Hindu scripture) Lakshmana tells Rama that he has a weapon of war that could destroy the entire race of the enemy, including non-combatants. Rama advises Lakshmana that destruction en masse is forbidden by the ancient laws of war, even if the enemy is unrighteous.[254]

In February 2015, 26 faith leaders representing many of the major faith traditions in the UK came together to sign a statement about nuclear weapons, agreeing that nuclear weapons 'violate the principle of dignity and worth of every human being which is common to each of our faith traditions'.

From a humanist, or 'non-theist' perspective, the dignity and worth of every human life is also central to any consideration of morality. A weapon that is so shocking in its ability to kill, maim and genetically damage future generations and the environment cannot meet the test of being morally acceptable.

Ethics of deterrence

If the use of nuclear weapons cannot be justified on moral grounds, what about the concept of nuclear deterrence? We have already seen that nuclear deterrence is nothing other than a threat to use them, and for that threat to be 'credible' the government must be ready and willing to actually use them. Moreover there must be, in effect, a declared intention to use them after deterrence has failed. We have also seen in Chapter 12 that in legal terms, a threat or conspiracy or intention to commit an illegal act such as murder is legally equivalent to having committed it and in many cases leads to an equivalent prison sentence.

Sir Michael Quinlan was himself the first to admit that nuclear deterrence rests solely on the willingness to actually use nuclear weapons. If it cannot be morally justified to use these weapons, it cannot be morally justified to threaten to use them, nor to possess them for possible future use nor to base a defence policy around the threat to use them. 'Security policies based around the threat of the use of nuclear weapons are immoral and ultimately self-defeating…' says the UK Multi-Faith Statement on Nuclear Weapons.[255]

But there is in fact a further moral argument against nuclear deterrence itself as a concept. For the whole concept of nuclear deterrence, as we have seen in Chapter 3, rests on the idea that at the very moment of intense crisis, when the very survival of the state is at stake, political leaders on both sides of a potential nuclear conflagration will be able to rationally weigh up the costs and benefits of different options for nuclear escalation and de-escalation and make the correct calculations that the theory of deterrence tells them they should make.

In a series of letters between Michael Quinlan and the theologian, Walter Stein, Stein makes the charge that this kind of thinking is 'deliberately irresponsible' because it assumes that rational decision-making will take place in a situation where there has been 'catastrophic loss of control', 'unparalleled pressures of time, shock and uncertainty,' resulting in 'critical vulnerabilities of command and control systems'. Stein calls this 'not just a mere occasion of sin, but a consent to the evils built into the strategy that are inescapable consequences of that strategy'.[256]

In other words, as we know in fact from the Cuba Missile Crisis, the concept of nuclear deterrence inevitably puts people in situations where they cannot be expected to make perfectly rational decisions and yet the survival of the human race depends precisely upon them making perfectly rational decisions under those very circumstances. That in itself is not only irrational but irresponsible, as Stein puts it, because we are simply setting ourselves up for a disaster, in this case the ultimate disaster.

Summary

All of world's major religions include in some form or other the basic principle, 'thou shalt not kill'. In Eastern religions, this has tended to be taken more literally than in the West, where philosophers and theologians have tried for centuries to define and codify the exceptions to this rule.

According to the various formulations of 'just war' theory, killing can only ever be justified, even in warfare, if certain conditions are met. Principle among these are the requirements to target only combatants and legitimate military targets, to limit the killing to that which is absolutely necessary for victory and not even to initiate hostilities unless there is a strong likelihood of success and other means short of war have been tried and failed.

Many of the just war criteria are already enshrined in the various conventions and protocols that form the laws of war in a strictly legal sense. But the moral criteria go beyond this, by challenging the very notion of a war which by definition no one can 'win.' Can the potential unleashing of all-out nuclear war, threatening the very survival of life itself ever be morally justified?

Can anyone, with any degree of confidence, claim that the use of a single nuclear weapon will not unleash a chain of events leading to an all-out nuclear war? Even the hypothetical case of a potentially 'legal' use of low-yield nuclear weapon to destroy invading ships while still on the high seas cannot meet this moral standard, since it is first of all unlikely in this day and age that such an attack would be 'successful' in and of itself. And secondly, it is impossible to predict what might follow as a result of such an attack.

Comparatively 'low-yield' nuclear weapons were removed from the European continent and eliminated from the arsenals of both sides was because it was realised that these made all-out nuclear war more likely rather than less likely. Low-yield nuclear weapons lower the threshold for using any nuclear weapons and once nuclear weapons are used, no one can predict where it will stop.

The use of low-yield nuclear weapons risks escalating a small-scale conflict into all-out nuclear war. The use of high yield nuclear weapons risks endangering all life on Earth. An 'airburst' nuclear attack against cities would result in the mass slaughter of innocent civilians whilst a 'groundburst' nuclear attack on purely military targets risks radioactive fallout killing, injuring, and causing genetic damage to people in faraway neutral countries and even in the country that fires the weapon.

Launching a nuclear weapon against a country which does not itself have nuclear weapons would be an act of aggression that should attract global condemnation, while launching nuclear weapons against another country with nuclear weapons could result in nuclear retaliation aimed at the UK.

Launching nuclear weapons in a 'first strike' means being willing to accept both the global condemnation and nuclear retaliation, while launching them in retaliation after being attacked is not only pointless but is also an act of pure revenge for which there can be no moral justification.

In seeking to justify the UK's possession of nuclear weapons, as opposed to the actual use of nuclear weapons, the argument is often made that possession prevents use. Indeed, it was Sir Michael Quinlan's belief that by preventing war, nuclear weapons were actually a moral 'good'. But as he himself pointed out, 'weapons deter by the possibility of their use, and by no other route'.[257]

Possession of nuclear weapons, in and of itself, is not a moral issue if there is no possibility to ever use them. However, the concept of nuclear deterrence depends not only on the 'possibility' of their use but on the *willingness* to use them, and indeed on the *intention* to use them if and when the circumstances are deemed appropriate. Otherwise it would be utterly pointless to have them and 'deterrence' would be meaningless.

Possessing nuclear weapons with the intention to use them, even if only in the extreme circumstance where the very survival of the state is at stake is a moral issue of immense proportions. It means that the UK as a state stands ready to destroy not only an 'enemy' population but also its *own* population in the belief that by doing so it would somehow 'protect' itself as a state. What moral code, anywhere, gives a state that kind of absolute supremacy over its own citizens?

Morality, surely, is not about laws or commandments or even moral codes. It is about the dignity and respect which we afford to each other as human beings. Nuclear weapons and all the language that goes with them are about as far removed from the universe of human morality as it is possible to be.

CHAPTER 23

Does Trident Fit the World of Today?

Those opposing Trident are sometimes labelled 'woolly minded idealists' living in 'Cloud-Cuckoo-Land', with no idea of what the real world is actually like. The real world is assumed to be one in which nuclear weapons play a necessary and important role in the affairs of state, and that it is therefore unrealistic to imagine a situation in which nuclear weapons would no longer be present. Much of this thinking goes back, not just to the Cold War, but the dark days of 1940, when Britain stood alone against Hitler.

> A British Prime Minister would never give up Britain's place as a nuclear weapon state as long as the memory of 1940, standing alone and the Battle of Britain, remained fresh...
> (Sir Frank Cooper, former permanent secretary of the MOD)[258]

The world of 1940 and the world of today

In 1940, Britain was an empire with over 50 colonial 'possessions' all over the world, including the whole of the Indian sub-continent, huge swathes of Africa and the Middle East and a large part of the Caribbean. It was still a period of history when countries went around claiming 'colonies', invading and occupying each other and fighting wars to increase their territorial possessions or to gain access to land and raw materials.

In 1940 there was no NATO, no OSCE, no EU and no UN. There was no World Court, no Geneva Convention, no Universal Declaration of Human Rights, no Amnesty International, no Oxfam, no Christian Aid. There was no body of knowledge known as peace research or peace studies, little understanding of mediation or conflict resolution or of the processes of interpersonal communication and negotiation.

Very few people in Britain had their own telephone in 1940. Most people had not ever been on an aeroplane. Immigration from former colonies in

Asia, Africa and the Caribbean had not yet begun, so even in London and Birmingham the population was overwhelming white and Christian.

That world is part of history. We now live in a shrinking world that is increasingly interconnected, with instantaneous communications, internet, mobile phones and television in every home. People see the world on their handheld phones and TV screens. They travel the world with ease.

The community of nations

The world of the 21st century is not just one in which we are all more closely connected with each other at a personal level. The problems facing the UK such as climate change, terrorism and even housing or the rise of income inequalities, are not problems that can be solved by the UK alone. The global economy links the UK intimately to what is happening economically in other countries, just as the climate of the UK is directly affected by the carbon produced by other countries (and vice versa).

When it comes to international disputes and crises, it is no longer the case that one country is left on its own to deal with them. The United Nations system, comprising not only the General Assembly and the Security Council, but another 33 specialised agencies, programmes and international bodies, monitors and supports the daily needs of billions of people around the world. For all its faults and shortcomings, the UN system and the body of international law it has created, make the world a far safer place for far more of the world's population than ever before in human history. We live in a world populated by over 40,000 non-governmental organisations. They work in every country of the world and help to hold governments to account, to monitor press freedoms, to protect human rights, to respond to international emergencies, to support families and communities in need and build a fairer and safer world for all.

What does this mean in terms of the UK's place in the world and reliance on nuclear weapons? Undoubtedly, the world remains an unstable and uncertain place. Wars continue to happen, along with terrorism, genocide and other forms of oppression, tyranny and violence. But is it up to the UK to respond to any of these unilaterally by itself (or in sole bilateral partnership with the US only)?

The reality is that the UK is part of a global community of around 200 independent states that need to work together to solve global problems and resolve disputes when they arise. The UK, as we have seen, is legally committed to the principles and procedures laid down in the UN charter for achieving this. This is the 'real world' of the 21st century. There is no place in this world for nuclear weapons and most countries have accepted that: 159 out of 193 countries in the world already live in nuclear-free zones which outlaw the presence of nuclear weapons. 121 countries have committed themselves to 'filling the legal gap' that allows the UK and other nuclear weapons states to claim their nuclear weapons are still 'legal'; 49 countries have the capacity to develop nuclear weapons but have chosen not to.

> Nuclear weapons are held by a handful of states, which insist that these weapons provide unique security benefits and yet reserve uniquely to themselves the right to own them. The situation is highly discriminatory and thus unstable; it cannot be sustained.[259]
> (Canberra Commission)

The emerging global norm

The UK is one of a very small number of countries fighting to retain nuclear weapons in the face of persistent and growing calls for their total elimination. These calls come from the vast majority of other states, but also from eminent and respected world leaders who have put their names to a growing list of commissions, reports, statements and initiatives demanding the total elimination of all nuclear weapons. The Canberra Commission, for instance, consisted of the sitting Australian Prime Minister at the time, Paul Keating, former President of France Michel Rocard, former US Secretary of Defence and architect of deterrence theory Robert McNamara, former UK Chief of Defence Staff Field Marshall Lord Carver and others of that professional standing.

Other mainstream, 'realpolitik' figures who have in recent years put their name to the goal of eliminating all nuclear weapons include former US Secretary of State Henry Kissinger, former Commander of US Strategic Air Command General Lee Butler, and former US Secretary of State George Schultz.

In the UK, senior military officers like Lord Carver, Lord Mountbatten, Commander Robert Green and Sir Hugh Beach have long signalled their opposition to Trident. More recently, however, former Chief of the Defence Staff Field Marshal Lord Bramall, General Lord Ramsbotham and Major-General Patrick Cordingley, erstwhile Commander of the 7th Armoured Brigade, among others, have added their names to the growing list of military professionals opposed to Trident.[260]

These are not woolly-minded pacifists or people with their heads in the clouds. These are people who have worked with nuclear weapons and engaged with nuclear deterrence, who now think better of it. While it is perhaps regrettable that most of these people made their views known about nuclear weapons after retiring from public life, nonetheless it is important that these voices are heard, especially by those who still support nuclear weapons and the theory of nuclear deterrence.

Summary

The final insult thrown at those who believe that a nuclear-free world is possible is that they are living in 'Cloud-Cuckoo-Land'. The 'real world', as we are told all too often, consists of states, the dynamics of state power, competition between states, and war, deterrence and nuclear weapons. But which of these is the 'real world'?

We live on a small, increasingly interconnected and interdependent planet with high-speed travel and trade that bring people from every corner of the globe together like never before. A community of nearly 200 independent states interact with each other on the basis of commonly agreed principles and practices that are laid down in a huge and growing body of treaties and international law.

None of this existed in 1940, when Britain stood alone against Hitler and developed the mindset for having its own nuclear 'deterrent'. The world was an utterly different place. In 1940, people still thought it was acceptable to have 'colonies' and for the British Empire to lord itself over a fifth of the world's population without their consent or participation. In 1940, people still accepted the idea that countries had a right to invade and occupy other countries purely to increase their own territory or gain access to raw materials.

But that is not the 'real world' of the 21st century and there is no going back to such a world. While there are still wars and conflicts and new forms of terrorism to contend with, these are vastly outnumbered by the number of peace treaties being signed, the number of military dictatorships which have been transformed into democracies, and the number of dialogues, discussions and negotiations which have averted wars and ended bloodshed across the globe.

Trident is no more of the 'real world' of today than colonialism, slavery or apartheid. In fact, politicians and civil servants in the UK and nuclear weapons states are living inside a 'bubble', where talk of 'needing' nuclear weapons for our security appears normal and talk of nuclear disarmament is scandalous.

The multilateral nuclear disarmament initiatives that have been repeatedly boycotted or voted against by the UK have had overwhelming support from the vast majority of other countries. A growing number of statesmen and women, including high ranking generals and others who have worked with and been responsible for nuclear weapons, have come out saying that nuclear weapons must go.

Pursuing nuclear disarmament is not 'Cloud Cuckoo Land'. It is the real world of the 21st century.

PART SEVEN

Wrapping it all up

CHAPTER 24

The Truth About Trident

SO WHAT IS the truth about Trident? The truth is that we live in a world that is not as it was in 1939–40, when Britain stood alone against Nazi Germany and prevented an invasion by a combination of wits, luck, geography, will power, enormous self-sacrifice and the skill of some RAF fighter pilots. The idea that Trident would protect us in a similar situation is not only outmoded but dangerous, since it assumes that the UK can act independently and to its own ends in a world that is increasingly interdependent and interconnected.

Trident is a weapon of mass destruction. Each Trident warhead is probably at least six times more powerful than the bomb dropped on Hiroshima, and one Trident submarine contains more destructive power than was dropped on Germany and Japan throughout the whole of WWII, *including* the bombs dropped on Hiroshima and Nagasaki. If the UK were ever to use such a weapon, even against purely military targets, it would cause millions of deaths and millions more injuries. The radioactive fallout would cause deaths and injuries, not only in the UK itself but around the world. Climate change affecting global food supplies could not be ruled out as another possible result.

The theory of nuclear deterrence rests on the threat to use these weapons if an aggressor were ever to threaten or attack the UK. That threat is only credible if there is the political and military will to actually use these weapons under those circumstances. No deterrent can be 100% effective and the longer we play the deterrence game, the greater the chances of a nuclear weapon being used, by accident or by design.

We know from WWII that mass destruction of cities does not in itself win wars or even dent the war-fighting capability of a determined adversary. There is therefore little reason to suppose that the threat of mass destruction of cities by nuclear weapons, any more than by conventional weapons, is an effective deterrent. Although Japan surrendered shortly after the atom bombs were dropped on Hiroshima and Nagasaki, there is strong evidence to suggest that these were not the deciding factor in ending the war.

Even during the darkest days of the Cold War, had an overwhelmingly larger and more powerful adversary like the Soviet Union *chosen* to invade and occupy the UK and/or the rest of Western Europe, nuclear weapons would probably not have stopped them. Certainly the UK's nuclear weapons would not have stopped them, since the Soviets had vastly more nuclear weapons at their disposal and vastly more people and infrastructure.

The Cold War is now over, and yes, the world is a dangerous and uncertain place – made especially so by the existence of more than 15,000 nuclear weapons, many of which could well be aimed right now at the UK. Do the 200 or so nuclear weapons on Trident make the UK safer in such an environment? Or is it closer to the truth to say that on balance, the UK's continued possession of nuclear weapons actually makes us, and the rest of the world, *less* safe?

The UK is a small island nation comprising less than 1% of the world's population and less than 0.2% of the earth's land mass (and that includes Scotland!). No matter how much destruction the UK might be able to wreak on some other country, the retaliation would potentially be equally devastating. In what sense does that ability to destroy make us 'secure'?

Security in today's world does not come from military might, or from threatening other countries with nuclear destruction. It comes from working effectively with others through multilateral institutions such as the UN to ensure that *all* countries are secure from threats like fascism, genocide, megalomaniacal attempts at global domination and other ideologies that potentially threaten all of us.

Only by working incessantly to ensure that *no* country has nuclear weapons can we be protected from the threat of nuclear weapons ourselves. By insisting that we have an inalienable right to possess nuclear weapons for our own security, we are merely encouraging other countries to follow our example. A world in which every other country possesses nuclear weapons for their own security is an infinitely more dangerous place than a world in which there are no nuclear weapons.

Does a nuclear-free world sound utopian? Perhaps if it does, it is worth pondering for a moment on the alternative. The longer the UK and other nuclear weapon states go on claiming that they need these weapons for their security, the greater the likelihood becomes of one of these weapons being used. This is not just because of the mind games involved in convincing oneself that these weapons are still 'credible' as a deterrent. It is a simple matter of statistics. The chances of an accident or miscalculation are always going to increase the longer a system this risky is kept in place.

If the detonation of a single nuclear warhead somewhere in the world triggers a 'launch on warning' retaliatory strike because it is assumed to have been an act of war by Russia or the US, even if launched by another country, then we are all finished as a human species. All-out nuclear war spells the end of human civilisation as we know it.

If, on the other hand, a nuclear detonation goes off somewhere and yet does *not* trigger all-out nuclear war, perhaps hundreds of thousands of people will be dead, depending on where it goes off. Millions more will be homeless, facing various forms of radiation sickness and other diseases. The world's humanitarian response agencies will be totally overwhelmed by the unprecedented scale of such a disaster. If the disaster happens in London, or Glasgow, or New York or New Delhi or Moscow or Tel Aviv or Beijing, the repercussions will be immense, not only on the immediate victims but on the surrounding infrastructure that a whole country may be dependent upon.

What is likely to be the overwhelming response of the world community to such an unprecedented disaster resulting from a single nuclear explosion somewhere in the world? With one voice the world will be crying out, 'Get rid of these weapons NOW before that can ever happen again!' Why wait for a catastrophe of unparalleled proportions before deciding to do what is already the obvious thing and get rid of these weapons once and for all? Either we do the right thing now or we wait until disaster strikes and we do it then. That is the choice before us.

In fact, the UK is already morally and legally obligated to eliminate its nuclear weapons. In signing the Non-Proliferation Treaty in 1968, the UK along with the other four recognised nuclear weapon states committed themselves to negotiating nuclear disarmament 'in good faith' and 'at an early date'. In 1995, the UK reiterated its commitment to this goal with an 'unequivocal undertaking' to fulfil its obligations under the NPT.

All of the arguments covered in the first half of this book are in fact irrelevant if it is accepted that the UK must disarm in accordance with its legal commitments. To argue that the UK 'needs' Trident when it has already agreed to get rid of it is nonsensical. The only question that should be on the table is how nuclear disarmament can best be achieved. Unfortunately, the UK continues to vote against multilateral disarmament initiatives, to boycott multilateral nuclear disarmament negotiations currently taking place and to obstruct the efforts of the vast majority of other countries to achieve a global ban on nuclear weapons. These actions do not indicate a country acting 'in good faith' to achieve nuclear disarmament 'at an early date'.

The deeper truth about Trident is that by renewing it for a further 30 years or more at enormous expense, the UK is signalling its defiance to the rest of the world and to the commitments made to them. It is saying to the world, 'we remain willing, indefinitely, to threaten the very survival of the planet in order to somehow 'defend' ourselves from unknown future threats'. What kind of partner does that make us in the community of nations? What message does it send, not just to other countries, but to our own communities and our own children? Can we retain Trident and still retain our dignity as human beings and our respect for other human beings on this small and precious planet of ours?

35 'Truths' About Trident

1. An all-out nuclear war between the US and Russia would have such catastrophic consequences that we cannot rule out the possibility that it would extinguish all life on earth.
2. A more 'limited' regional nuclear war, for instance between India and Pakistan, North and South Korea, or Israel and Iran, would still cause such devastation and climactic changes that there is the possibility of up to two billion people dying from starvation alone.
3. Even the 40 warheads from one Trident submarine, if used, could cause global climate changes that would affect the UK as well as every other country. That is in addition to killing more than 5 million people if aimed at 'centres of state power' in Russia, for example.
4. The theory that nuclear weapons are in and of themselves purely a 'deterrent' is unproven and riddled with contradictions.
5. A deterrent can fail, and is increasingly likely to be used in order to remain 'credible' as a deterrent.
6. Deterrence depends on the leaders of another country being sufficiently sane and rational to make a calculated decision that attacking the UK would have more costs than benefits, while at the same time assuming that our own leaders under the same circumstances will be insane and irrational enough to follow through with a nuclear attack if they call our bluff.
7. Use of Trident against Russia, for instance, would almost certainly result in a devastating nuclear attack on the UK, since they have many thousands more nuclear weapons.
8. Nuclear weapons were probably not the main cause of Japan's surrender in WWII and in general, the bombing of cities, whether with conventional bombs or nuclear weapons, is not what wins wars.
9. If bombing of cities does not win wars, then the threat of bombing cities, as in nuclear deterrence, is unlike to deter a potential aggressor

from attacking the UK.

10. Nuclear weapons are probably not the cause of relative 'peace' between the major powers since 1945 or the reason the Soviet Union never attacked the West. There are many other more plausible reasons.
11. The longer countries like the UK continue to maintain nuclear weapons and to argue they are 'necessary' for our defence, the more likely other countries will seek to obtain their own.
12. A world awash with nuclear weapons is an infinitely more dangerous one than a world with no nuclear weapons at all.
13. Trident makes the UK more of a target, for nuclear attack as well as for terrorism.
14. A nuclear war involving the UK but not involving the US is extremely unlikely but even this could have devastating global consequences.
15. Trident is not independent but heavily dependent on ongoing US support.
16. Trident does not guarantee Britain a seat at the top table. Britain plays a leading role in the world because it is a major industrial nation with a long history.
17. To use a nuclear weapon would be illegal under international law as it would cause disproportionate and indiscriminate harm to civilians, long-term damage to neutral countries, unnecessary and prolonged suffering to combatants and genetic damage to future generations. To threaten an illegal act is legally tantamount to the same thing.
18. It is absurd to think that the UK and other countries can continue to develop, build and deploy nuclear weapons indefinitely without them ever being used.
19. Nuclear accidents, mishaps and errors of judgment are occurring all the time and it is only luck that has prevented a major catastrophe so far. The longer we maintain these weapons the greater the chance of an accident becomes.
20. The full cost of renewing Trident, including running costs for 30 more years of 'continuous at-sea' patrols, is over £100 billion and could easily come to more than £200 billion according to the government's own projections.
21. The cost of renewing Trident is out of all proportion to other government expenditure and cannot be justified at a time when other

social needs are not being funded.

22. Jobs 'lost' to any cancellation of Trident are needed more than ever for developing and building renewable energy sources for the future as well as for meeting many other social needs. These are jobs requiring similar skills and would require a fraction of the investment currently planned for Trident.

23. Renewal of Trident threatens the break-up of the UK because the people of Scotland are strongly opposed to it being based there.

24. The UK's voting record at the UN and in other multilateral forums makes it clear that the UK is not acting 'in good faith' to achieve nuclear disarmament.

25. The UK has agreed to an 'unequivocal undertaking' to eliminate its nuclear weapons.

26. The renewal of Trident is not a mere 'replacement' of existing equipment but an 'upgrading' to counter advances in anti-submarine warfare and deep sea detection. Upgrading Trident fuels an ongoing arms race that threatens to continue escalating and could make the new subs obsolete before they are even launched.

27. Britain's unilateral disarmament of 300 warheads was necessary because these were mostly obsolete and useless as weapons.

28. We know nuclear disarmament is possible because it has already been done in places like South Africa.

29. Cancelling Trident would potentially have an electrifying effect on other countries and spur global efforts for the complete elimination of all nuclear weapons

30. Getting rid of all existing nuclear weapons and effectively monitoring all potential nuclear activity to prevent any country building a nuclear arsenal is perfectly doable and most of the mechanisms are already in place.

31. The Labour Party did not lose the 1983 election because of its commitment to disarmament but because the SDP split the Labour vote. It won the 1964 election with a commitment to disarmament (which it then reneged on) and there is no reason it cannot win the 2020 election on a similar commitment to disarm.

32. Nuclear weapons are morally indefensible according to all major world religions as well as from a humanist perspective. They cannot meet the test of a 'just war'.

33. Trident is not a defence and does not keep us safe. All it can do is cause massive destruction and death in the aftermath of an attack on the UK, it cannot prevent such an attack.
34. War never has been an efficient or effective way to deal with conflicts between or within states. The sooner we commit to peaceful ways of resolving conflicts the safer we will all be.
35. The dictum 'if you want peace, prepare for war' has led to 25 centuries of war, not 25 centuries of peace. If we want peace, we must prepare for peace and rule out war – and especially nuclear war – as an option.

In a speech which went largely unnoticed, at the height of the Cold War in 1979, the late Admiral of the Fleet, Lord Louis Mountbatten of Burma, made his views on this matter very clear:

> As a military man who has given half a century of active service, I say in all sincerity that the nuclear arms race has no military purpose. Wars cannot be fought with nuclear weapons. Their existence only adds to our perils because of the illusions which they have generated. There are powerful voices around the world who still give credence to the old precept, 'if you desire peace, prepare for war'. This is absolute nuclear nonsense…

'I am not asserting this without having deeply thought about the matter,' he added, going on to say:

> When I was Chief of the British Defence Staff, I made my views known. I have heard the arguments against this view but I have never found them convincing. So I repeat in all sincerity, as a military man I can see no use for any nuclear weapons which would not end in escalation, with consequences that no one can conceive.[261]

APPENDIX I

Treaty on the Non-Proliferation of Nuclear Weapons (NPT)

The States concluding this Treaty, hereinafter referred to as the Parties to the Treaty,

Considering the devastation that would be visited upon all mankind by a nuclear war and the consequent need to make every effort to avert the danger of such a war and to take measures to safeguard the security of peoples,

Believing that the proliferation of nuclear weapons would seriously enhance the danger of nuclear war,

In conformity with resolutions of the United Nations General Assembly calling for the conclusion of an agreement on the prevention of wider dissemination of nuclear weapons,

Undertaking to co-operate in facilitating the application of International Atomic Energy Agency safeguards on peaceful nuclear activities,

Expressing their support for research, development and other efforts to further the application, within the framework of the International Atomic Energy Agency safeguards system, of the principle of safeguarding effectively the flow of source and special fissionable materials by use of instruments and other techniques at certain strategic points,

Affirming the principle that the benefits of peaceful applications of nuclear technology, including any technological by-products which may be derived by nuclear-weapon States from the development of nuclear explosive devices, should be available for peaceful purposes to all Parties to the Treaty, whether nuclear-weapon or non-nuclear-weapon States,

Convinced that, in furtherance of this principle, all Parties to the Treaty are entitled to participate in the fullest possible exchange of scientific information for, and to contribute alone or in co-operation with other States to, the further development of the applications of atomic energy for peaceful purposes,

Declaring their intention to achieve at the earliest possible date the cessation of the nuclear arms race and to undertake effective measures in the direction of nuclear disarmament,

Urging the co-operation of all States in the attainment of this objective,

Recalling the determination expressed by the Parties to the 1963 Treaty banning nuclear weapons tests in the atmosphere, in outer space and under water in its Preamble to seek to achieve the discontinuance of all test explosions of nuclear weapons for all time and to continue negotiations to this end,

Desiring to further the easing of international tension and the strengthening of trust between States in order to facilitate the cessation of the manufacture of nuclear weapons, the liquidation of all their existing stockpiles, and the elimination from national arsenals of nuclear weapons and the means of their delivery pursuant to a Treaty on general and complete disarmament under strict and effective international control,

Recalling that, in accordance with the Charter of the United Nations, States must refrain in their international relations from the threat or use of force against the territorial integrity or political independence of any State, or in any other manner inconsistent with the Purposes of the United Nations, and that the establishment and maintenance of international peace and security are to be promoted with the least diversion for armaments of the world's human and economic resources,

Have agreed as follows:

Article I

Each nuclear-weapon State Party to the Treaty undertakes not to transfer to any recipient whatsoever nuclear weapons or other nuclear explosive devices or control over such weapons or explosive devices directly, or indirectly; and not in any way to assist, encourage, or induce any non-nuclear-weapon State to manufacture or otherwise acquire nuclear weapons or other nuclear explosive devices, or control over such weapons or explosive devices.

Article II

Each non-nuclear-weapon State Party to the Treaty undertakes not to receive the transfer from any transferor whatsoever of nuclear weapons or other nuclear explosive devices or of control over such weapons or explosive devices directly, or indirectly; not to manufacture or otherwise acquire nuclear weapons or other nuclear explosive devices; and not to seek or receive any assistance in the manufacture of nuclear weapons or other nuclear explosive devices.

Article III

1. Each non-nuclear-weapon State Party to the Treaty undertakes to accept safeguards, as set forth in an agreement to be negotiated and concluded with the International Atomic Energy Agency in accordance with the Statute of the International Atomic Energy Agency and the Agency's safeguards system, for the exclusive purpose of verification of the fulfilment of its obligations assumed under this Treaty with a view to preventing diversion of nuclear energy from peaceful uses to nuclear weapons or other nuclear explosive devices. Procedures for the safeguards

required by this Article shall be followed with respect to source or special fissionable material whether it is being produced, processed or used in any principal nuclear facility or is outside any such facility. The safeguards required by this Article shall be applied on all source or special fissionable material in all peaceful nuclear activities within the territory of such State, under its jurisdiction, or carried out under its control anywhere.

2. Each State Party to the Treaty undertakes not to provide: (a) source or special fissionable material, or (b) equipment or material especially designed or prepared for the processing, use or production of special fissionable material, to any non-nuclear-weapon State for peaceful purposes, unless the source or special fissionable material shall be subject to the safeguards required by this Article.

3. The safeguards required by this Article shall be implemented in a manner designed to comply with Article IV of this Treaty, and to avoid hampering the economic or technological development of the Parties or international co-operation in the field of peaceful nuclear activities, including the international exchange of nuclear material and equipment for the processing, use or production of nuclear material for peaceful purposes in accordance with the provisions of this Article and the principle of safeguarding set forth in the Preamble of the Treaty.

4. Non-nuclear-weapon States Party to the Treaty shall conclude agreements with the International Atomic Energy Agency to meet the requirements of this Article either individually or together with other States in accordance with the Statute of the International Atomic Energy Agency. Negotiation of such agreements shall commence within 180 days from the original entry into force of this Treaty. For States depositing their instruments of ratification or accession after the 180-day period, negotiation of such agreements shall commence not later than the date of such deposit. Such agreements shall enter into force not later than eighteen months after the date of initiation of negotiations.

Article IV

1. Nothing in this Treaty shall be interpreted as affecting the inalienable right of all the Parties to the Treaty to develop research, production and use of nuclear energy for peaceful purposes without discrimination and in conformity with Articles I and II of this Treaty.

2. All the Parties to the Treaty undertake to facilitate, and have the right to participate in, the fullest possible exchange of equipment, materials and scientific and technological information for the peaceful uses of nuclear energy. Parties to the Treaty in a position to do so shall also co-operate in contributing alone or together with other States or international organizations to the further development of the applications of nuclear energy for peaceful purposes, especially in the territories of non-nuclear-weapon States Party to the Treaty, with due consideration for the needs of the developing areas of the world.

Article V

Each Party to the Treaty undertakes to take appropriate measures to ensure that, in accordance with this Treaty, under appropriate international observation and through appropriate international procedures, potential benefits from any peaceful applications of nuclear explosions will be made available to non-nuclear-weapon States Party to the Treaty on a non-discriminatory basis and that the charge to such Parties for the explosive devices used will be as low as possible and exclude any charge for research and development. Non-nuclear-weapon States Party to the Treaty shall be able to obtain such benefits, pursuant to a special international agreement or agreements, through an appropriate international body with adequate representation of non-nuclear-weapon States. Negotiations on this subject shall commence as soon as possible after the Treaty enters into force. Non-nuclear-weapon States Party to the Treaty so desiring may also obtain such benefits pursuant to bilateral agreements.

Article VI

Each of the Parties to the Treaty undertakes to pursue negotiations in good faith on effective measures relating to cessation of the nuclear arms race at an early date and to nuclear disarmament, and on a treaty on general and complete disarmament under strict and effective international control.

Article VII

Nothing in this Treaty affects the right of any group of States to conclude regional treaties in order to assure the total absence of nuclear weapons in their respective territories.

Article VIII

1. Any Party to the Treaty may propose amendments to this Treaty. The text of any proposed amendment shall be submitted to the Depositary Governments which shall circulate it to all Parties to the Treaty. Thereupon, if requested to do so by one-third or more of the Parties to the Treaty, the Depositary Governments shall convene a conference, to which they shall invite all the Parties to the Treaty, to consider such an amendment.

2. Any amendment to this Treaty must be approved by a majority of the votes of all the Parties to the Treaty, including the votes of all nuclear-weapon States Party to the Treaty and all other Parties which, on the date the amendment is circulated, are members of the Board of Governors of the International Atomic Energy Agency. The amendment shall enter into force for each Party that deposits its instrument of ratification of the amendment upon the deposit of such instruments of ratification by a majority of all the Parties, including the instruments of ratification of all nuclear-weapon States Party to the Treaty and all other Parties which, on the date the amendment is circulated, are members of the Board of Governors of the International Atomic Energy Agency. Thereafter, it shall enter into force for any other Party upon the deposit of its instrument of ratification of the amendment.

3. Five years after the entry into force of this Treaty, a conference of Parties to the Treaty shall be held in Geneva, Switzerland, in order to review the operation of this Treaty with a view to assuring that the purposes of the Preamble and the provisions of the Treaty are being realised. At intervals of five years thereafter, a majority of the Parties to the Treaty may obtain, by submitting a proposal to this effect to the Depositary Governments, the convening of further conferences with the same objective of reviewing the operation of the Treaty.

Article IX

1. This Treaty shall be open to all States for signature. Any State which does not sign the Treaty before its entry into force in accordance with paragraph 3 of this Article may accede to it at any time.

2. This Treaty shall be subject to ratification by signatory States. Instruments of ratification and instruments of accession shall be deposited with the Governments of the United Kingdom of Great Britain and Northern Ireland, the Union of Soviet Socialist Republics and the United States of America, which are hereby designated the Depositary Governments.

3. This Treaty shall enter into force after its ratification by the States, the Governments of which are designated Depositaries of the Treaty, and 40 other States signatory to this Treaty and the deposit of their instruments of ratification. For the purposes of this Treaty, a nuclear-weapon State is one which has manufactured and exploded a nuclear weapon or other nuclear explosive device prior to 1 January 1967.

4. For States whose instruments of ratification or accession are deposited subsequent to the entry into force of this Treaty, it shall enter into force on the date of the deposit of their instruments of ratification or accession.

5. The Depositary Governments shall promptly inform all signatory and acceding States of the date of each signature, the date of deposit of each instrument of ratification or of accession, the date of the entry into force of this Treaty, and the date of receipt of any requests for convening a conference or other notices.

6. This Treaty shall be registered by the Depositary Governments pursuant to Article 102 of the Charter of the United Nations.

Article X

1. Each Party shall in exercising its national sovereignty have the right to withdraw from the Treaty if it decides that extraordinary events, related to the subject matter of this Treaty, have jeopardized the supreme interests of its country. It shall give notice of such withdrawal to all other Parties to the Treaty and to the United Nations Security Council three months in advance. Such notice shall include a statement of the extraordinary events it regards as having jeopardized its supreme interests.

2. Twenty-five years after the entry into force of the Treaty, a conference shall be convened to decide whether the Treaty shall continue in force indefinitely, or shall

be extended for an additional fixed period or periods. This decision shall be taken by a majority of the Parties to the Treaty.1

Article XI

This Treaty, the English, Russian, French, Spanish and Chinese texts of which are equally authentic, shall be deposited in the archives of the Depositary Governments. Duly certified copies of this Treaty shall be transmitted by the Depositary Governments to the Governments of the signatory and acceding States.

IN WITNESS WHEREOF the undersigned, duly authorized, have signed this Treaty.

DONE in triplicate, at the cities of London, Moscow and Washington, the first day of July, one thousand nine hundred and sixty-eight.

Note: On 11 May 1995, in accordance with Article X, paragraph 2, the Review and Extension Conference of the Parties to the Treaty on the Non-Proliferation of Nuclear Weapons decided that the Treaty should continue in force indefinitely (see Decision 3).

APPENDIX II

Summary of Advisory Opinion of the International Court of Justice on the Legality of the Threat or Use of Nuclear Weapons, 8 July 1996

THE COURT
(1) By thirteen votes to one,
Decides to comply with the request for an advisory opinion;
IN FAVOUR: President Bedjaoui; Vice-President Schwebel; Judges Guillaume, Shahabuddeen, Weeramantry, Ranjeva, Herczegh, Shi, Fleischhauer, Koroma, Vereshchetin, Ferrari Bravo, Higgins;
AGAINST : Judge Oda;
Replies in the following manner to the question put by the General Assembly:
A. Unanimously,
There is in neither customary nor conventional international law any specific authorization of the threat or use of nuclear weapons;
B. By eleven votes to three,
There is in neither customary nor conventional international law any comprehensive and universal prohibition of the threat or use of nuclear weapons as such;
IN FAVOUR President Bedjaoui; Vice-President Schwebel; Judges Oda, Guillaume, Ranjeva, Herczegh, Shi, Fleischhauer, Vereshchetin, Ferrari Bravo, Higgins;
AGAINST Judges Shahabuddeen, Weeramantry, Koroma;
C. Unanimously,
A threat or use of force by means of nuclear weapons that is contrary to Article 2, paragraph 4, of the United Nations Charter and that fails to meet all the requirements of Article 51, is unlawful;
D. Unanimously,
A threat or use of nuclear weapons should also be compatible with the requirements of the international law applicable in armed conflict, particularly those of the principles and rules of international humanitarian law, as well as with specific obligations under treaties and other undertakings which expressly deal with nuclear weapons;
E. By seven votes to seven, by the President's casting vote,
It follows from the above-mentioned requirements that the threat or use of nuclear weapons would generally be contrary to the rules of international law applicable in

armed conflict, and in particular the principles and rules of humanitarian law;
However, in view of the current state of international law, and of the elements of fact at its disposal, the Court cannot conclude definitively whether the threat or use of nuclear weapons would be lawful or unlawful in an extreme circumstance of self-defence, in which the very survival of a State would be at stake;
IN FAVOUR: President Bedjaoui; Judges Ranjeva, Herczegh, Shi, Fleischhauer, Vereshchetin, Ferrari Bravo;
AGAINST: Vice-President Schwebel; Judges Oda, Guillaume, Shahabuddeen, Weeramantry, Koroma, Higgins;

References

Ainslie, John, 'Sharpening Trident', 2009: [www.swordofdamocles.org].

Ainslie, John, 'Unacceptable Damage: Damage criteria in British nuclear planning', February 2013.

Ainslie, John, 'If Britain fired Trident: the humanitarian consequences of a nuclear attack by a Trident submarine on Moscow', *Scottish CND*, Glasgow, February 2013.

Ainslie, John, 'Substandard: The Trident Whistleblower and the Safety of British Submarines', *Scottish CND*, Glasgow, May 2015.

Ainslie, John 'United Kingdom: Status of UK's Nuclear Forces,' in *Assuring Destruction Forever Reaching Critical Will*, March 2012, (www.reachingcriticalwill.org).

Ainslie, John, 'No place for Trident', *Scottish CND*, Glasgow, 2014.

All Saints Church Kings Heath Social Action Group *The Replacement of Trident* briefing paper, Birmingham (undated).

Aldridge, Robert, *Counterforce Syndrome*, 1978.

Arkin, WM and Handler, Joshua, 'Naval Accidents 1945–1988', *Neptune Papers*, No. 3, IPC, London, 1989.

Brehm, Maya, Moyes, Richard and Nash, Thomas 'Banning Nuclear Weapons' *Article 36* London, February 2013 [www.article36.org/wp-content/uploads/2013/02/Report_web_23.02.13.pdf].

Baker, Rt Rev John Austin, Bishop of Salisbury et al, *The Church and the Bomb*, Hodder and Stoughton, London, 1982.

Baum, Seth D, 'Winter-Safe Deterrence: The Risk of Nuclear Winter and Its Challenge to Deterrence' in *Contemporary Security Policy* 36(1) 14 March 2015.

Baylis, John and Stoddal, Kristian, *The British Nuclear Experience, The Roles of Beliefs, Culture and Identity,* Oxford University Press, Oxford, 2014.

Baylon, Caroline, Brunt, Roger and Livingstone, David, 'Cyber Security at Civil Nuclear Facilities: Understanding the Risks,' *Chatham House, The Royal Institute of International Affairs,* London, September 2015.

Blunt Crispin, 'Figures show crippling costs of renewing Trident' 25 October 2015 [http://www.blunt4reigate.com/news/figures-show-crippling-costs-renewing-trident].

Borrie, John 'A Limit to Safety: Risk, 'normal accidents' and nuclear weapons' *ILPI-UNIDIR Vienna Conference series* 2014.

Boulton, Frank 'Dangers associated with civil nuclear power programmes'

in *Medicine Conflict and Survival,* 31 (1) 2016 pg 6, pgs 100–132 (forthcoming).
British Bombing Survey Unit, *The Strategic Air War Against Germany 1939–45*, BBS, 1945.
Church of Scotland, *Taking Out Moscow: Conversations About Trident*, St Andrew Press, 1991. ISBN 9780861531486 (out of print).
Campaign for Nuclear Disarmament, *Trident Mythbuster* CND Briefing May 2015.
Chalmers, Malcolm and Walker, William, *Unchartered water: UK, nuclear weapons and the Scottish Question,* Tuckwell Press, 2001.
Church of England Board for Social Responsibility, *Church and the Bomb*, Hodder and Stoughton, London, 1982.
Churchill, Winston, *The Iron Curtain speech* Fulton, Missouri 5 March 1946.
Coates, Ken, ed., *The Carnage Continues, and Now for Trident*, Spokesman, 2006.
Corbyn, Jeremy 'Defence Diversification' August 2015.
Cox, John, *Overkill*, Penguin, Harmondsworth, 1977.
Darnton, Geoffrey Ed., *The Bomb and The Law, London Nuclear Warfare Tribunal; Evidence, Commentary and Judgment*, Alva and Gunnar Myrdal Foundation, Stockholm, 1989.
Fenwick, Toby, 'Trident: An alternative proposal for UK nuclear deterrence' *CentreForum* February 2015.
Fromkin, David, 'The Strategy of Terrorism' in *Foreign Affairs*, July 1975, Council on Foreign Relations, USA.
Gaddis, John, *The Cold War: A New History*, Penguin, London, 2005.
Gill, David, *Britain and the Bomb,* Stanford University Press, California, 2014.
Glasstone, Samuel and Dolan, Philip J. eds *The Effects of Nuclear Weapons* Third Edition, United States Department of Defense Washington DC, 1977.
Green, Robert, *The Naked Nuclear Emperor*, DSC, Christchurch, NZ, 2000.
Green, Robert, *Security Without Nuclear Deterrence,* Second Edition, Disarmament and Security Centre, Christchurch, NZ, 2014.
Hall, Xanthe, 'Time for Nuclear Sharing to End' *OpenDemocracy.net*, 8 October 2015 (www.opendemocracy.net /can-europe-make-it/xanthe-hall/time-for-nuclear-sharing-to-end).
Hallett, Graham, *European Security in the Post-Soviet Age*, 2007.
Hambling, David, *The Inescapable Net: Unmanned Systems in Anti-Submarine Warfare*, BASIC, 2016
Hammond, Jeremy 'Rogue State: Israeli Violations of UN Security Council Resolutions', in *Foreign Policy Journal*, 27 January 2010: [http://www.foreignpolicyjournal.com/2010/01/27/rogue-state-israeli-violations-of-u-n-security-council-resolutions/].
Hasegawa, Tsuyoshi, *Racing the Enemy: Stalin, Truman and the Surrender of Japan,* Harvard University Press, Boston, 2005.
HM Government 'National Security Strategy and Strategic Defence and Security Review 2015: A Secure and Prosperous United Kingdom' November 2015.
HM Treasury, Spending Review and Autumn Statement, cm 9162, November 2015:

[https://www.gov.uk/government/uploads/system/uploads/attachment_data/file/479749/52229_Blue_Book_PU1865_Web_Accessible.pdf].

Hennessy, Peter, *Silent Deep* London, Allen Lane, 2015.

Holy See *Pacem In Terris* Encyclical of Pope John XXIII on establishing universal peace in truth, justice, charity and liberty, 11 April 1963.

Holy See *Laudato Si'* Encyclical letter of the Holy Father Francis on Care for our Common Home, 24 May 2015.

House of Bishops, *Who is My Neighbour*, 2015.

Ingram, Paul, *Trident: the need for comprehensive risk assessment* BASIC 23 November 2015.

Ingram, Paul 'Measuring the Financial Costs,' in *Background Papers to the Trident Commission*, BASIC, 2014.

International Law and Policy Institute, 'NATO and a Treaty Banning Nuclear Weapons', [nwp.ilpi.org/?p=2317].

Jamison, Brian, *Britannia's Sceptre: Scotland and the Trident System* Argyll, 2006.

Johnson, Rebecca and Zelter, Angie, *Trident and International Law: Scotland's Obligations*, Luath Press, Edinburgh, 2011.

Kile, Shannon and Kristensen, Hans, 'British Nuclear Forces' in *SIPRI Yearbook* 2015, SIPRI, Stockholm, 2015.

Kristensen, Hans M, Norris, Robert S, Oelrich, I 'From Counterforce to Minimal Deterrence: A New Nuclear Policy on the Path Toward Eliminating Nuclear Weapons *Federation of American Scientists & The Natural Resources Defense Council* April 2009.

Kristensen, Hans 'British submarines to receive upgraded US nuclear warhead,' *Federation of American Scientists*, 1 April 2011 [http://blogs.fas.org/security/2011/04/britishw76-1/].

Lewis, Patricia, Williams, Heather, Pelopidas, Benoît and Aghlani, Sasan, 'Too Close for Comfort: Cases of Near Nuclear Use and Options for Policy' *Chatham House, The Royal Institute of International Affairs* London, April 2014.

Mills, Claire, *Replacing the UK's Nuclear Deterrent*, House of Commons Library, Briefing Paper, No. 7353, 1 March 2016.

Myritten, Henri, 'Disarming Masculinities' *Disarmament Forum,* 4, UNIDIR: Geneva 2003.

NATO, 'Strategic Concept for the Defence and Security of the Members of the North Atlantic Treaty Organization' Adopted by Heads of State and Government at the NATO Summit in Lisbon 19–20 November 2010.

Norris, Robert S., Burrows Andrew S., and Fieldhous, Richard W, *Nuclear Weapons Data Book*, Westview Press, Boulder July/August 1994.

Oertel, Janka 'The United Nations and NATO' unpublished draft paper prepared for the ACUNS 21st Annual Meeting, Bonn, Germany, 5–7 June 2008.

Ogilvie-White, Tanya, *On Nuclear Deterrence: The Correspondence of Sir Michael Quinlan*, International Institute of Strategic Studies, London, 2011, p. 11.

Parliamentary Office for Science and Technology, 'Chernobyl Fallout', *Information*

for Members Briefing Note 45, July 1993, POST, London.
Pinker, Steven, *The Better Angels of Our Nature: Why Violence Has Declined*, Viking, New York, 2011.
Quinlan, Michael *Thinking about nuclear weapons*, RUSI, London, 1997.
Religions for Peace, *Resource Guide on Nuclear Disarmament for Religious Leaders and Communities*, NY, 2013.
Republic of the Marshall Islands *Application Instituting Proceedings Against the United Kingdom*, International Court of Justice, 24 April 2014.
Ritchie, Nick, *Trident in UK Politics and Public Opinion* British American Security Information Council July 2013.
Richie, Nick, *A Nuclear Weapons Free World? Britain, Trident and the Challenge Ahead*, Palgrave MacMillan, London, 2012.
Ritchie, Nick *Response to the Trident Commission Concluding Report* University of York 23 July 2014.
Rogers, Paul, *Guide to Nuclear Weapons*, Berg, Oxford, 1988.
Rogers, Paul, *The Role of British Nuclear Weapons After The Cold War*, British American Security Information Council, 1995.
Rowe, Dorothy, *Living With the Bomb*, Routledge and Kegan Paul, London, 1985.
Sandia National Laboratories, *Official List of Underground Nuclear Explosions (UNEs) in Nevada*, July 1994, [http://nuclearweaponarchive.org/Usa/Tests/Nevada.html].
Schell, Jonathan, *The Fate of the Earth*, Stamford University Press, 1982.
Schell, Jonathan, *The Unfinished Twentieth Century: The Crisis of Weapons of Mass Destruction*, Verso, London, 2011.
Schlosser, Eric, *Command and Control*, Penguin, London, 2013.
Scientists for Global Responsibility, *Newsletter* 35 Winter 2008.
Schneidmiller, Chris, 'Limited Nuclear War Could Deplete Ozone Layer, Increasing Radiation' *Global Security* Newswire 24 February 2011 [http://www.nti.org/gsn/article/limited-nuclear-war-could-deplete-ozone-layer-increasing-radiation/].
Sebald, WG *On the Natural History of Destruction*, Modern Library, New York, 1999.
Simon, Steven, Bouville, Andre, Land, Charles, 'Fallout from Nuclear Weapons Tests and Cancer Risks' in *American Scientist*, Jan-Feb 2006, vol.94, no. 1, pp 48ff.
Simma, Bruno, 'NATO, the UN and the Use of Force: Legal Aspects' *EJIL* 10 (1) *1999*.
Simpson, Tony, ed, 'Trident Undone', *The Spokesman*, vol 127, 2015.
Siracusa, Joseph M, *Nuclear Weapons: A Very Short Introduction*, OUB, Oxford, 2015.
Solomon, Fredric and Marston, Robert Q., *The Medical Implications of Nuclear War*, National Academy Press, Washington, 1986.
Speech at Brookings Institute, quoted in 'Scottish Independence would be Cataclysmic for the West' *Herald Scotland*, 8 April 2014, [http://www.

heraldscotland.com/news/13154575.George_Robertson__Scottish_independence_would_be_cataclysmic_for_the_west/].

Stein, Walter Ed., *Nuclear Weapons: A Catholic Response,* Burns and Oates, London, 1963.

Street, Tim, 'Politics of British Nuclear Weapons', Oxford Research Group

Trident Commission, *Concluding Report*, BASIC, 2014 [www.basicint.org/tridentcommission].

Trenin, Dmitri, 'The Drivers of Russia's Foreign Policy' *APPG Global Security and Non-Proliferation* meeting held 3 November 2015.

Twigge, Stephen and Scott, Len, 'The Other Other Missiles of October: The Thor IRBMs and the Cuban Missile Crisis' in *Electronic Journal of International History* (3) 2000.

UK Government, *The Future of the United Kingdom's Nuclear Deterrent* HMSO Norwich December 2006.

UK Ministry of Justice '2012 Compendium of re-offending statistics and analysis' *Ministry of Justice Statistics bulletin* 12 July 2012.

UK Ministry of Defence, FOI Request ICO Case Reference FD50444068 27 February 2013.

UK Ministry of Defence, FOI Request by Nukewatcher May 2006.

UK Ministry of Defence, *The Future of the United Kingdom's Nuclear Deterrent,* Fact Sheet Four, 1 December 2006.

UK Mission to the UN, *Intervention at Vienna Conference on the Humanitarian Impact of Nuclear Weapons* 8–9 December 2014 [www.gov.uk/government/world-location-news/uk-intervention-at-the-vienna-conference-on-the-humanitarian-impact-of-nuclear-weapons].

United Nations GA 53rd session, 79th plenary meeting 4 December 1998, New York.

United Nations GA 70th session, Promotion of multilateralism in the area of disarmament and non-proliferation A/C.1/70/L.9, 15 October 2015, New York.

United States Department of Energy, *United States Nuclear Tests July 1945 through September 1992,* DOE/NV--209-REV 15, December 2000.

US NRC, *Reactor Safety Study: An Assessment of Accidental Risks in US Commercial Nuclear Power Plants*, 1975. WASH-1400, NUREG 75/014 [http://www.barringer1.com/mil_files/NUREG-75–014-Report-&-Executive-Summary.pdf].

US Strategic Bombing Survey (USSBS), *Overall Report: European War*, 30 Sept 1945.

Vinthagen, Stella and Kenrick, Justin, *Tackling Trident*, Irene, 2012.

Walker, William, 'Trident – not in our backyard' in *Surging for Oil* eds Lykiard, A, Gorbachev, M and Rogers, P, Spokesman Books, Nottingham, 2007.

Walker, William, 'Trident's Replacement and the Survival of the United Kingdom' *Survival* 57 (5) October – November 2015.

Webber, Phil and Parkinson, Stuart, *UK Nuclear Weapons: A Catastrophe in the*

Making? Scientists for Global Responsibility, 2015.
Webber, Phil, 'Could one Trident submarine cause nuclear winter?' 2008 [http://www.sgr.org.uk/climate/NuclearWinterTrident_NL35.pdf].
Wilson, Richard, 'Resource Letter EIRLD-2: Effects of Ionizing Radiation at Low Doses *American Journal of Physics* 80 (1) 2012.
Wilson, Ward, *Five Myths About Nuclear Weapons*, Houghton Mifflin Harcourt, 2013.
YouGov/*The Times Trident Survey* results 25–26 January 2015 [https://d25d2506sfb94s.cloudfront.net/cumulus_uploads/document/ksx1tw2rj8/TimesResults_150126_Trident_Website.pdf].
Zelter, Angie, *Trident on Trial: The Case for People's Disarmament*, Luath Press, Edinburgh, 2001.
Zelter, Angie, ed, *World in Chains*, Luath Press, Edinburgh, 2014.
Stephen Zunes [http://fpif.org/united_nations_security_council_resolutions_currently_being_violated_by_countries_other_than_iraq/].

Endnotes

Chapter 1

1 According to *SIPRI Yearbook*, 2015, UK's nuclear stockpile decreased from 225 to approximately 215 warheads during 2015. See Shannon Kile and Hans Kristensen, 'British Nuclear Forces' in *SIPRI Yearbook* 2015 p. 485.

2 HMG, National Security Strategy and Strategic Defence and Security Review 2015, Cm9161, p. 34.

3 http://www.lockheedmartin.com/content/dam/lockheed/data/space/documents/tridentdiid5/SWFLANTBrochure810.pdf

4 HMG, op cit, p. 34.

5 Part of the Trident D5 missile component is the Mark4A 're-entry vehicle' (RV). This fits up to 14 warheads that can be independently sent to different targets as the missile begins its descent. Multiple Independently-targeted Re-entry Vehicles (MIRV) were a major advancement in the nuclear arms race because it meant that anti-ballistic missile systems on the other (ie Russian) side could not know where, or indeed how many places, the warheads were heading towards.

6 See Peter Hennessy, *Silent Deep London*, Allen Lane, 2015 p. 673 ff.

7 The destructive power of nuclear weapons is normally measured in terms of thousands of tonnes (KT) or millions of tonnes (MT) of conventional explosive (TNT) that would be needed to produce the equivalent 'bang'.

8 See *SIPRI Yearbook* 2015, p. 485.

9 See Hans Kristensen, 'British submarines to receive upgraded US nuclear warhead,' *Federation of American Scientists*, 1 April 2011: [https://fas.org/blogs/security/2011/04/britishw76–1/].

10 The then Defence Secretary Malcolm Rifkind announced that Trident would also have a 'sub-strategic' role in 1992. See Milan Rai, *Tactical Trident*, Drava Papers, London, 1994.

11 US Department of Energy, *United States Nuclear Tests: 1945–1992*, DOE/NV--209-REV 15, December 2000: [http://www.nv.doe.gov/library/publications/historical/DOE_NV%20--%20209%20Rev%2016.pdf].

12 Secretary of State for Defence Des Browne formally abandoned the sub-strategic role for Trident in a speech at Kings College, 25 January 2007. This was confirmed in an FCO policy paper, 'Lifting the Nuclear Shadow', 2009, in which it was stated that 'the UK believes that the use of any nuclear weapon would be strategic in nature and has consequently stopped using the term sub-strategic…' (p. 28.)

13 Estimate of the total tonnage of bombs dropped in WWII is approximately three million tonnes, or 3MT.

14 Earlier, the figure of 12.5 KT was used as an estimate but it is more common now to use the figure of 15KT, which is the average of 12–18KT. The truth is no one knows the exact figure.

15 In 1997, the official register claimed 202,118 killed from the Hiroshima bomb. See http://www.warbirdforum.com/hirodead.htm

16 Temperature of the interior of the sun is estimated to be 7–10 million degrees C, while the interior of a nuclear weapon fireball is estimated to be between 30–100 million degrees C.

17 See Samuel Glasstone and Philip Dolan, eds, *Effects of Nuclear Weapons*, US Department of Defense, Washington, DC, 1977, p 390. Chapter 3 goes into much more detail about the radiological effects of a nuclear explosion.

18 John Ainslie, *Unacceptable Damage*, Feb 2013: [http://www.banthebomb.org/images/stories/pdfs/UnacceptableDamage.pdf].

19 Normal air pressure at sea level is 14.7 psi, so overpressure is how much pressure is applied additional to that.

20 http://www.cdc.gov/niosh/docket/archive/pdfs/NIOSH-125/125-ExplosionsandRefugeChambers.pdf.

21 Glasstone and Dolan op cit, p. 78.

22 Ainslie, op cit.

23 See Webber, Phil and Parkinson, Stuart, 'UK Nuclear Weapons: A Catastrophe in the Making?' *Scientists for Global Responsibility*, 2015, p. 6. Also Webber, Phil, 'Could one Trident submarine cause nuclear winter?' 2008 [http://www.sgr.org.uk/climate/NuclearWinterTrident_NL35.pdf].

24 See Hefland, Ira, *Nuclear Famine: Two Billion People at Risk?*, International Physicians for the Prevention of War, 2013.

25 Webber, 2008, op cit.

26 See Peter Hennessy op cit, p. 478.

27 Quoted in John Ainslie, *If Britain Fired Trident*, Scottish CND, 2013, p. 3.

28 Ibid.

29 According to the NSS/SDSR and other UK statements in 2015, 120 warheads are considered 'operationally available' and 'up to 40' warheads are on each submarine, meaning that the government considers three submarines to be operationally available to launch their missiles if needed.

30 With the exception of a country which it considers to be in breach of the nuclear non-proliferation treaty.

Chapter 2

31 In the US, the 'rad' is still used as a unit of radiation dose. In the rest of the world this has largely been replaced by the 'Gray'. One rad is 1/100th of a Gray.

32 The equivalent unit in the US is the 'rem', which is 1/100th of a Sievert.

33 US Dept of Defense, *Effects of Nuclear Weapons*, 1977, p. 607.

34 See Dennis Heresi, 'Dr Louise Reiss, Who Helped Ban Atomic Testing, Dies at 90', in *New York Times*, 10 January 2011 [www.nytimes.com/2011/01/10/science/10reiss.html?r=0].

35 Glasstone and Dolan op cit.

36 Glasstone and Dolan op cit.

37 [http://www.telegraph.co.uk/news/uknews/9156393/Chernobyl-sheep-movement-restrictions-finally-lifted.html].

38 International Physicians for the Prevention of Nuclear Weapon estimate that 430,000 people have already died as a result of nuclear tests, and a further 2 million will eventually die as a result of cancers and other long-term effects, based on data from US National Research Council and UN Committee on the Effects of Atomic Radiation. See IPPNW, *Radioactive Heaven and Earth*, p. 164.

39 Boulton, Frank, 'Dangers associated with civil nuclear power programmes: weaponisation and nuclear waste' in *Medicine, Conflict and Survival*, Vol. 31, 2015, pp. 100–122.

Chapter 3

40 UK Mission to the UN, Intervention at Vienna Conference on the Humanitarian Impact of Nuclear Weapons 8–9 December 2014 [www.gov.uk/government/world-location-news/uk-intervention-at-the-vienna-conference-on-the-humanitarian-impact-of-nuclear-weapons].

41 'To talk about a 'nuclear deterrent' implies acceptance of the doctrine of deterrence, which not all do. Referring to a 'nuclear weapons programme' might be a suitable alternative,' from *BBC News Style Guide:* [http://www.bbc.co.uk/academy/journalism/article/art20130702112133560].

42 US Department of Defence, dictionary of military terms: [www.militaryfactory.com/dictionary/military-terms-defined.asp?term_id=1657].

43 There is considerable controversy around the figures used, but for example, see [http://news.bbc.co.uk/1/hi/uk/4457402.stm].

44 See Ministry of Justice, *Compendium of Re-Offending Statistics and Analysis*, 12 July 2012.

45 Then French President Francois Mitterrand, in his memoirs, said that Mrs Thatcher threatened to nuke Argentina if he did not give her the codes for the French-made missiles threatening British ships. Quoted in Tony Simpson, ed, Trident Undone, p. 34.

46 Ogilvie-White, Tanya, *On Nuclear Deterrence: The Correspondence of Sir Michael Quinlan*, International Institute of Strategic Studies, London, 2011, p. 11.

Chapter 4

47 Richard Moyes, Phil Webber and Greg Crowther, *Humanitarian Consequences*, Article 36, London, 2013.

48 Quoted in NSS/SDSR 2015.

Chapter 5

49 General MacArthur estimated Operation Olympic would cost the US 23,000 lives in the first 30 days. Admiral Nimitz estimate was 49,000 and General Norstad claimed it would cost 'half a million' US lives. In his memoirs, President Truman claimed it would have cost at least 250,000 lives but perhaps that was meant to include Japanese military and civilian deaths.

50 Figures vary, but these are generally accepted numbers. See, for instance, [http://www.historynet.com/battle-of-okinawa-operation-iceberg.htm].

51 US Strategic Bombing Survey, *Summary Report: Pacific War*, 1946.

52 The RAF was already a separate wing of the British military, but during WWII all US bombing was conducted by the US Army Air Force (USAAF) and only in 1947 was the USAF established.

53 Statistics from Ward Wilson, *Five Myths About Nuclear Weapons*, Houghton Mifflin Harcourt, 2013.

54 Hasegawa, Tsuyoshi, *Racing the Enemy: Stalin, Truman and the Surrender of Japan*, Harvard University Press, Boston, 2005, p37. See also Wilson, op cit, Chapter 1 and Weber, Mark, 'Was Hiroshima Necessary', *Institute for Historical Review*, Vol. 16, no 3, p4: [http://www.ihr.org/jhr/v16/v16n3p-4_Weber.html].

55 Hasegawa, op cit, p. 108.

56 Ibid, p. 71.

57 Truman did not let Stalin sign the Potsdam Proclamation demanding that Japan surrender unconditionally or 'face devastating consequences' because at this point he was hoping the atom bomb would end the war and leave the Soviets out of it.

58 Ibid p. 73.

59 'The evidence is compelling that Soviet entry into the war had a strong impact on the peace party. Indeed, Soviet attack, not the Hiroshima bomb, convinced political leaders to end the war by accepting the Potsdam Proclamation', Hagesawa, p. 198.

60 Wilson, op cit, p. 58.

61 USSBS, Overall Report: European War, 30 Sept 1945, p. 72.

62 Ibid, p. 166.

63 Chapter 15 of British Bombing Survey Unit, *The Strategic Air War Against Germany 1939–45*, 1945.

64 Quoted in Gian Gentile, 'Advocacy or Assessment? The US Strategic Bombing Survey of Germany and Japan' in *Pacific Historical Review*, vol 66, no 1, Feb 1997, p. 53.

65 As is usual when it comes to war casualties, the numbers vary enormously.

66 See [http://www.gallup.com/poll/4924/bush-job-approval-highest-gallup-history.aspx].

67 From Wilson, op cit, p77.

Chapter 6

68 As quoted by Margaret Thatcher at Soviet State banquet in Moscow, 30 March, 1987.

69 The Peace Research Institute Oslo (PRIO) counts any violent conflict with more than 1,000 killed in a given year as a 'war' and has totted up more than 258 of these since 1945.

70 Between them, US, UK, France, Russia/Soviet Union, China, Israel, India, Pakistan and North Korea have been involved in at least 44 wars since 1945.

71 Following the Russian revolution of 1917 and their withdrawal from WW1 in March 1918, there was an Allied invasion of Russia to try to topple the Bolsheviks, involving troops from Britain, France, the USA, Greece, Japan, China, Poland and Italy.

72 Quoted in Rob Green, *The Naked Nuclear Emperor*, p. 65.

73 See Vladislav Zubok and Constantine Pleshakov, *Inside the Kremlin's Cold War*, Harvard University Press, Cambridge, Ma, 1996, p. 32. Also John Gaddis, *The Cold War: a New History*, Penguin, New York, 2005, p. 11 ff.

74 There was alleged Soviet support to the Spanish Civil War and to attempted coups in Greece and Italy.

75 Steven Pinker uses a formula to calculate war deaths, genocides and other historical data as a proportion of the total human population at the time. This gives a very different picture than looking at absolute figures, since 40 million dead in WWII is much more than 2 million dead at the hands of Genghis Khan, for instance. But since the world population at the time of Genghis Khan is estimated to have been only a fraction of what it was in the 20th century, Pinker calculates that Genghis Khan killed more of the world's population than Hitler did.

76 USA, UK, France, Russia, China, India, Pakistan, Israel and North Korea (although it is doubted that North Korea has the means to deliver one).

77 Spain did not join NATO until 1982.

78 Also Afghanistan, North Vietnam, North Korea as well as the Eastern European states, all allied to the Soviet Union and/or China.

79 There is no hard evidence that the mujahedeen were being funded by the CIA prior to the Soviet invasion, however the US was funding anti-Soviet forces in virtually every country of the world during the Cold War, so it seems unlikely that they would have avoided Afghanistan, where the pro-Soviet government was repressive and unpopular and there were armed groups already trying to overthrow it.

80 This is disputed but the US installed intermediate range nuclear missiles in Turkey within easy reach of Moscow in 1960. These became operational in 1962 just prior to the Cuban missile crisis. See Ward Wilson, *Five Myths About Nuclear Weapons*, Houghton Mifflin Harcourt, 2013.

81 In fact, Pakistan began testing nuclear weapons in 1983, but these tests did not involve a nuclear detonation and were kept secret until 2000, so they can hardly have acted as a 'deterrent' for Pakistan prior to the public nuclear test detonation in 1998.

82 President Singh of India was encouraged by the international community not to use nuclear weapons on Pakistan. This was not popular in India and he lost the following election.

Chapter 7

83 BBC1, *Andrew Marr Show*, 8 November 2015. Transcript quoted.

84 NSS/SDSR, Cm9161, p. 24.

85 NATO, 'Active Engagement, Modern Defense: Strategic Concept for the Defense and Security of the Members of the NATO Alliance', 2010, p.10.

86 US Officials continue to highlight their 'appreciation' for the UK's Trident Fleet although it is unclear what this means in practice.

87 NSS/SDSR pp. 85–86.

88 [http://large.stanford.edu/courses/2015/ph241/holloway1/docs/SI-V10-I1_Kesler.pdf].

89 [http://www.acq.osd.mil/dsb/reports/ResilientMilitarySystems.CyberThreat.pdf].

90 [http://www.theguardian.com/uk-news/2015/nov/24/trident-could-be-vulnerable-to-cyber-attack-former-defence-secretary-says].

91 [http://www.computing.co.uk/ctg/news/2436369/yes-trident-really-could-be-vulnerable-to-a-cyber-attack-warn-experts].

92 See Milan Rai, op cit.

93 [http://www.theguardian.com/politics/2003/dec/06/military.freedomofinformation].

94 NSS/SDSR, op cit, p. 16.

95 See for example [https://zgeography.wordpress.com/2014/02/19/geographic-and-demographic-cleavages-ukraine/].

96 US funding for pro-Western Ukrainian organisations came from USAID, the National Endowment for Democracy, the Open Society Foundation, the US embassy and big name US backers like John McCain. Some have claimed CIA involvement. See 'Brokering Power: US role in Ukraine coup hard to overlook' in *RT*, 19 Feb 2015: [https://www.rt.com/news/233439-us-meddling-ukraine-crisis/].

97 See Rob Green, op cit.

Chapter 8

98 Trident Commission, Concluding Report, BASIC, 2014 [www.basicint.org/tridentcommission].

99 Ibid p. 12.

100 See David Hambling, *The Inescapable Net: Unmanned Systems in Anti-Submarine Warfare*, BASIC, 2016.

Chapter 9

101 Speech at Brookings Institute, quoted in 'Scottish Independence Would be Cataclysmic for the West' Herald Scotland, 8 April 2014, [http://www.heraldscotland.com/news/13154575.George_Robertson__Scottish_independence_would_be_cataclysmic_for_the_west/].

102 NSS/SDSR p. 34.

103 Memo to the Foreign Affairs Select Committee, 26 November 2015.

104 See Janka Oertel, 'The United Nations and NATO' unpublished draft, 3/6/08, pg 2 and Bruno Simma, 'NATO, the UN and the Use of Force: Legal Aspects', *European Journal of International Law*, Vol. 10, No. 1, 1999, pp. 1–22.

105 International Law and Policy Institute, 'NATO and a Treaty Banning Nuclear Weapons', [http://nwp.ilpi.org/?p=2317], accessed 15 December 2015.

106 See [http://www.flanderstoday.eu/politics/federal-parliament-joins-call-ban-nuclear-weapons].

107 [http://www.thelocal.de/20120905/44779].

Chapter 10

108 HM Government 'National Security Strategy and Strategic Defence and Security Review 2015: A Secure and Prosperous United Kingdom' November 2015. p. 34.

109 Ibid, p. 35.

110 Now that underground as well as above ground nuclear testing has stopped, testing continues at a 'sub-critical' level where there is no nuclear explosion and also at a 'virtual' level where complex computer simulations are used to calculate the results of different nuclear weapon designs.

111 HM Government, op cit, p. 35.

112 The Supreme Allied Commander of NATO is always an American general, while the Secretary-General of NATO, or political head, is usually a European.

113 See Hennessey, op cit, pp. 211–212.

114 Cmnd 8517, quoted in FOI request: [http://web.archive.org/web/20051229080220/http://www.mod.uk/linked_files/publications/foi/rr/nuclear190705.pdf].

115 See *Hansard*, 28 March 2007, column 1524W: [http://www.publications.parliament.uk/pa/cm200607/cmhansrd/cm070328/text/70328w0002.htm#07032871000435].

116 See John Ainslie, *Sharpening Trident*, 2009: [www.swordofdamocles.org].

117 See Robert Aldridge, *Counterforce Syndrome*, Institute of Policy Studies, 1978. According to Aldridge, a former Trident and Polaris design engineer at Lockheed, it is the increased CEP of Trident, made possible through GPS, that makes it a 'first strike' weapon capable of destroying Soviet nuclear missile silos.

118 See http://www.theregister.co.uk/2007/07/18/drop_sa_say_satnav_lovers/.

119 See Hennessy, op cit, p. 655.

Chapter 11

120 Tony Blair, *A Journey*, Hutchinson, London, 2010, pp635–636.

121 Some suspect that Israel conducted its only nuclear test with South Africa in 1979 although this has never been confirmed. Mordechai Vanunu, a worker at the Israeli Damona nuclear plant revealed in 1986 that Israeli had a well-established nuclear weapons programme, although this is still officially denied by the Israeli government.

122 This number does not include all the resolutions about Israel that have been vetoed by the US over the years. Well over half of all US vetoes in the UN Security Council have been about Israel. Stephen Zunes in his report lists 32 Israeli violations of UN Security Council resolutions (up to 2002): [http://fpif.org/united_nations_security_

council_resolutions_currently_being_violated_by_countries_other_than_iraq/], while Jeremy Hammond lists 80 security resolutions ignored by Israel in 'Rogue State: Israeli Violations of UN Security Council Resolutions', in *Foreign Policy Journal*, 27 January 2010: [http://www.foreignpolicyjournal.com/2010/01/27/rogue-state-israeli-violations-of-u-n-security-council-resolutions/].

123 See full text of the NPT treaty in Appendix 1.

124 Referring to the N5 recognised by the NPT would then allow us to refer to the N9 as the currently known actual NWS, the N8 as the 'declared' NWS, etc. just as we have the G7, G8 etc.

125 As mentioned in Chapter 9, France has nuclear weapons but these are not assigned to NATO.

126 It was the G7 before Russia was invited to join, and Russia's membership was suspended in 2014 so it may revert to being called G7 again. The OECD is the Organisation for Economic Cooperation and Development. See definition of other acronyms at the front of the book.

Chapter 12

127 See previous chapter. I refer here to the 'N5' to distinguish the 5 recognised nuclear weapon states from the 5 permanent members of the UN Security Council, known as the 'P5'. Although these are the same countries, this was not always so and may not be so in the future.

128 'I want clearly to spell out to the House what we are not doing. We are not upgrading the capability of the system. We are not producing more usable weapons…' *Hansard*, 14 March 2007, column 302: [http://www.publications.parliament.uk/pa/cm200607/cmhansrd/cm070314/debtext/70314–0005.htm].

129 There was also a second element to this bargain, which was the promise to share peaceful nuclear power generation technology with all countries so they could also benefit from this.

130 See full text of NPT in Appendix 1.

131 Speech by Lord Mulley, UK Minister for Disarmament, at Geneva during plenary of Eighteen Nation Disarmament Committee, 1968.

132 See Appendix 1.

133 Most recently in reference to the bombing of Syria, claimed by David Cameron as an act of self-defence under Article 51 when in fact Article 51 allows for no such thing.

134 International Court of Justice, *Legality of the Threat or Use of Nuclear Weapons, Advisory Opinion*, 8 July, 1996 [http://www.icj-cij.org/docket/files/95/7495.pdf], p. 258.

135 Ibid, p. 258.

136 Ibid, p. 259.

137 Under the Criminal Justice Act of 2003, the threat to kill 'where the defendant intends the victim to fear it will be carried out' carries a maximum life sentence.

138 Ibid, p. 246.

139 Ibid, p. 264.

Chapter 13

140 Written statement to the House of Commons, HCWS4, Safety at HM Naval Base Clyde, 28 May 2015: [http://www.parliament.uk/documents/commons-vote-office/May%20 2015/28%20May/1-Defence-Clyde.pdf].

141 This was at RAF Lakenheath in 1956, when a US nuclear bomber crashed into a storage hut containing three nuclear weapons but fortunately not their plutonium cores, which were stored in another hut at the time.

142 See Eric Schlosser, *Command and Control*, Penguin, London, 2013. Also Lewis, Patricia, Williams, Heather, Pelopidas, Benoît and Aghlani, Sasan, 'Too Close for Comfort: Cases of Near Nuclear Use and Options for Policy' Chatham House, The Royal Institute of International Affairs London, April 2014.

143 [http://www.theguardian.com/world/2013/may/08/us-airforce-nuclear-missiles].

144 Schlosser, op cit, p. 472.

145 According to papers released in 2013 under a FOI request.

146 Schlosser, op cit, p. 246.

147 See Thule Forum, 'Broken Arrow: the B-52 Accident…' [http://www.thuleforum.com/broken_arrow/].

148 [http://www.aerospaceweb.org/question/weapons/q0268.shtml].

149 [http://www.theguardian.com/world/2001/apr/05/kursk.russia].

150 See [www.pravdareport.com/russia/politics/09–10–2012/122396-submarine_reagan_gorbachev-0].

151 *Hansard,* Written Questions, 2 November 2009, Column 649W [http://www.publications.parliament.uk/pa/cm200809/cmhansrd/cm091102/text/91102w0008.htm].

152 Quoted in Chatham House, 2014. [http://www.publications.parliament.uk/pa/cm200809/cmhansrd/cm090402/text/90402w0024.htm].

153 Ibid.

154 [http://www.heraldscotland.com/news/13173071.Nuclear_bomb_convoys_travelling_across_the_UK_suffer_70_safety_lapses/].

155 UK Ministry of Defence, FOI Request by Nukewatcher, May 2006.

156 See Schlosser, op cit, pp. 470–471.

157 Ainslie, op cit, p 19–20.

158 [http://www.bbc.co.uk/news/uk-politics-26463923.

159 http://robedwards.typepad.com/files/the-nuclear-secrets.pdf].

160 Quoted in [http://www.savetheroyalnavy.org/parliamentary-debate-in-wake-of-trident-safety-allegations/].

161 Patricia Lewis et al, op cit.

162 Ibid, pp. 16–17.

163 This is evident from Reagan's memoirs and other Western intelligence reports, although no archives have been forthcoming from the Russian side to confirm what Soviet leaders were thinking. See Chatham House, op cit, pp. 13–16.

164 Ibid.

165 http://thebulletin.org/three-minutes-and-counting7938.

166 US NRC, *Reactor Safety Study: An Assessment of Accidental Risks in US Commercial Nuclear Power Plants*, 1975. WASH-1400, NUREG 75/014. [http://www.barringer1.com/mil_files/NUREG-75–014-Report-&-Executive-Summary.pdf].

Chapter 14

167 From LibDem report, September 2006.

168 Keith Hartley figure, BASIC briefing, March 2012.

169 The figure of £100 billion was quoted in the LibDem's party manifesto for the 2010 election and described by a former advisor to the Defence Secretary as a 'plausible' figure for the total lifetime costs of Trident replacement.

170 See reply to parliamentary questions: [http://www.blunt4reigate.com/news/figures-show-crippling-costs-renewing-trident]. This was before the much higher NSS/SDSR figures came out, so £167 billion is already an out of date figure.

171 See *Hansard*, 4 August 1980, v990, cc 323–69. This figure had risen to £7.5 billion by March 1982, when the decision was taken to use the more advanced D5 missiles rather than the originally planned C4 missiles on the Trident submarines. By the late 1980s the estimate had risen to £10 billion and the final bill in 1994 came to £12.52 billion, according to a House of Commons report, although again it very much depends on who is counting, what they are counting, and how they are counting it. [http://researchbriefings.parliament.uk/ResearchBriefing/Summary/CBP-7353].

172 In 1994 it was claimed that the final bill of £12.52 billion was only slightly more than £5 billion in 1980 prices and therefore there had been no cost overrun, but that is not how the costs were explained to parliament in 1980. See *Hansard* above.

173 The Astute programme was budgeted in 1997 at £2,578 million and by 2007 had cost £3,798 million, according to the National Accounting Office report of 2008.

174 NSS/SDSR figures, p. 36.

175 Paul Ingram, 'Measuring the Financial Costs' in *Background Papers to the Trident Commission*, BASIC, 2014, p 21.

176 See Ritchie, op cit, p. 160–161.

177 Ibid, p 22.

178 Ibid.

179 These are broken down for 2005–2006 in a written parliament answer by then Defence Secretary Des Browne. *Hansard*, Written Questions, 24 July 2006, column 776W.

180 See MOD, Annual Report and Accounts 2014–15, HC32, 16 July 2015, pp. 162–163.

181 Robert S. Norris, Andrew S. Burrows and Richard W. Fieldhous, *Nuclear Weapons Data Book*, Westview Press, Boulder July/August 1994, pg. 68.

182 Written answer to parliamentary question, see Crispin Blunt MP's website 'Figures show crippling costs of renewing Trident' 25 October 2015 [http://www.blunt4reigate.com/news/figures-show-crippling-costs-renewing-trident].

183 HM Treasury, Spending Review and Autumn Statement, Cm 9162, November 2015: [https://www.gov.uk/government/uploads/system/uploads/attachment_data/file/479749/52229_Blue_Book_PU1865_Web_Accessible.pdf].

184 Ibid, p. 100.

Chapter 15

185 Ritchie op cit, p113.

186 Figures from Ritchie op cit, p. 108.

187 Ibid.

188 See STUC, *Trident and Jobs: The Case for a Scottish Defence Diversification Agency*, 2014.

189 See CAAT, *Arms to Renewables*, London, 2015.

Chapter 16

190 Lord Ashcroft, 'Trident and Scotland Poll' May 2013 [www.conservativehome.blogs.com/files/trident-poll-summary.pdf].

191 Ibid.

192 YouGov *The Times*, survey results, 27 January 2015.

193 William Walker, 'Trident's replacement and the survival of the UK,' in *Survival*, IISS, Vol. 57, no 5, Oct-Nov 2015, pp. 7–28.

194 See Rebecca Johnson and Angie Zelter,eds, *Trident and International Law Scotland's Obligations,* Luath, Edinburgh, 2011, p. 24.

195 Ibid, see pp. 19–24.

196 John Ainslie, 'No place for Trident', Scottish CND, Glasgow, 2014. See also Malcolm Chalmers and William Walker, *Unchartered Water: UK, nuclear weapons and the Scottish Question*, Tuckwell Press, 2001 p. 16 – the safety requirement is for warhead storage to be 134km from any housing and 1.6 km from any housing because of risks involved in handling the high explosives.

197 Ibid, p. 17.

198 Ibid, p. 18.

Chapter 17

199 From HM Government, National Security Strategy and Strategic Defence Review, 2015, Cm 9161, p. 36.

200 This was in answer to questions during launch of the Trident Commission report, House of Commons, 1 July 2014.

201 [https://www.gov.uk/government/uploads/system/uploads/attachment_data/file/28423/120426_2011_ukni_workshop_final_rpt.pdf].

202 See Frank Boulton 'Dangers associated with civil nuclear power programmes' in *Medicine Conflict and Survival*, 31 (1) 2016 pg 6, pgs 100–132 (forthcoming).

203 Ibid.

204 See [http://www.nti.org/treaties-and-regimes/conference-on-disarmament/] for a complete breakdown of what the CD has done in each of its sessions since 1998.

205 [http://reachingcriticalwill.org/images/documents/Disarmament-fora/1com/1com15/eov/L13_N5.pdf].

206 The UK voted 'yes' on UN General Assembly resolution A/C.1/66/L.41 on 'United Action Towards the Total Elimination of Nuclear Weapons', which included 'Welcoming also the recent announcements on overall stockpiles of nuclear warheads by France, the United Kingdom of Great Britain and Northern Ireland and the United States of America...' [http://www.reachingcriticalwill.org/images/documents/Disarmament-fora/1com/1com11/res/L41.pdf].

207 [http://reachingcriticalwill.org/images/documents/Disarmament-fora/1com/1com12/eov/L46_France-UK-US.pdf].

208 [http://www.article36.org/nuclear-weapons/documents-suggest-uk-boycott-of-key-nuclear-weapons-meeting-was-driven-by-p5-partners/].

209 [http://www.nuclearinfo.org/article/non-proliferation/vienna-conference-maintains-momentum-humanitarian-initiative-nuclear].

210 See http://cpr.unu.edu/why-the-2015-npt-review-conference-fell-apart.html.

211 Many countries opposed an 'indefinite extension' of the NPT when this came up at the 1995 review conference, since it would mean leaving the situation in situ where five countries have nuclear weapons and the other 182 countries do not. Since the five NWS had made little progress towards fulfilling their Article VI obligation to disarm, the 1995 conference sought a number of assurances from them that this would happen if they allowed the NPT to be extended indefinitely. The Middle East NFZ was part of that bargaining which took place.

Chapter 18

212 In answer to questions, launch of Trident Commission report, 1 July 2014.

213 See Rob Gree, *The Naked Nuclear Emperor,* DSC Christchurch 2000, p. 10.

214 The subsequent Chevaline update to Polaris actually downgraded the warhead to 40 KT, but there were two of them per missile plus other decoys.

215 This is apparently only possible through the use of real time weather and other targeting data from US satellites.

216 Nick Richie, *A Nuclear Weapons Free World? Britain, Trident and the Challenge Ahead*, Palgrave MacMillan, London, 2012 p. 12.

217 In the 1974–79 Labour government, David Owen argued that the ability to kill one million Russians ought to be sufficient as a deterrent. He was outnumbered by those in cabinet who pointed out that Russia lost more than 20 million in WWII and still survived as state. Therefore, it was argued that 1 million dead was not enough.

218 According to Bruce Blair, nuclear security expert at Princeton University, in *Zero Alert for Global Nuclear Forces*, Brookings Institution, 1995, p. 87.

219 Ritchie, p. 310.

220 See Aldrich, op cit.

Chapter 19

221 According to survey by Z/Yen research, as quoted in the *Financial Times*, 23 September, 2015. [http://www.ft.com/cms/s/0/eb72290c-61ce-11e5–9846-de406ccb37f2.html#axzz3uzCELXAm].

222 see [http://www.globalfirepower.com/country-military-strength-detail.asp?country_id=united-kingdom].

223 These were reinstated in 2014 against ISIS targets in Syria.

Chapter 20

224 Ward Wilson, op cit.

225 See, for instance, Mike Bowker and Robin Brown, eds, *From Cold War to Collapse,* Cambridge University Press, Cambridge, 1993, p. 102.

226 Tony Blair, op cit, pp. 635–636.

Chapter 21

227 See [http://www.nuclearfiles.org/menu/key-issues/nuclear-energy/history/dec-truma-atlee-king_1945–11–15.htm].

228 See Stone, Dan, ed, *Oxford Handbook of Postwar European History*, Oxford University Press, 2012, p. 448. Atlee's foreign secretary, famously said, 'we've got to have this thing over here, whatever it costs. We've got to have the bloody Union Jack on top of it.'

229 David Gill, *Britain and the Bomb*, Stanford University Press, 2014, p. 21.

230 See Ritchie, op cit.

231 The main issue which led to the SDP split was the EU, because at the same 1980 Labour conference, the party also committed itself to withdrawing from the EU. The second most important issue was over NATO, where once again, the party conference voted to withdraw from NATO. The nuclear issue was certainly one of the other issues which divided the Labour party but there were many others.

232 'Working Together for Britain,' Liberal-SDP Alliance manifesto, 1983: [http://www.politicsresources.net/area/uk/man/all83.htm].

233 Ibid.

234 'The New Hope for Britain,' Labour Party manifesto, 1983: [http://www.politicsresources.net/area/uk/man/lab83.htm#Disarmament] and Butler, p. 63.

235 That does not mean we would have had a Labour government but there would have had to be negotiations about forming a coalition government of some kind.

236 See Bill Gidding, *Labour's Love Lost* at [http://boldprose.com/?p=85].

237 From the 'EdStone' which Ed Milliband erected to symbolise what the Labour Party stood for at the 2015 election.

Chapter 22

238 Quoted during 'Talking Trident' debate at Rich Mix, London, in July 2014, organised

by BASIC and WMD Awareness Group.

239 Quinlan, Michael, *Thinking about nuclear weapons*, RUSI, London, 1997 pp45–47.

240 Church of England Board for Social Responsibility, *Church and the Bomb*, Hodder and Stoughton, London, 1982.

241 Ibid, p. 160.

242 Ibid, p. 143.

243 St Petersburg Declaration of 1868 [http://www.weaponslaw.org/instruments/1968-saint-petersburg-declaration].

244 As outlawed by the Hague Declaration of 1899, which was not signed by the UK until 1907 and was never signed by the US.

245 Geneva Protocol, 1925, came into force in 1928. Further treaties prohibiting all biological weapons came into force in 1972 and chemical weapons in 1993.

246 Quoted in above.

247 Quran, 2:190.

248 According to the Sunni tradition, these are the instructions which Abu Bakr al-Siddiq, the first Caliph, gave to his armies. See [http://www.juancole.com/2013/04/islamic-forbids-terrorism.html].

249 Quran, 2:190.

250 Quran 8:61.

251 Shevuot 35b. See [http://www.jlaw.com/Articles/war3.html].

252 'Purity of Arms' doctrine of the Israeli Defence Force (IDF).

253 Hinduism, Buddhism, Jainism, Sikhism, Taoism, Confucianism and Shintoism.

254 Religions for Peace, *Resource Guide on Nuclear Disarmament for Religious Leaders and Communities*, NY, 2013, p. 6.

255 http://endnuclearweapons.org.uk.

256 Quoted in Ogilvie-White, p. 125.

257 Michael Quinlan, *Thinking About Nuclear Weapons*, RUSI, London, 1997.

Chapter 23

258 Quoted in Hennesey, op cit, p. 678.

259 Rotblat, Joseph Ed., *Nuclear Weapons: Road to Zero,* Westview Press, Boulder CO, 1998, pg. 4.

260 Letter to *The Times*, 21 April 2010.

Chapter 24

261 Speech by Admiral of the Fleet, Earl Mountbatten of Burma, on the occasion of the award of the Louise Weiss Foundation Prize to the Stockholm International Peace Research Institute, Strasbourg, 11 May, 1979. Reproduced in pamphlet form by CND, London, 1979.

Quakers in Britain

The Quaker commitment to peace arises from the conviction that love is at the heart of existence and that all human beings are unique and equal. This leads Quakers to put their faith into action by working locally and globally to change the systems that cause injustice and violent conflict.

Quakers share a way of life, not a set of beliefs. Their unity is based on shared understanding and a shared practice of silent worship, where they seek a communal stillness. Quakers seek to experience the Spirit directly, within themselves and in their relationships with others and the world around them. They meet together for worship in local meetings, which are open to all who wish to attend. Quakers try to live with honesty and integrity. This means speaking truth to all, and engaging actively and creatively with decision-makers.

Since the 17th century, Quakers have worked to bring this world into conformity with the Kingdom of God as they understand it. This has meant being at the forefront of campaigns to abolish the transatlantic slave trade, to find peaceful alternatives to war, for restorative justice, to achieve equal rights for women and to build a fairer and more sustainable society for all.

Website: http://www.quaker.org.uk/
Twitter: @BritishQuakers
Facebook: facebook.com/QuakersinBritain/
Email: enquiries@quaker.org

Some other books published by **Luath Press**

World in Chains – the impact of nuclear weapons and militarisation from a UK perspective

Angie Zelter

ISBN 978–1-910021–03–3 PBK £12.99

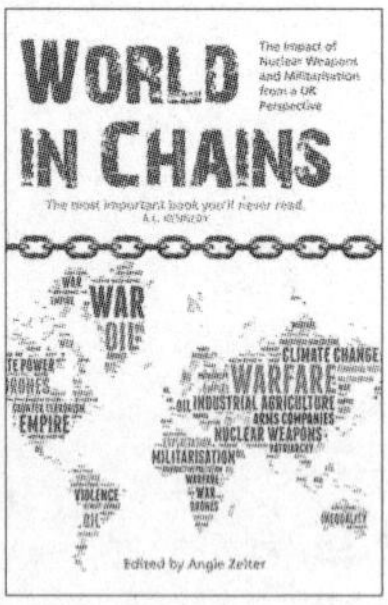

World in Chains is a collection of essays from well-reputed experts in their field, all of which deliver engaging and analytical critiques of nuclear warfare. They point to the changes needed to re-structure society, so that it is based on compassion, co-operation, love and respect for all. Their words inspire us to resist the growing militarisation and corporatisation of our world.

In the past I have often wondered why obviously unethical or inhumane horrors were able to take place, what people were doing at the time to prevent them or what kind of resistance was happening, how many people knew and tried to stop the genocide, slavery, poverty and pollution… I want those who come after my generation to know that, yes, we do know of the dangers of nuclear war, of climate chaos, of environmental destruction. This book will show you that there were many people working to change the structures that keep our world in chains. ANGIE ZELTER

'The most important book you'll never read.' AL KENNEDY

Faslane 365: A year of anti-nuclear blockades

Edited by Angie Zelter

ISBN: 978–1-906307–61–5 PBK £12.99

The Faslane campaign has been fantastic, it has encouraged people to act as the opposition to a government of false consensus and arrogance. Trident is an expensive stupid nuclear toy that creates an arms race, threatens to destabilise arms reduction treaties and lurches us into an uncertain future. It is a redundant dinosaur of the cold war era that has no place and serves no purpose, other than to aggrandise the military prowess of Britain's rulers. So when a state is uncivil, civil disobedience to the state becomes merely good manners. To everyone who locked themselves to the gates of Faslane, who blocked the roads, who dressed as pixies or swam across the loch to reach the submarines, I salute your lessons in civic etiquette. MARK THOMAS, comedian and political activist

Faslane 365 is the story of the people and ideas that embodied the 365 day blockade of Fasland Naval Base, home of Britain's nuclear submarines. Combining poems, anecdotes, articles and observations, it details the preparation and demonstration of the blockades, documents Scotland's history of anti-nuclear resistance, analyses Britain's nuclear policy, examines the campaign's impact on Faslane's local community, and considers the international ramifications of disarmament. With contributions from AL Kennedy, Adrian Mitchell, Eurig Scandrett and many others.

Trident on Trial: The case for the people's disarmament

Angie Zelter

ISBN: 978–1-906307–61–5 PBK £12.99

This is the story of global citizenship in action, a story of people's power and the right of individuals to prevent their state from committing very great wrongs. This book is about the women and men who are taking responsibility to prevent mass murder. It is about people's disarmament. I hope it will inspire you to join us. ANGIE ZELTER

When three women – Ellen Moxley, Ulla Roder and Angie Zelter – boarded a research laboratory barge responsible for the concealment of Trident when in operation, they emptied all the computer equipment into Loch Goil. Their subsequent trial ended with acquittal for the 'The Trident Three' on the basis that they were acting as global citizens preventing nuclear crime. This led to what is thought to be the world's first High Court examination of the legality of an individual state's deployment of nuclear weapons. However the High Court failed to answer a number of significant questions.

Trident on Trial is Angie Zelter's personal account of Trident Ploughshares, the civil-resistance campaign of People's Disarmament. The book also includes profiles of and contributions by people and groups who have pledged to prevent nuclear crime in peaceful and practical ways...

This fine book should be read by everyone, especially those who have the slightest doubt that the world will one day be rid of nuclear weapons. JOHN PILGER

Trident and international Law: Scotland's Obligations

Edited by Rebecca Johnson and Angie Zelter

ISBN: 978–1-906817–24–4 PBK £12.99

As a further generation of nuclear-armed submarines is developed, *Trident and International Law* challenges the legality of UK nuclear policy, and asks who is really accountable for Coulport and Faslane.

Although controlled by the Westminster Government, and to some extent by the US Government, all of the UK's nuclear weapons are based in Scotland. The Scottish Government therefore has responsibilities under domestic and international law relating to the deployment of nuclear weapons in Scotland.

Public concern expressed over these responsibilities led to the Acronym Institute for Disarmament Diplomacy, the Edinburgh Peace and Justice Centre and Trident Ploughshares organising an international conference, 'Trident and International Law: Scotland's Obligations'. This book presents the major documents and papers, with additional arguments from renowned legal scholars. The conclusions deserve careful consideration.

Gross violations of international obligations are not excluded from the purview of the Scottish Parliament. HE JUDGE CHRISTOPHER WEERAMANTRY

Details of books published by Luath Press can be found at:

www.luath.co.uk

Luath Press Limited

committed to publishing well written books worth reading

LUATH PRESS takes its name from Robert Burns, whose little collie Luath (*Gael.*, swift or nimble) tripped up Jean Armour at a wedding and gave him the chance to speak to the woman who was to be his wife and the abiding love of his life. Burns called one of the 'Twa Dogs' Luath after Cuchullin's hunting dog in Ossian's *Fingal*.

Luath Press was established in 1981 in the heart of Burns country, and is now based a few steps up the road from Burns' first lodgings on Edinburgh's Royal Mile. Luath offers you distinctive writing with a hint of unexpected pleasures.

Most bookshops in the UK, the US, Canada, Australia, New Zealand and parts of Europe, either carry our books in stock or can order them for you. To order direct from us, please send a £sterling cheque, postal order, international money order or your credit card details (number, address of cardholder and expiry date) to us at the address below. Please add post and packing as follows: UK – £1.00 per delivery address; overseas surface mail – £2.50 per delivery address; overseas airmail – £3.50 for the first book to each delivery address, plus £1.00 for each additional book by airmail to the same address. If your order is a gift, we will happily enclose your card or message at no extra charge.

Luath Press Limited
543/2 Castlehill
The Royal Mile
Edinburgh EH1 2ND
Scotland
Telephone: +44 (0)131 225 4326 (24 hours)
Email: sales@luath. co.uk
Website: www. luath.co.uk